Rupert Stadler
Walter Brenner
Andreas Herrmann

How to Succeed
in the Digital Age

Rupert Stadler
Walter Brenner
Andreas Herrmann

How to Succeed
in the Digital Age

Strategies from 17 Top Managers

Frankfurter Allgemeine Buch

Bibliographical information from the German National Library:
The German National Library has catalogued this publication in
the German National Library registry; detailed bibliographical
data is available at http://dnb.-d.nb.de

Publishers:
Rupert Stadler
Walter Brenner
Andreas Herrmann
How to Succeed in the Digital Age:
Strategies from 17 Top Managers

Frankfurter Societäts-Medien GmbH
Frankenallee 71 – 81
60327 Frankfurt am Main
Geschäftsführung: Hans Homrighausen

Frankfurt am Main 2014

ISBN 978-3-95601-078-1

Frankfurter Allgemeine Buch

Copyright	Frankfurter Societäts-Medien GmbH
	Frankenallee 71 – 81
	60327 Frankfurt am Main
Cover design	Anja Desch, F.A.Z.-Institut für Management-, Markt- und
	Medieninformationen GmbH, 60327 Frankfurt am Main
Typesetting	Jan Hofmann

Table of Contents

About this Book

"Your customers are the real treasure," according to a Chinese proverb, *"and your wares are just the straw."* If you go by this ancient piece of wisdom from one of the fastest-growing economies on the planet today, then you will heed it as a call to increase your "treasure trove" of customers. And by extension, innovative products and services would come second in importance to the customer. Taken to its logical conclusion, this concept would mean that, alongside the explicit verbal wishes expressed by customers, it would also be the data they generate – either consciously or not – that would represent the true treasure trove of the future. Which leads us to the fundamental question of how important a role customer data can play for a company.

When developing business models for the digitized world, there is no avoiding customer profiling if you want to offer tailor-made products and services. Who with whom? Where? When will a customer need something, search for it or use it? Today, the users of both physical and virtual products are already personalizing them to meet their individual needs and, by doing so, are generating a large amount of data. And the service provider who owns the best data can then also offer the best services. Google, for example, recognized this fact years ago. Today, the California-based company has surged into the lead as the world's largest Internet search engine, and its trove of customer data has expanded at an explosive rate. In the meantime, Google has used this platform to launch dozens of other services that go above and beyond the classical web-based search engine. At the same time, though, it is vital for companies to treat their customers' personal information responsibly and ensure that it is not collected without informed consent from the parties involved.

The art of creating added value from data is prized outside the digital world as well in the real world of classical brick-and-mortar businesses that deal with real, flesh-and-blood customers. This is already leading to new and technologically sophisticated products and services that are a constant source of amazement. But even the most finely honed product offerings will fail if customers do not embrace them as warmly as developers and producers had hoped. So what will fascinate the customer of tomorrow?

One thing is certain: No company can afford to bask in the glow of today's successes. The rapid revolution in the IT world has shown us just how quickly things can change and shift in any industry. The computing power of the first generation of industrial computers grew in massive leaps and bounds. But it could not keep up with personal computers, a parallel development a thousand times more powerful just three decades later. Many customers opted for decentralized and networked solutions instead of relying on a central data processing system. And today, we are seeing a similar market shift in the personal computing world to tablet computers and those other versatile, stand-out performers of the mobile IT world: smartphones.

The relentless advance of networking has not slowed down. The rapid spread of the Internet and mobile communication represents one of the biggest changes facing us in all areas of life – and also for modern corporate management. Nowadays, intelligent functions can be integrated into both products and services, whether through an Internet connection or, for example, by placing mini-transponders in products that send out a specific radio frequency, allowing the product to be located and identified. Information and communication technology solutions like these would have been unimaginable even a few years ago. They have changed the way we live and work, and comprise the basis for new business models in a digital, networked world. And these changes are happening so fast that they can rightly be called a revolution. It is an upheaval that is affecting every industry, every individual and our society as a whole.

In the course of a lengthy discussion in St.Gallen about the difference between customer satisfaction and customer excitement, the three editors of this book came up with the idea of addressing this complex set of issues and to seek answers to the following questions: How can we establish a lasting relationship between a brand, its customers and products? And how will the customer and product relationships of the future change in a digital era of new technologies and an all-encompassing network? Following a period of exciting and intensive research with 17 CEOs, top managers and leading researchers, we have presented the answers in this book.

Each chapter from our authors examines a very different approach to answering these questions. They show how companies operating at the global level are both reacting to and actively shaping the changing world of customer and product relations. The customer plays – quite rightly – the starring role. Customers' involvement in social networks, which can be created and nurtured not only in the real, but also the virtual sense, will continue to shape the interaction between the company and the customer of the future.

The opportunity for an entirely new way of interacting with customers and employees is based above all on new perspectives. The authors of this book allow the reader to share in the insights they have gained from these perspectives – and their individual ideas of what networking might look like in the future.

In this book, we have brought together visions for the future from the worlds of finance, services, Information Technology (IT), telecommunications, the media, energy, the chemical industry and various industrial sectors. The one motif that unites them all? The "human factor."

In this book, articles based on real-world applications stand side by side with theoretical perspectives. One insight, among others, that emerges is that 21st-century society is undergoing one of the largest social revolutions in the history of humankind. Companies will be well advised to adapt their ways of doing business to the needs of this new world – or risk missing the boat entirely. New systems of relationships and data streams will change both structures and processes, and will engender a new management model for the digital and networked world in which there is a close relationship between the customer, the company and the company's products or services. And this relationship will generate data. Above and beyond this, we will see an exchange between customers with other customers, products with other products, services with other services and companies with other companies. The relationship levels and data streams within this triangle will comprise the core of the management model (see graphic[1]) that above all will explain the changes that will result from this digitization and networking.

The management model for the digital, networked world

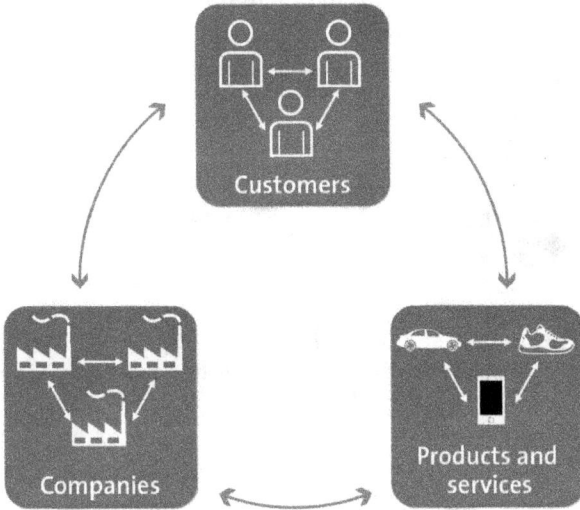

---

[1] This management model will be covered in more detail in the next section by the authors Walter Brenner and Andreas Herrmann

New social networks where the real and virtual worlds mix call for new management models. Today we are hearing a lot about Generation Y. Their successors, Generation Z, will in turn leave their mark, with an entirely different set of wants and needs than those we have today. Consequently, there is much discussion about "social management" and the need for business leaders to recognize its importance.

At present, we can only guess what life will actually look like in the year 2030 or 2050. But one thing is clear: Customer and product relations of the future will, to a great extent, be shaped by collaborative innovation. Creativity will no longer be the sole purview of the provider. Collaborative innovation will happen when we give our employees, partners and customers the necessary creative space, if they are given the chance to work together with us to create new products and services and if we listen to them.

We as the publishers want to take the opportunity here to thank all of the authors for collaborating with us in creating this book. Moreover, our project would not have been possible without the tireless efforts of numerous project contributors, notably Saskia Zelt from the Institute of Information Management with the University of St.Gallen, and Dietmar Scherer from Audi. And we would also like to thank you, our readers, in advance, for your active role in this project. Because it wouldn't have made sense to write a book about the digital revolution without creating an accompanying website and blog where our readers can leave their feedback, criticism and praise to guide us when producing the next edition: www.success-in-the-digital-age.com

Ingolstadt, Germany, and St.Gallen, Switzerland, February 2014
The Publishers Rupert Stadler, Walter Brenner, Andreas Herrmann

The Authors

Prof. Dr. Walter Brenner was born in 1958. Since April 1, 2001, he has been a professor of information management and the managing director of the Institute for Information Management at the University of St.Gallen . He previously held professorships at the University of Essen and the Freiberg University of Resources in Germany. His research activities focus on the industrialization of information management, the management of IT service providers, customer relationship management, applications of new technologies and design thinking. He also works as an independent consultant in the field of information management and the readiness of companies for the digital, networked world.

Prof. Dr. Andreas Herrmann was born in 1964. He worked with AUDI AG from 1991 until 1993. He then pursued post-doctoral studies at the University of Mannheim, which he completed in 1996. Starting in 1997, he held the Marketing Chair at the University of Mainz. He joined the faculty at the University of St. Gallen in 2002, initially as the director of the Institute for Media and Communications Management. In 2005 he was appointed head of the Center for Business Metrics, and since 2009 has jointly headed the Center for Customer Insight with Prof. Torsten Tomczak. Prof. Herrmann is also a co-founder and advisory board member of the consulting firms 2hm and 4hm. He has published 15 books and more than 250 journal articles.

The authors wish to thank Saskia Zelt and Christophe Vetterli for their assistance.

The Management Model in the Digital, Networked World

Walter Brenner, Andreas Herrmann,
University of St.Gallen

With every footfall on the forest floor, the runner moves one step closer towards achieving the target distance or time. Despite the athlete's apparently very low-tech activity in the woods, the run is no longer measured with a map or timed by a stopwatch, at least not in the original – or one could almost say, old-fashioned – sense. Surrounded by trees, the runner is embedded in the digital, networked world. Distance, altitude, time, the momentary and average speed, heart rate and calorie consumption are all measured using sensors in the runner's shoes, heart rate monitor and smartphone, transmitted to the network and linked to the corresponding profile data. The smartphone has a digital trainer inside. As for headphones, it's no longer just music that they're playing into the runner's ears. Now it's the voice of a coach with instructions on pacing for optimal training results. After completing a run, athletes can compare the data with past training sessions and customize their training schedules to meet their needs and achieve better performance. Suitable online nutrition plans can also help to achieve new personal bests. Runners can post their latest race results on social media platforms such as Facebook to harvest "likes" and comments from friends and club mates. Solitary training becomes a very public matter, with virtual "trainers" and fans. One prominent example is Ironman Zurich, an endurance triathlon event. Participants have a chip attached to their ankle that transmits a signal when they cross a timing mat. However, it is not only the organizers and triathletes who can see the data. The results are made instantly accessible worldwide in real time through the official Ironman website.

The digital, networked world will also change the soccer fields of the future. Players' shoes will be fitted with sensors that detect every movement, the distance covered, the speed and the force behind a shot. But it won't be just the shoes – the nets will also be equipped with advanced technology. The sport's global governing body, FIFA, has recently announced plans to introduce goal line technology (FIFA.com 2012). This will provide referees with a reliable basis for their decisions, and will put fans – virtually – right in the middle of the action where they can track every move. Trainers and commentators will have new ways of analyzing matches and results. But there are unresolved questions such as: Who ultimately owns the data? Who can use it? Does the data belong to the player, the club, the tournament organizer, the media partner, the sponsor, the sports equipment manufacturer, or can data pertaining to public figures even be seen a public good? While debate on these issues rages, the new technologies have already become routine for recreational soccer players, whose shoes now constantly update their social network contacts on all of their supposedly amazing feats.

And it's not only in the world of sports that networking and digitization are making their presence felt: They are also becoming part of everyday life. One example is the latest generation of televisions, both in terms of technology and services. The television is becoming an outsized monitor that functions as a control center, encouraging users to interact within the digital, networked world. Now it is possible to surf the web, take part in Skype conferences or sort out recent holiday photos while relaxing on the couch. A smartphone can be used to control a television, but that's not all: It can also manage a number of functions within the user's home. We can now use online services to play and record TV shows and movies. With Apple TV, for example, customers can watch video content on an iPad or a TV screen. Apps for mobile end devices can send a full-size picture to a regular television as well. Social networks and services such as Facebook and YouTube can also be integrated into the television experience.

Now that they find themselves in this digital, networked world, companies must learn to make optimal use of the opportunities and potential of the 21st century social revolution, because the digitization and networking process is just getting started. The following discussions will examine the effects this will have on relationships between customers and companies and on products and services. After looking at current trends and development paths, we will present the management model for the digital, networked world. We then offer a systematic classification of the relationships within the model, illustrated by examples.

Trends and Development Paths in the Digital, Networked World

This section discusses different trends and development paths that are identifiable in the digital, networked world. These include *networking, customization, real time, data utilization and analysis, service orientation and ongoing legal uncertainties.*

Networking

The Internet has become a communication medium that interactively links products, customers and companies. Individuals are networking through social media, and the boundaries between the physical and virtual world are becoming blurred. As of January 2012, Facebook had 845 million active users. If it were a country, it would be the third most populous nation on earth. The digital world allows round-the-clock networking, erasing the boundaries set by time and geography. But the uses of social media platforms like Facebook now extend far beyond the networking of individuals. Companies are using them to get closer to their customers than ever before, and business models such as on-dango.com, which integrate product sales into Facebook, have turned it into the world's largest shopping mall. Terms such as "The Internet of Things"[1] have been coined to describe the intelligent networking of physical objects with the digital world. Computers are being absorbed by objects, and products are being enhanced with artificial intelligence (Fleisch and Friedemann 2005). Companies are using this networking to integrate suppliers, partners and even customers into the product development process. Driving the intermeshing of these areas is the availability of information through mobile end devices such as smart-phones. Today, almost everyone can access the Internet no matter where they are.

Customization

In the digital world, changes are no longer shaped by hierarchies – i.e. organizations – but rather by individuals. The individual person now wields an unprecedented level of influence on the economy, society and politics (Tapscott and Williams 2006). Via social media such as Facebook, Twitter, YouTube, blogs and forums, everyone can make his or her voice heard. With this new-found confidence, customers are increasingly emboldened to demand customization of products and services. The manner of consumption is shifting from passive to active, and is turning customers themselves into producers. As a result, customers are being offered individualized products and services, and are getting involved in the design and even the development process of

---

1 This term originated with research in the Auto ID Lab at the Massachusetts Institute of Technology (MIT) (http://web.mit.edu/newsoffice/2012/auto-id-cloud-of-things-big-data.html).

products. When shopping on amazon.com, customers can check under "Recommendations for You" for ideas based on their past purchases. New car buyers can now use configuration tools on a smartphone to customize their vehicles, and athletes can design their own running shoes at miadidas. As a result, every car and running shoe can now be unique.

Real Time

The quantity of data available in real time for a vast range of uses is increasing all the time. Real time tracking of Amazon orders is now routine, for example, and the Premier Inn app lets hotel customers look for nearby hotels, carry out a real-time check for vacancies and, if desired, make a booking. Networking in the digital world also takes place in real time. For example, motilo.com provides a digital space for Facebook friends to get together for real-time shopping, put together outfits and purchase them. Real-time document processing has also arrived. Regardless of geographical separation, GoogleDocs lets two or more people share a document so that they can all work simultaneously on the same document without versioning. In the future, real-time communication between cars and their surroundings ("car-to-X communication") will prevent traffic jams through the exchange of real-time information on traffic conditions, including environmental data such as the weather or the state of the road surface.

Data Utilization and Analysis

Networking generates data that contains vital information for companies about the needs and usage habits of customers. Some of these data are deliberately created by customers, while other information is unconsciously generated by them as they surf the Internet or simply use digitally embedded products. Social media monitoring solutions such as Radian6 by salesforce.com enable companies to search social networks and blogs to learn what networked consumers are saying about them or their products. This enables them to react quickly to customer responses.

New business models now make it possible to analyze consumers' online behavior and make the results available to the advertising market (Biermann 2010). Google and other companies gain access to large quantities of customer data by using such services as GoogleMail, GoogleCalendar, GoogleDocs and Google+ to become embedded in their customers' lives. At present, Google uses the collected data mainly for targeted online advertising.

Service Orientation

Consumers are increasingly looking for all-round service packages to complement products. Such services can help to set a company apart from the competition while creating added value for the customer. The traditional manufacturer thus becomes a service provider and is forced to rethink its business model. For example, adidas no longer merely sells athletic apparel. With its miCoach app, it supports athletes by helping them to create training plans and to track their training results as preparation for competitions. In the networked homes of the future, refrigerators won't just keep food at the desired temperature; they'll send a reminder to purchase items before they run out. Heidelberg, the world's leading manufacturer of printing presses, now supplements the sales of its machines with services that improve their quality and availability. Every printing press contains more than 2,500 sensors that transmit data to the company via Internet. This allows remote scheduling or ordering of maintenance and service work, thus complementing the product itself with additional services.

Ongoing Legal Uncertainty

Another aspect of digitization and the associated spread of networking is the ongoing state of legal uncertainty. It is still very difficult to enforce the fundamental right to data protection, partly due to the lack of comprehensive solutions to protect digital privacy. Data are no longer created in closed systems, but rather in networks, and are thus available everywhere and at all times. Networking permits collaboration and remote access, which can also make it possible for unauthorized persons to invade a user's privacy. But there is more at stake than the menace of criminal attacks. There are also real concerns regarding the limits set for law enforcement agencies and secret services. An example familiar to the German public is the ongoing debate surrounding the Bundestrojaner, or "Federal Trojan" used by authorities to spy on suspects. Under the ruling by the Federal Constitutional Court, monitoring must be limited to the data from current communications. In practice, however, it has become evident that this trojan can siphon off any chosen data or software – undetected by the user. Investigators can also activate a computer's microphone and camera to monitor what is happening in the room. This could enable them to tamper with investigations in any way desired and to falsify digital evidence. Consequently, digital privacy has no clear boundaries.

Data storage locations may also vary, so that data captured by a device within a given country's boundaries could possibly be stored on servers at a number of locations around the world. As a result, the data would be subject to the prevailing laws and legal opinion in the country or countries where the servers are located. It remains an unresolved issue whether the virtual world needs laws that, instead of being based on national boundaries, take the form of separate rights within digital boundaries. A further issue is the fact that, in the social network Facebook, for instance, users surrender all control over their personal information to Facebook without receiving any commitment to protect it. It appears that the benefits to the social network itself are regarded as more important than the risks from the loss of control over a user's own data.

The Management Model in the Digital, Networked World

The world is making the transition from an industrial society to an information society. Over the past few years a digital, networked world has taken shape, encompassing the relationships between all objects in the physical and virtual worlds. Customers leave digital "fingerprints" whenever they use the Internet to search for information or complete a transaction. The "digital citizen" is not an anonymous subject in a statistical subset, but rather a representation of a real human being, described by individual data points (Negroponte, 1995). Customers and prospective customers knowingly and unknowingly generate data in open and closed systems, and this information is increasingly available in real time. It opens up new information sources for identifying customer needs. The possession of these data and the ability to use them are crucial to securing market advantages and gaining a competitive edge. But it is not only for companies that the growing volume of data opens up new opportunities for data analysis. Today's customers are confident and well-informed. They build their own networks to link the various aspects of their lives and improve their everyday existence. They increasingly expect a direct interaction with products and the company and also want the products and services they order to be tailored to their individual needs. The new networking of customers, products and companies is yielding new types of relationships that represent both an opportunity and a challenge for companies. And this challenge is no longer one to be dealt with by the marketing department – it is now a top management priority.

The management model in the digital, networked world – as described in the introduction to this book – focuses on the relationships between the three objects: The customer, the company, and products and services. Figure 1 shows how these three objects are embedded in their environment. The model illustrates how data are captured, exchanged and analyzed between these objects, and how data from their surrounding environment can flow into their relationships and become an integral part of them.

The model is based on the St.Gallen management model (Rüegg-Stürm 2003; Ulrich and Krieg 1972), which sees the company as a complex system and takes both integrated and holistic approaches to describing its management. Under the St.Gallen model, developments in the environmental spheres – jointly referred to under this model as the environment, consisting of society, nature, technology and the economy – comprise the framework for company decisions. For example, the environmental sphere of nature is concerned with climate conditions and trends and their impact on the company. The model under discussion here extends the definition of the environment to include data from the environment and the exchange of such data with customers, products and companies. Examples include current temperature data, GPS coordinates, or infrastructure data such as the locations of bank cash dispensers or traffic guidance system data. They help to optimize the utilization of products and services and, in some cases, are actually essential for making products and services possible or useful – for instance the data for measuring the mileage covered by a running shoe. Without incorporating GPS data, the sensor in the shoe would not have the same added value for the runner. As a result, the environment is no longer just a framework for corporate decision making, and instead becomes an integral part of products and services, directly interacting with the customer-product-company relationship construct. The integration of environmental data will play a vital role in the future, and will facilitate further innovations in the product and company environment.

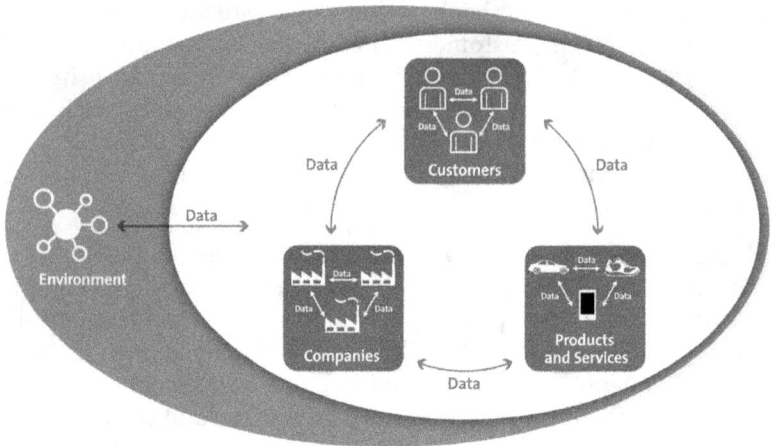

Figure 1: The management model in the digital, networked world

The relationships in the model can be placed in two categories. First, the objects of the model relate to components in their own group. For example, customers are in contact with other customers through such channels as social networks or communities. Second, the objects interact with those in the other groups, so that an exchange takes place between customers, the company and the product or service. Today this could mean a customer exchanging ideas with a company through social media while networking with various products and services via smartphone. These relationships are defined by the exchange of data, including the utilization of data from the environment.

The relationships within the triangle comprised of the customer, product/service and company have changed over time. The networking of customers, products and companies through the Internet has led to an increased volume of data generated within the relationships. This goes beyond the conventional exchange of data, for instance through the settlement of a product purchase with a company. These new data make the interaction between customers, products and companies possible and can also be used to analyze and develop new or improved services.

Large quantities of data are also generated within a company, including quality data from production operations, and cost data on production processes and support processes. Consequently, modern business intelligence systems will be used more in the future to make these data available for analysis at various levels. Today decisions can already be made in real time with the aid of these systems. Manufacturing is no longer possible without the production, analysis and exchange of data. Communication about design or manufacturing plans takes place between departments, employees and even machines. In addition, a large volume of data is generated through communications among employees. Apart from conventional communication via e-mail, there are many platforms for the exchange of information in the digital world. Employees communicate on various topics in blogs and forums. An internal Wiki gives them access to a broad internal knowledge base specific to the company. The rise of information and communication technology (ICT) is also leading to the spread of machine-to-machine communication, which can be described as a data transfer between end devices without human intervention. This includes communications either among such end devices as manufacturing machinery, vehicles and smartphones, or between such devices and a control center (Fleisch and Friedemann 2005). As a result, data can be exchanged between products and companies without any conscious interaction on the part of the customer.

These new types of relationships and the customer-related data they generate can also serve as a central information source. The Institute for Information Management at the University of St.Gallen has carried out three projects with Audi on the basis of the Design Thinking method (http://dthsg.com; Brenner and Witte 2011; Kelley 2001). The objective of the first project was to identify ways of boosting customer loyalty through the use of vehicle data. The solution, Audi IMA, addresses global traffic safety needs. The development of a preventive maintenance solution as a mobile application enables car owners to monitor the condition of their vehicle around the clock. This solution is backed by an exchange of data between the car and the manufacturer. The second project addresses two decisive obstacles that have so far limited the success of peer-to-peer carsharing concepts – trust and convenience. Under the "flemo" concept (flexible mobility), it is possible for participants to rent out their own car to a limited, invitation-only group of participants. This means that car owners can configure their very own car sharing community. The participants can then use the "FlemoBox" to unlock the door or activate the automatic payment process. The third project was launched against the backdrop of the constantly shifting mobility needs. The Seamless Mobility prototype combines a travel planning concept encompassing all modes of transport with a rewards system, under which users receive so-called Love Points, for instance for promoting the Audi brand. The points can be cashed in at a later date within the system, for example for a service upgrade on the member's vehicle.

These examples underscore the importance of data. In applications, the quality is crucial. Data are generated, among other means, through the networking and the changes in the object relationships. It is therefore becoming more important to place data in the right context and to analyze and use them intelligently. From the perspective of the company, this means that "the classical boundaries of the enterprise begin to blur, to change inwardly and outwardly, and in some areas even to dissolve" (Picot et al. 2003). This results in changes on all levels, from strategy and processes right through to the company's systems.[2] Companies must adjust their management to the needs of the new world to ensure that they are ready to make the switch from the one world to the other when the time comes.

Relationships in the Digital, Networked World

Customers in the Digital, Networked World

Information is freely available in the World Wide Web. As a result, products on offer are subject to careful scrutiny, and manufacturers now face consumers who are better informed all the time. The digital natives – defined as those born after 1980, who have consequently grown up with digital technologies such as the Internet (Prensky 2001) – are becoming more numerous. They see the physical and virtual worlds as closely linked, and take for granted a lifestyle in which they are constantly networked (Palfrey and Gasser 2008). As a result, customers chat, post, tag, tweet, poke, like and communicate in different ways and in different groups. Platforms such as forums and review portals are sometimes organized by customers themselves and in other cases are launched by companies to facilitate communication among customers. For example, the HolidayCheck rating portal allows customers to review hotels, upload holiday photos and compare travel products. Companies such as Bazaarvoice offer solutions to leverage the potential of this customer feedback. These solutions build social networks where customers can talk about the brand and thus provide authentic support in enhancing the brand value in the form of opinions and stories. The LEGO Group is just one of the companies that have created customer networks. In addition to product information provided by the company itself, the LEGO Club serves as a platform for club members to communicate about models with videos, photos and comments. This yields a wealth of data on the customers' consumption

---

2 Further discussions on the topic of business engineering can be found in Österle and Winter (2000), and are not explicitly included in the scope of this article.

habits, their preferences and their needs. But the data also provide added value for the customers themselves, who use them to form opinions and decide what products to buy. The W3b analysis by Fittkau and Maass (2009) shows more than half of users surveyed used customer reviews as an information source before making a purchase decision. Moreover, a 2009 study of 200 online shoppers conducted by E-Commerce Center Handel (ECC), a think tank and consultancy dedicated to e-commerce, showed that the inclusion of customer reviews in online stores made prospective buyers 38.7 percent more likely to make a purchase (ECC Handel 2010).

The Constumer's Relationship to the Product

Customers no longer merely consume and use everyday products and services; now they embed them with the digital world and are engaged in a constant exchange of information. For example, new technologies let customers control products from remote locations. With T-Entertain, Deutsche Telekom's web-based television service, users can use an app or web browser to set up the receiver at home in their living room to record a program. Siemens HomeControl app gives homeowners remote access to certain Siemens products and lets them adjust their home heating, air conditioning, ventilation and lighting via smartphone. With near field communication (NFC), customers who buy a Lipton beverage from a vending machine can recommend their choice to Facebook friends on the spot. For many customers, the smartphone itself serves as a "central management unit" for their everyday lives. They use their handheld device to obtain information from their surroundings such as weather forecasts, traffic updates and locations of cash dispensers, and to control other products using apps. Through the data exchange between the customer and product, the product can interact with the customer. And while the product is in use, data are collected – including customer data. Apps such as Smart Alarm are already measuring the user's sleep cycle by tracking movements detected by an iPhone placed under the pillow. With this information, the app selects the ideal wake-up time, optimally attuned to individual sleep phases. Next-generation windows are fitted with handles with special sensor technology that transmits by radio the angle at which they are opened and tilted as well as status data indicating whether they are closed and locked. With its smart floor concept, Vorwerk has introduced a carpet that uses RFID technology for the intelligent control of service robots.

Customers and Their Relationships with Companies

As illustrated by the examples of review portals and communication via social networks, the information on the purchase decision and the factors determining customer loyalty is no longer entirely under the company's control. Companies reach out to customers through various channels. However, the notion that the rise of the digital world means the end of face-to-face customer contact is a fallacy. Especially in the age of unlimited communication opportunities, it's obvious that, for building customer loyalty, personal contact is irreplaceable. Even the proprietors of a general store in bygone days understood how their business worked as a central hub of trade and communication, creating ideal conditions for building long-term customer relationships. We are seeing a surge in popularity of brick-and-mortar retail concepts. Parents have come to appreciate the Apple Store's babysitting service, and Deutsche Bank has realized that the latest tablet devices make it easier to talk with young customers at bank branches. Of course this is not to say that companies can ignore the events and customer loyalty possibilities of new media, which enable them to reach customers anywhere and anytime. For bank customers, this means that, in addition to having service available at the branch, they expect access via Internet and telephone. Companies therefore have to serve several channels at once, with each complementing the others. In the world of new media, a company with no online presence can in fact be deemed non-existent. Having a Facebook page, Twitter account or blog is now commonplace for companies, and is no longer a distinguishing feature.

New sales channels, enabled by new technologies, now complement conventional online shopping, which today accounts for a substantial share of consumer spending. They combine bricks-and-mortar retail concepts with e-commerce. One example is the Homeplus Virtual Store concept by Tesco, as seen in subway stations in South Korea. Posters on the station walls show life-sized pictures of supermarket shelves. Shoppers use a smartphone app to scan the bar codes. This places the desired goods in a virtual shopping basket. After the transaction is completed, the selected items are packed and dispatched, and the customer receives them soon after arriving home. The subway station thus becomes a supermarket, and busy commuters can use their travel time to get their grocery shopping done.[3] Another example: Users of the Xbox game console can now contact the support team directly via Twitter. The answer to the problem comes back via Twitter as well, and is accessible to other users. And this is not an isolated case: Other companies, such as Samsung, have also set up Twitter-based customer support.

---

3   Video clip showing the Homeplus Subway Virtual Store concept: www.youtube.com/watch?v=nJVoYsBym88

In addition, companies are actively involving their customers in the development or expansion of their services. More and more customers are playing a role in the innovation processes of companies and contributing their wishes and ideas right from the start (Gassmann, Enkel and Chesbrough 2010). Websites such as myStarbucks Ideas and Dell Ideastorm let customers post their suggestions for product innovations and improvements. The community votes on the user input and decides which ideas will be pursued further and developed. In this way, companies gain access to a much broader knowledge base than they could ever exploit within their own walls – and they learn first-hand about their customers' needs. At the same time, customers can satisfy their increased desire for customization and their wish to have a say in the design process. Today's companies not only have customers, but also followers who become genuine fans on social media platforms.

Data from the outside environment are also gathered, for example when a customer walks into a real branch office and "checks in" on Facebook, thus sharing a preference with other users. Some companies, such as Starbucks, use location tracking to combine the online check-in in stores with coupon campaigns for free beverages. This enhances the brand's social media profile. Other companies – Apple, for instance – build closed systems around their products (iPhone, iPad, MacBook, etc.) in the digital world to raise barriers to entry, keeping competitors out.

But it is not only the data consciously produced by customers at locations determined by the company that make a difference. For example, the logistics company FedEx runs special software to monitor social media. One of its uses is as an indirect means of identifying customer complaints, to which FedEx can then respond. The examples above, such as Radian6, and Predictive Behavioral Targeting show how unstructured data can be structured and put to good use.

Products as an Integral Part of Digitization and Networking

Products can also be networked with other products. This generates added value for customers through the exchange of data. For example, the networking of the iPhone with the owner's car makes it possible to listen to a playlist while driving or access iPhone contacts for navigation purposes. The Samsung Smart TV uses apps to turn a television into an interactive monitor. In addition, social media networks can be accessed through the television, and various devices, including audio equipment, are linked to it. With the Miele@home system solution, Miele household appliances – which are equipped with appropriate communication modules – constantly exchange information such as energy consumption data. In the automotive world, car-to-X communication is opening up the possibility of car-to-car and car-to-surroundings communication. In the future, vehicles will send each other warnings of traffic jams ahead, and driver assistance systems will get steadily better at communicating with the outside world. Today we already have cars that recognize road signs and alert the driver if he or she is exceeding the speed limit. Similarly, cars can use lane markings to detect when the vehicle is in danger of veering off the road. Data communication can thus make a very real difference in helping to avoid accidents and even save lives.

The Relationship between Products and Companies

Companies and products exchange data. For example, updates can be installed automatically, and error reports about the product can be transmitted directly to the company. When a Microsoft program crashes, error analysis is carried out online, providing information to improve the product. Products generate data while in use that can be analyzed to show how customers are actually using them. For instance, Nike collects information generated by its Nike+ series of products that is matched with the data provided when the customer registers the product. Apple is in constant contact with Apple devices and retrieves such information as the physical location. It is not always transparent which data a company can retrieve and for what purpose. The possibilities are boundless. Even usage-related data such as driving style or the mileage covered may help insurance companies to offer individual, consumption-related insurance models geared to driving habits. As the insurance company is not the manufacturer, other devices or interfaces to the car are needed to collect this information.

Companies in the Digital, Networked World

Innovations often come about in cooperation with other companies, supported by networking technologies ranging from communication platforms to the networking of production processes across company boundaries. Just as they do when companies exchange ideas with customers, communication platforms in open and closed systems help to develop ideas and improvements and also to foster innovations. SAP uses the SAP Community Network (SCN) to interact not only with customers, but also with partners, employees and experts. Digitization has also transformed the cooperation among companies along the value chain. Logistics firms have become more important with the increase in online shopping. Companies are networking with their customers both in B2B dealings and in the retail segment. The BASF WorldAccount platform gives customers of the chemical industry giant access to the world of BASF. Siemens and other companies use information technology to connect to partners in the production process. This has primarily resulted in a broadening of the perspective of companies. Instead of limiting their viewpoint to their own value chain, their scope now embraces the needs of the end customers with the aim of offering them better primary products in the future. For example, ThyssenKrupp involves end customers in the innovation process. Moreover, many data points can be found along the value chain. In the future, these data will be available for use even by companies not involved in manufacturing a product.

The Significance of Data and Their Analytical Potential

The year 2010 marked the first time that the total volume of data produced and replicated within a single year broke the zettabyte barrier (1 zettabyte equals 1,000,000,000,000,000,000,000 gigabytes). In 2011, this amount increased to 1.8 zettabytes (Enriquez 2011). A basic distinction is made between structured and unstructured data. The former have an identical structure, as in the case of records in a database. By contrast, unstructured data, such as texts, image files, audio or video files, lack any unified structure. It is especially in the area of unstructured data that the quantity is growing relentlessly, above all in the form of audio and video files. Every minute, 48 hours of new video material is uploaded to YouTube (Bonset 2011).

However, the quantity of data created by individuals by uploading documents, photos, music and video is dwarfed by the amount of information captured about these people in the digital universe. Every user has a so-called "digital shadow" (Gantz and Reinsel 2011), mostly stored in an unstructured form. Companies are also faced with a flood of data in what is known as the "big data" phenomenon. But new tools for capturing, searching and analyzing these data make it possible to structure them, and thus to generate added value for companies.

Data are also collected in product configuration tools and sales support systems (Stadler et al. 2012). These systems generate data about customers' perceptions of products, their preferences for individual items or the ones they actually choose. In the past, this information was unavailable, or could be obtained only through enormous market research efforts.

The real value of these systems lies in the fact that they provide information on customer behavior. From records of where customers click in product configurators or what terms they search for on the Internet, all of these data reflect genuine information needs and buying decisions by customers. As a result, they comprise a record of real behavior, as opposed to mere opinions and attitudes, which are usually tainted by social and political factors.

A key limitation of conventional market research is that, as a rule, consumers can be asked only about their likely future behavior. The resulting information is vague, because for many buyers, their real behavior is only determined when they face the concrete purchase or consumption situation. Another drawback is that market researchers are often interested in capturing customers' emotional responses, which are generally prefiltered. In addition, people rarely reveal their true motivations, and instead give reasons that they believe are socially or politically acceptable. Consequently, these systems permit direct access to real behavior, which solves many problems of classical market research.

A further advantage: Collecting these data costs nothing. In many cases, these behavioral data are stored in the systems of manufacturers or dealers, and only await analysis. This means a significant reduction in data capture expenses. The data can also be obtained much more quickly than before. It makes real-time market research a reality, resulting in new opportunities for the testing of products and services. Moreover, it is possible to capture process data. For example, analysis can reconstruct users' click sequences in a product configurator, and special software tools can capture mouse movements. This information – known as click stream analysis – delivers valuable insights into customers' reflections and thought processes about the various offerings of the manufacturer or dealer. The mouse cursor often moves to the options a customer is considering. Consequently, the path taken by the pointer across the screen can ultimately be seen as a record of the customer's reasoning.

Studies show that process data can help to arrive at a deeper understanding of customer decisions. Process data provide insights into how customers interact with products and services. As a result, they shed light on all processes arising between a customer's consideration of a product and the final decision to choose that product or an alternative. The new information systems in particular generate valuable information that will yield substantial benefits for market research in the future.

It is still uncertain how the utilization of these data and the possibilities for influencing decisions will affect individual behavior. There is widespread debate about whether personalized search queries, for example, will result in algorithms being handed control of user decisions. Even now, a complete profile of an individual's living situation can be determined by just 20 data points. Information on shopping habits, travel destinations, communication channels and other details is already available on networks. This makes it possible to predict future behavior and influence decisions. Because of customers' increasing reliance on recommendations, they run the risk of turning over the entire decision making process to an algorithm (Meckel 2011).

Summary and Outlook

The transition from an industrial to an information society poses new challenges for companies that will force them to rethink their business models. As the boundaries of a company's own organization become blurred, changes must be made to its management approach along with adjustments to strategies, processes and systems. The world is becoming a networked place, and the physical and virtual worlds are merging into a digital world. This networking embraces not only individuals and companies, but also products and services. This interconnectivity in the digital world creates added value for the customer. One day, for example, Internet services will be a standard feature of cars.

Within the digital world, it is becoming much more common for data – both structured and unstructured – to be generated at multiple locations. Apart from data actively provided by customers, for example in online profiles, each customer leaves a "digital fingerprint" in the network through their purchases or the opinions they express. In addition, data on customers' lifestyles and habits are generated through the use of products and services integrated into the digital world. The ownership of such data and the ability to utilize them may become a decisive competitive advantage for a company. Data are increasingly being generated in real time, and information technology is overcoming the limitations of geography and time. The mobility made possible by technology and the resulting availability of information through various devices allows everyone to carry the Internet everywhere "in their pocket."

Now, more than ever before, the focus is on the customer. Customers no longer see themselves as mere consumers. Today they want to have a say in the planning and design of products and services. Through social media networks, they can make their voices heard and play a

formative role in shaping business. They network with other customers, products and services as well as companies. By reviewing products,
they influence the decisions of other customers through social networks. Online shopping no longer has to be a solitary endeavor, as platforms now let users engage in real-time shopping with others through
links to social media networks. Customer contact can take the form of
face-to-face encounters in stores or online in chat mode. It is essential
for companies to provide both options. New sales channels are transforming subway stations into supermarkets, where shoppers use their
smartphones to scan barcodes on posters showing pictures of food
items.

Products interact with customers and other products and generate
value through the exchange of data. For example, users can set up
their favorite smartphone apps on their receivers at home. The car is
no longer just a mode of transport. It also functions as a navigator
through the digital world. Moreover, new information technologies
will make driving safer than ever before. Communication between vehicles and their surroundings and car-to-car communication will fundamentally transform the driving experience. Companies will engage
in a dialog with their customers about products and services via social
media, and thus stay closely attuned to customer needs. But we will
also see new possibilities for company-to-company communication as
well. Innovation is no longer a process carried on quietly within a company organization. Instead it is carried out jointly with partners and
customers. It may thus be necessary for relationships or aspects of relationships that are neglected today to undergo reappraisal and further
development.

Bibliography

Biermann, Kai. "Browser enttarnen ihre Nutzer."
www.zeit.de/digital/datenschutz/2010-01/browser-fingerabdruck-eff. January 30, 2010.

Brenner, Walter, and Christoph Witte. Business Innovation – CIOs im Wettbewerb der Ideen.
Frankfurt am Main: Frankfurter Allgemeine Buch, 2011.

Bonset, Sébastien. "YouTube Statistik: Jede Minute kommen 48 Stunden Video hinzu."
http://t3n.de/news/youtube-statistik-minute-kommen-48-stunden-video-hin- zu-343031.
November 15, 2011.

ECC Handel, editorial team. "Positive Kundenbewertungen in Online-Shops erhöhen die
Kaufwahrscheinlichkeit deutlich."
http://www.ecckoeln.de/News/Positive-Kundenbewertungen-in-Online-Shops-
erh%C3%B6hen-die-Kaufwahr.
January 19, 2010.

Enriquez, Juan. "The Glory of Big Data."
http://www.popsci.com/technology/article/2011-10/glory-big-data.

FIFA.com, Blatter editorial team. "Die Zeit für Technologie ist gekommen."
http://de.fifa.com/aboutfifa/organisation/marketing/qualityprogramme/news/
new-sid=1660734/index.html. July 5, 2012.

Fittkau & Maas Consulting GmbH. "Nutzermeinungen im Internet beeinflussen Kaufver-
halten erheblich." http://www.w3b.org/e-commerce/nutzermeinungen-im- internet-
beeinflussen-kaufverhalten-erheblich.html. December 8, 2009.

Fleisch, Elgar, and Friedemann Mattern (editor). Das Internet der Dinge. Berlin, Heidelberg,
New York: Springer-Verlag, 2005.

Gantz, John, and David Reinsel. "The Digital Universe Study: Extracting Value from Chaos."
IDC, 2011.

Gassmann, Oliver, Ellen Enkel, and Henry Chesbrough. "The Future of Open Innovation."
R&D Management (2010), Vol 40. Nr. 3: 213-221.

Kelley, Tom. The Art of Innovation: Lessons in Creativity from IDEO, America's Leading
Design Firm. Innovation Edition. New York: Crown Business Publishing, 2001.

Meckel, Miriam. NEXT: Erinnerungen an eine Zukunft ohne uns. Reinbek: Rowohlt Verlag,
2011.

Negroponte, Nicolas. Being Digital. New York: Vintage Books, 1996.

Österle, Hubert, and Robert Winter (editor). Business Engineering – Auf dem Weg zum
Unternehmen des Informationszeitalters, second printing. Berlin, Heidelberg, New York:
Springer-Verlag, 2003.

Palfrey, John, and Urs Gasser. Born Digital. Understanding the First Generation of Digital
Natives. New York: Basic Books, 2008.

Picot, Arnold, Ralf Reichwald, and Rolf T. Wigand. Die grenzenlose Unternehmung: Information, Organisation und Management. Fifth printing. Wiesbaden: Gabler, 2003.

Prensky, Marc. "Digital Natives, Digital Immigrants." On the Horizon (2001), Vol. 9. No. 5: 1-6.

Rüegg-Sturm, Johannes. Das neue St.Galler Management-Modell. Grundkategorien einer
integrierten Managementlehre. Der HSG-Ansatz. Second printing. Bern: Haupt Verlag,
2003.

Stadler, Rupert, Dieter Kopitzki, Andreas Herrmann, Lucas Beck, and Reto Hofstetter.
"Defaults als Navigationshilfen in Produktkonfiguratoren – ein Beispiel aus der Automobilindustrie." Marketing Review St.Gallen, Vol. 29. No. 2: 42-46, 2012.

Tapscott, Don, and Anthony D. Williams. Wikonomics: die Revolution im Netz. Munich: Carl
Hanser Verlag, 2007.

Ulrich, Hans, and Walter Krieg. Das St. Galler Managementmodell. Bern: Haupt Verlag, 1972.

The Research Chairs

The Professor Walter Brenner Research Chair

The Institute for Information Management is a part of the University of St.Gallen. It is dedicated to the study of the interface between companies and information technology. The research chair of Professor Walter Brenner studies the fields of information management and innovation. The core issues of information management relate to those responsible for IT as well as aspects of corporate management and the use of information and communication technology. Among the key methodologies in innovation research is the Design Thinking method. It is based on a customer-centric approach and the construction of prototypes. Many projects go far beyond the limits of classical information management and result in innovative products and services.

For more information: http://www.iwi.unisg.ch

The Professor Andreas Herrmann Research Chair

The Customer Insight Research Center is part of the University of St.Gallen, and has four research chairs dedicated to purchasing, consumption and decision-making behavior of customers. Among the topics studied at the Prof. Andreas Herrmann Research Chair are customer perceptions of product design, the facets that influence customer expectations of product utility, and the emotional responses triggered by design elements. Other projects seek to understand customers' decision-making behavior in mass-customization systems. As more and more products are configured online, it becomes necessary for the product experience to be communicated, in a sense, in the virtual world. Moreover, customers must make numerous decisions on various product features, which poses entirely new challenges for the communication of product information.

For more information: http://www.fci.unisg.ch

The Author

Prof. Dr. Miriam Meckel was born in 1967 and studied media and communication sciences, sinology, political science and law at the University of Münster (Germany) and the University of Taipei (Taiwan). Following her studies, she worked as an on-air presenter, reporter and editor for news and news magazines at both public and private German broadcasters (ARD, VOX and RTL). In 1999, she joined the faculty at the University of Münster as a professor of communication sciences. In 2001, Meckel was appointed as the state secretary serving the office of the premier of the German state of North Rhine-Westphalia, initially as a government spokesperson, and subsequently as the state secretary for Europe, international affairs and media. Since 2005, she has served as a professor of corporate communications and as the director of the Institute for Media and Communications Management at the University of St.Gallen, Switzerland, and as a faculty associate at the Berkman Center for Internet & Society at Harvard University in the USA.

Serendipity as an Innovation Strategy

Miriam Meckel, University of St.Gallen

"It's the customer, stupid!" This twist on the catchy slogan from former U.S. President, Bill Clinton, perfectly captures the change in direction taken by companies in recent years. The customer has become the central focal point for corporations, and ever more integrated into a company's strategy. Meeting the customer's expectations has now become both a strategic challenge and an operational requirement. The Internet and especially social networks have made it possible for us to collect and evaluate information on these expectations at ever-increasing levels of detail. But is this a process that can continue endlessly, or would customers be better off if companies were to surprise and inspire them? "It's serendipity, stupid!" could be the new battle cry for the algorithmically powered, social Internet of "Big Data" analysis. Surprises would actually be a customer benefit. Let's take a closer look at what has happened in customer relations, the role played by the Internet and how companies use it – and must constantly redefine the way they use it – to stay attuned to changing times and to their customers.

Customer Relations 2.0: Listening to and Understanding the Customer

Four factors play an important role in effective, customer-oriented relations:

1. *The conditions for communication* are becoming more flexible in terms of transparency, participation and decentralization. Modular processes are replacing rigid structures and systems and creating new standards of communication. Users are, in part, taking control over these communication processes and are in turn even changing the identity of the company.

2. *The inputs* are, increasingly, becoming part of all corporate processes in the form of user-generated content. Information is embedded in a network of social connections that determines its value and significance.

3. *The mechanisms* are, to a large extent, technology driven and based on the collaboration and cooperation among an unlimited number of participants in the Internet. And they are continuously being expanded by new technological innovations (for example, open innovation, augmented reality, 3-D printing, etc.). In these collaborative processes, information – and someday, material components, too – can be arbitrarily recombined, and also vetted and cataloged by an often large number of users.

4. *The emergent results* come about through the interplay of users. It is also the users that determine the usefulness and relevance of these results depending on the needs of the moment.

Web 3.0

The customer calls the shots and can be involved in (almost) everything. That was the secret behind Web 2.0. For the Web 3.0 generation, we may have to take this idea further.

So far, nobody has come up with a truly clear and unifying definition of Web 3.0. But we can interpret it as a third evolutionary stage of the World Wide Web; it's a stage in which the technology actually "understands" the information (the semantic web) and is capable of creating logical connections – just like human beings. Another feature of Web 3.0 will be the ability to deliver exactly what customers like, want and need automatically, becoming a personalized Web through the analysis of their generational data, search and behavioral history (Colomo-Palacios, Varajão, Soto-Acosta 2012). And ultimately, our lives will become increasingly defined by technology and networked: Communication won't just be with our smartphones, but also with our home's heating and security systems. Or with our cars. We'll be able to ask our mislaid glasses "Where are you?" and they will transmit a reply, indicating their location (ubiquitous computing, the Internet of things).

What this Transition in the Web and Digital Technology Means for Customer Relations

Peer2Peer and Crowdsourcing: the Economy of Collaboration

The new forms of communication via the Internet are also bringing changes to our networked society and all of its subsystems: business, politics and culture. The emergence of a networked society will change our access to information, knowledge structures and the courses of action open to us. Linear structures will give way to reflexive ones and hierarchies will be replaced by networks. Which means that networking will represent far more than just technological links between countless computers across the globe. Instead, it refers to a different form of procedural self-organization. Communication in networks displays a higher degree of complexity than in hierarchies. Connections and combinations thereof will become more numerous and multifaceted. In short, especially for the networked society, all processes are becoming more complex and more contingent on one another.

Manuel Castells (2001) postulated that a network's performance is dependent upon two traits: on the one hand, its connection status – the ability to establish and maintain an error-free connection between its individual components – and, on the other hand, its consistency, or the extent to which the goals of the network and each component are aligned. "Business firms and, increasingly, organizations and institutions are organized in networks of variable geometry whose intertwining supersedes the traditional distinction between corporations and small business, cutting across sectors, and spreading along different geographical clusters of economic units" (Castells 2001, 502). In this sense, not only our economic system is changing, but also our entire society. The driving force behind this change is the development of technology that makes this networking possible.

The coordination mechanisms embedded in the networking process are not limited to communication conditions. They also characterize the changing set of circumstances facing markets and companies in the networked society. Up until now, we have made a basic distinction between two organizational modes: the company and the market. Both work together, albeit despite employing differing coordination approaches. Companies coordinate resources (for example, employees and capital), generally, in hierarchical structures under the leadership of the management. Markets coordinate supply and demand through the price.

Web 2.0 introduced a new type of coordination mechanism: Communities coordinate the production of information and communication-based goods in a self-organizing and emergent process via crowdsourcing (Howe 2006). These goods are user-based and organized according to an open-source principle. Yochay Benkler (2006) described this networked economy as "the rise of non-market production to much greater importance," in which "every...effort is available to anyone connected to the network, from anywhere, [which] has led to the emergence of coordinate effects, where the aggregate effect of individual action… produces the coordinate effect of a new and rich information environment" (page 4 f.).

Consequently, the more recent developments in the networked society extend far beyond the issue of participation in markets based solely on technical access. There is also an emphasis on participation in the actual creation process of these information and communication goods in a "culture of participation" (Schonfeld, 2005).

The network philosopher, David Weinberger (2002) introduced an important aspect into this discussion – one that presents a particular difficulty for companies. As the centralized control of content management disappears, a more loosely joined collection of content and connections (links and network nodes) is emerging, and on a scale that is so far unprecedented. In this Web, there are countless numbers of individual documents ("small pieces loosely joined") that can be joined and configured in arbitrary ways. And what the Web initially did with content, it is now doing with our institutions and structures – and with us, too: "We are the true 'small pieces' of the Web, and we are loosely joining ourselves in ways that we're still inventing" (page X.).

For companies, these developments are a direct challenge to established parameters such as hierarchies, functional areas of job responsibility, top-down processes and a company's organizational coherence. And the customer's role is also becoming ever more flexible: He or she is still the buyer, but may also sometimes act as a producer, service provider or innovator.

This is also evident in the fact that the economy of peer production is characterized by three parameters that all signal an obvious link to customer orientation and the integration of customers into important company processes (Meckel 2008):

1. *Participation:* Everyone can participate in all communication processes – independently of hierarchies or institutional affiliations. For many of the movers and shakers and also users of the Web, this represents the democratization of the world of information as well as goods and services on offer.

2. *Emergent networking:* With each contribution, every participant changes the content and the quality of the whole, based on the concept, "My productivity increases when you're in my network, and yours increases when I'm in yours."

3. *Transparency:* All processes behind the production and deployment of information and opinions in the network are absolutely trans-

parent and, therefore, open to scrutiny. Every contribution can be discussed, reviewed in detail, confirmed or challenged.

This network-driven transformation brings with it a great deal of potential for innovation. But it also harbors problems. It is above all the following trends that pose a challenge to companies and institutions and which are forcing companies to adapt their corporate strategies and implementation tools:

1. *Acceleration:* Viral communication (Langner 2005) allows for the accelerated dissemination of information in networks. This makes it possible to give millions of people access to important information, such as an advertisement for a product launch, to name just one of many examples, in just seconds through social networking platforms (such as YouTube, Facebook and others). Apple has consistently taken advantage of these possibilities to produce effective viral communication campaigns for the launch of each new product (Maisch and Meckel 2009). But companies can't limit themselves to using these accelerated processes for their own marketing purposes; they have to be just as quick in reacting to the demands of the market. One example: When ice cream producer, Langnese, decided to discontinue the "Nogger Choc" ice cream bar in 2001, a grassroots online campaign by fans of that popular treat soon pressured the company into reversing its decision (http://www.rp-online.de/digitales/internet/nogger-choc-ist-surueck.1.2186774).

2. *Disorder and Restructuring:* As was already the case in Web 2.0 – again with reference to the ideas of Internet philosopher David Weinberger (2007) – every piece of information and every bit of digital flotsam initially belongs under the heading "miscellaneous." For people accustomed to the two-dimensional "tidiness" of the analog world, this system at first results in utter chaos that needs to be restructured. In the digital world, every piece of information and every digital product can undergo changes in their categorization and their importance to a given user or customer every second. In effect, the network offers up chaos that needs to be constantly reconfigured into new categories and systems, but always remain contingent. Only users who can understand and shape these fluctuations will be able to derive innovative potential and competitive advantages from them.

3. *Information as a collective and collaborative commodity:* The business world has, up until now, treated information as an asset to utilize but also to protect – and possibly to hide from the view of unauthorized users outside of a company. By contrast, in Web-based peer production, the approach to information is increasingly based on the

open-source principle. A company needs to view its wealth of information (excepting, perhaps, things like patents) as a dynamic, emergent commodity that becomes more useful and productive the more it is made available and the more people can access it. Creativity and innovation have a greater tendency to occur in a setting where information can be connected with other information (for example, through mash ups and tagging), so that something entirely new and unknown can be created. "Smart businesses will allow their customers to organize and comment on their data," says David Weinberger (Heuer 2007, 88). In view of the traditional concepts of property rights and copyrights, this paradigm shift in the handling of information will certainly be one of the biggest challenges to the way companies do business.

All of these three development trends are posing new challenges for companies. Social networking in the broader sense is changing the role and meaning of information as the driver of key corporate functions: from research and development and from production through to the value chains and across entire business models. "Peer production in some cases threatens to decimate the information advantage of companies and markets" (Schonfeld 2005). But above all, it threatens the established order for the interpretation of corporate information. Later, we will look at areas where companies might be able to take on leadership functions again.

Big Data: All the Things We Know About Our Customers

In connection with the new rules of the game, from peer production to crowdsourcing, a new opportunity is taking shape. It is hidden in the term "big data," and places the concept of customer orientation on an unprecedented foundation of quantitative/empirical analysis possibilities. Here, too, the definition of the term is in flux, but we can basically state that "big data refers to datasets whose size is beyond the ability of typical database software tools to capture, store, manage and analyze." (McKinsey Global Institute 2001, 1). The data sets being analyzed are characterized through four "V's":

Volume (The amount of data),

Variety (Data typology based on raw data from structured and unstructured data sources through to social media analytics),

Velocity (The speed at which new data is generated and the accompanying analysis processes), and finally....

Value (How can data be used to generate true added value for one's own company, processes, services and products?) (Zikopoulos et al. 2012).

Big data is an overarching concept representing a new approach to dealing with data, and has so far been utilized in an increasingly effective manner by IT and Internet companies such as Amazon, Facebook and Google. It involves the analysis of millions of individual bits of data generated in the Internet through users' online communication, information searches and general behavior. This makes it possible to identify the defining structures of the preferences and behaviors of even the smallest communities and target groups.

Big data offers companies a wide spectrum of possibilities for implementing its data analysis capabilities in their business strategies. The result: the ability to focus more effectively on customer needs. According to initial explorations by the McKinsey Global Institute (2011), there are five main aspects:

1. Data must be made universally available throughout the entire company to make it accessible across the various corporate functions. This means processing it in a standardized format and storing it on appropriate platforms;

2. Companies must experiment with different analysis options under the conditions of big data to identify the best areas of application and use them in the company's interest;

3. Big data allows for a more detailed segmentation of customer and stakeholder groups, so that even the smallest interest groups – and their wants and needs – can be effectively analyzed and addressed;

4. Companies will need to become more familiar with the use of automated, algorithm-based analysis processes; this will, in turn, allow for a transfer of decision-making processes from humans to machines, i.e. software, in various spheres of activity (from risk management to pricing and sales, from marketing to data-driven automated recommendation systems);

5. Companies will need to incorporate the big data concept in the development of new products, services and even business models. The knowledge that can be gained from large-scale data analysis (customer, user, response and location-based data) will generate signals pointing to new possibilities and the strategic challenges of a necessary adaptation or change.

This development will unfold at different rates of speed in different industries. And while companies in the IT, information and technology sectors are already well versed in the use of big data, there will certainly be a time lag before companies in branches such as real estate, construction or wholesale retail utilize the potential of this technology. But ultimately, the key is to realizing that when big data becomes a part of routine business operations, intuition and other more or less irrational methods for making management decisions may be doomed to extinction as corporate leadership tools. It is no longer acceptable to use intuition or inadequate data resources to determine precisely measurable criteria for business success.

Two important aspects need to be taken into consideration at every step of the way in the implementation of big-data strategies: both of which could have far-reaching, long-term consequences, possibly culminating, for example, in the end of the top-down innovation process:

1. Brought to its logical conclusion, comprehensive analysis with forecasting capacity will gradually shrink the discretionary aspects of management decision-making. At some point in the distant future, it is conceivable that a CEO would do little more than rubber-stamp the data analysis by implementing whatever is unearthed through the analysis of complex data using algorithms.

2. Customer resistance to these changes is to be expected – especially from consumers who aren't ready or willing to relinquish all of their personal data and thus become fully transparent to companies – or who are only willing to do so under the terms of clearly spelled-out privacy policies. Data protection is a topic that will continue to dog the development of big data.

Digital Manufacturing: The Third Industrial Revolution

Until now, we have generally assumed that the rules of peer production and crowdsourcing – as well as the analytical capacity of big data – applied only to information products and elements. So: The customer communicates his or her preferences and interests, or a company analyzes these preference and interests using big data. But the actual implementation in the form of material goods has remained the output of an often complicated industrial infrastructure within the company.

This is made possible by technological advances in the digitization of industrial production combined with nanotechnology and more flexible materials. For years, highly complex and specialized products and their components – for example, hearing aids, dental implants, aircraft or car parts – have been produced using three-dimensional printing technology (3-D printers). It is indeed possible to use a 3-D printer to produce just about anything that can be made with advanced fibers (carbon fibers, for example) and modeled by software (Business Week, January 9, 2012). And while this technology generated only relatively modest global revenues of $1.4 billion in 2011 and is currently used mainly for the production of prototypes, the potential of what is being called the "third industrial revolution" (Economist, April 21, 2012) is much bigger.

One obvious plus of this technology is the real cost advantage it would provide at the production level (of material goods) – even with specialty items produced in relatively small quantities – an example of Chris Anderson's long tail theory (Anderson 2006). But at second glance, the process reveals other exciting possibilities closely related to the new economy based on collaboration and data analysis. For example: If the production process is increasingly taking place at the customer's location in the form of 3-D printing, this will completely alter the economic significance and meaning of salaries and wages; it will even change the answer to the question of outsourcing entire production runs. It will then be immaterial whether a product is produced in Ingolstadt, Shanghai or Dhaka. And many repetitive and redundant production steps will be rendered obsolete – or will be performed by individuals on computers and implemented on 3-D printers. Decisions on new product designs will be made on the basis of a company's market advantage, taking into account customer needs in an ongoing interaction with the customer and in accordance with the new viral production processes. However, these developments will mean that producers of physical products will also have to deal with the copyright issues that have so far mainly been a concern in the digital economy.

When discussing innovation strategy, one topic is especially exciting: Theoretically speaking, there will be a shift in the business models of many individual companies and even entire branches away from the production of single products or product lines to the development and marketing of specialized designs. One example: Let's imagine that the 3-D printer of the future is a portable device, or one that is available for use everywhere. Wherever our travels take us, we won't have to worry about what to pack. Once I've arrived at my hotel and settled into my room, I can do a bit of online shopping to decide which tie or scarf and shoes I want to wear for the evening event, and then print them out after selecting and downloading the designs.

In this future scenario, the customer will become an employee on a completely different scale. Ultimately, under these conditions, the bulk of the processes will be in the customer's hands (including parts of the supply chain previously kept under the strict control of the company). The customer will play an active role in product design and may even decide whether a new product makes it to the market – a decision which might, of course, be too much for some consumers. In the course of collaborative decision making, the customer can develop an idea for a new product and quickly turn it into a prototype. In the words of Grant Rochelle, Senior Director Manufacturing Industry Marketing with Autodesk, the 3-D design firm, "The factory of the future could be me, sitting in my home office" (Economist, April 4, 2012).

Serendipity as an Innovation Strategy

Trapped in a Rut: The Problem of Overcustomization

These are all exciting developments that get entrepreneurial thinkers all fired up when they succeed in breaking up conventional structures, mindsets and routines. And this brings us to an issue that must be re-examined under the conditions we have described to define new contexts for customer orientation.

In retrospect, it verges on amazing to consider that companies have been coming to grips with the challenges of customer-relationship management or a special form of one-to-one marketing for more than a decade. The four-step process presented as the path to success – first identify the customer; then differentiate between customer segments; then interact with the customer; and, finally, adapt your corporate strategy accordingly (Peppers, Rogers and Dorf 1999) – always focused on improving opportunities for customers to provide effective feedback to companies about their wishes, needs and interests. They would in turn receive communications and offers tailored to their needs. The new technological developments we're seeing today will make this even easier. Because in the meantime, customers can do (almost) everything themselves: It's customer integration at its best.

After a decade of honing and perfecting this strategy, we're now faced with a problem caused by the technology being perfected: overcustomization. Although this issue has so far only been seen as a side issue by companies in terms of costs – for example, in the area of enterprise resource planning – it could also become a problem for the customer, too.

With the collaborative integration of customers into more and more company processes, the all-encompassing analysis of their likes, dislikes and behaviors using big data, and the customization of product offers, customers are seeing more of their wants and needs being taken into consideration. When the resulting customized designs are delivered as templates by the company to the customers, they will be able to complete the physical production themselves. As a result, in the long term, one very important parameter for the innovation process and for lasting customer satisfaction will be dropped from the equation: serendipity.

In a world where companies can be right on target in calculating, forecasting and catering to individual product utilization patterns, preferences, and the full range of predictive data about decisions and courses of action, the world of chance discoveries will have no air to breathe. Serendipity will simply be dropped from the equation. And for companies, this harbors a danger that can be summed up by "success breeding failure;" from a more specialized viewpoint, this describes how the unguided innovation processes that go beyond familiar tastes, desires and familiar solutions will simply grind to a halt.

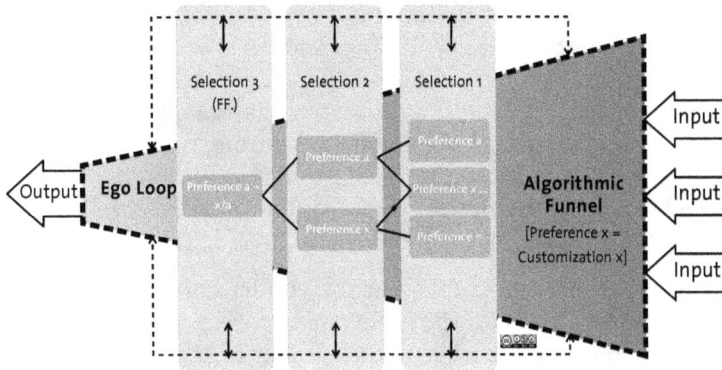

Figure 1: The mechanism of over-customization as illustrated using an "Algorithmic Funnel"

For customers, the problem lies elsewhere: falling into the comfort-zone trap of getting too cozy with service and product offers tailored exactly to your individual set of preferences, and feeling completely satisfied with what the company is providing. With the personalized Internet, we've already witnessed how extensive data mining for this purpose has resulted in a process that narrows down our options online. Increasingly, search engines and Internet providers only show us what they think we want to see and filter out information and offers they believe are of no interest to us (Pariser 2011).

With the customer-relationship management being driven by overcustomization, customers increasingly end up living in their own little world of perfectly analyzed preferences. And the feedback mechanism underlying the algorithmic analysis funnel based on big data customization will result in a sort of "global short-sightedness" on the part of the customer, with the possibilities being prescreened to exclude any options outside his or her pattern of likes and needs (Meckel 2011). At some point, we end up with monotony in a world perfectly tailored to the customer's wants: success breeds boredom.

Serendipity: The Complementary Innovative Power of the Unexpected

The antidote to this state of affairs is serendipity – unplanned discovery through happenstance (Merton and Barber 2004). It can be a decisive factor not only for innovation; it may also prove vital in establishing new customer behavior patterns and creating new products. It's how a failed experiment to develop a new kind of glue resulted in a product success story: the Post-It Note. And it's how a brand new way of brewing tea was invented: Thomas Sullivan, a New York tea merchant at the start of the 20th century, in search of a cheaper way to ship tea than in the tin containers prevalent at the time, tried little silk bags. When the tea was delivered to the customers, they poured hot water over the bags, thinking the design was intentional. And voilà! The tea-bag was born (see Gassmann and Friesike 2012, 91 ff.).

These examples may be simple, but they underscore the potential importance of serendipity for the innovation process. A problem that has – at least to some extent – been on the radar of academic researchers for quite some time (Deschamps 1995; Holbrook 2003; Snowden 2003), is now, owing to the mechanisms triggered by technological innovations, a major new challenge. Especially when we're dealing with complex, adaptable systems, coincidences or the element of surprise can become very important. Although we cannot adequately address this issue here, it is reasonable to ask how the predictability of decisions and behavior will coexist in the long term with the more recent results in various disciplines that show that highly networked and complex systems produce results that are neither linear nor predictable (Holbrook 2003).

If we see this as an inherent contradiction, the trends we have described could then take effect only in subsystems and organizations with a low level of complexity. Or they could emerge from a complex, networked system only as a more simple construction. In our times, both of these options have become almost inconceivable, and only take us back to the objection that taking serendipity out of customer relationships, based on the over-customization principle, cannot be a good idea. In both cases, this means going backwards in terms of strategic finesse and the development relationship management with customers (and other stakeholders). When the outcomes that can be expected and predicted begin to encompass all possibilities, the result is boredom, which contradicts the human vision of basic freedom to choose and decide.

Rethinking the Firm: The Company as Digital Trendsetter

So what is the upshot of all of this for the company operating in the age of perfected, digital customer relations? All of the possibilities presented by customization and customer integration seem to be pushing the company more and more into the background as the organizational form responsible for the development, production and delivery of products. But in truth, they harbor a new role for them: as trendsetters in an over-analyzed, totally calculated world in which someone else generally knows first what I want and what I'll do.

In 1892, the American psychologist, William James, held a speech for teachers in Cambridge, Massachusetts. "All our life, so far as it has definite form, is but a mass of habits," he told them. In one of his other works, The Power of Habit, James compared habit to water: "Water, in flowing, hollows out for itself a channel, which grows broader and deeper; and, after having ceased to flow, it resumes, when it flows again, the path traced by itself before" (James 1890). At that time, that was a negative commentary, because those in whose "channels" the water repeatedly followed the same course, were unconsciously cheated of the possibility to divert the water. It was about teaching people to use the power of habit to liberate themselves from the loss of control of their own free will, for which they were not to blame (Duhigg 2012).

Nowadays, with the results of research on the brain, some actually doubt whether such a thing as free will even exists, and whether humans can actually make decisions of their own accord (Geyer 2004). And on the other hand, methods such as one-to-one marketing, neuromarketing, personalized recommendation systems and many more are designed to make the human decision-making process ever more predictable. In other words, we've already had the ability to redirect the water, so to speak, for quite some time now. And often, the customer is aware of that fact. The water might have become faster, slicker and more colorful, but it's still just water. And with the exception of deeply rooted habits, it can also be redirected. Or we can add eye-catching elements to the flow. But to accomplish this, some kind of impetus needs to be deliberately added, because everything else is more or less automatic.

When the day comes when the customer is so much in control of his or her wishes and is also the person who brings them about that there is no longer any room for coincidence or surprise, then it may be the task of a new breed of customer-relationship managers to reintroduce serendipity to the mix. There are various possible ways for making this happen:

1. Companies and enterprises will need to reintegrate the element of surprise and intuition into their own organizational structures to make their defined processes – regardless of how complex – subject to disruption.

2. Human-generated recommendations – for example, via direct customer contact – will then become a special and valuable form of customer management that would offer customers a real alternative and thus serve to retain customer loyalty.

3. Companies will need to re-evaluate their automated analysis and calculation processes in their IT infrastructure on a regular basis for opportunities for factoring in planned serendipity, thus avoiding "customization overkill."

If these methods are successful, then companies can take on a new role in relation to their customers: They will become random generators in a world weighed down by calculation and prediction overkill. The goal will be to liberate people from the self-imposed loss of control over their own lives through the all-encompassing calculation of desires and actions on the basis of big data. Who could have imagined that we would have to think about this one day?

Bibliography

Anderson, Chris. The Long Tail. Why The Future of Business is Selling Less of More. New York: Hyperion, 2006.

Benkler, Yochay. The Wealth of Networks. How Social Production Transforms Markets and Freedom. New Haven: Yale University Press, 2006.

Bottcher, Dirk: "Das große Brabbeln." Brand Eins. 2/2012: 74-79.

Castells, Manuel. The Information Age: Economy, Society and Culture. Vol. I. The Rise of the Network Society. Oxford, UK: Blackwell, 2001.

Colomo-Palacios, Ricardo, Joao Varajao, and Pedro Soto-Acosta. Customer Relationship Management and the Social and Semantic Web: Enabling Clients Conexus. Hershey: IGI Publishing, 2012.

Deschamps, Jean-Philippe. "Managing Innovation: From Serendipity to Process." Prism, Issue 2. www.adlittle.com/prism-articles.html?&no_cache=1&view=141. 1995.

Duhigg, Charles. The Power of Habit. Why We Do What We Do and How to Change. London: Random House, 2012.

Gassmann, Oliver, and Sascha Friesike. 33 Erfolgsprinzipien der Innovation. Munich: Hanser, 2012.

Geyer, Christian (editor). Hirnforschung und Willensfreiheit. Zur Deutung der neuesten Experimente. Frankfurt: Suhrkamp, 2004.

Heuer, Steffan. "Ordnung durch Unordnung." Brand Eins. 7/2007: 88-91.

Holbrook, Morris B., "Adventures in Complexity: An Essay on Dynamic Open Complex Adaptive Systems, Butterfly Effects, Self-Organizing Order, Coevolution, the Ecological Perspective, Fitness Landscapes, Market Spaces, Emergent Beauty at the Edge of Chaos, and All That Jazz." Academy of Marketing Science Review 2003, no. 6. http://www.amsreview.org/articles/holbrook06-2003.pdf. 2003.

Howe, Jeff. "The Rise of Crowdsourcing." Wired Magazine. www.wired.com/

wired/archive/14.06/crowds.html. June 14, 2006.

James, William. The Principles of Psychology, Chapter IV: Habit. Available online at http://psychclas- sics.yorku.ca/James/Principles/prin4.htm. 1890.

Langner, Sascha. Viral Marketing: Wie Sie Mundpropaganda gezielt auslösen und Gewinn bringend nutzen. Wiesbaden: Gabler, 2005.

McKinsey Global Institute. "Big Data: The next frontier for innovation, competition, and productivity." (May 1, 2011). http://www.mckinsey.com/insights/mgi/research/technology_and_innovation/big_data_the_next_frontier_for_innovation . May 1, 2011.

Meckel, Miriam. "Aus Vielen wird das Eins gefunden. Wie Web 2.0 unsere Kommunikation verändert." Politik und Zeitgeschichte 39 (2008): 17-23.

Meckel, Miriam. "Weltkurzsichtigkeit. Wie der Zufall aus unserem digitalen Leben verschwindet." Der Spiegel, no. 38/2011: 120-121.

Meckel, Miriam, and Bettina Maisch. "Innovationskommunikation 2.0 – Das Beispiel Apple iPhone." Marketing Review St.Gallen (2009), Vol. 26. No. 2: 42-46.

Merton, Robert K., and Elinor Barber. The Travels and Adventures of Serendipity. Princeton, Oxford: Princeton University Press, 2004.

Pariser, Eli. The Filter Bubble. What the Internet is Hiding from You. New York: Penguin Press,

2011.

Peppers, D., Rogers, M. and Dorf, B.: "Is your Company ready for one-to-one Marketing?" Harvard Business Review, 1, (1999): 151-160.

Schonfeld, E. "The Economics of Peer Production. Could the Culture of participation threaten the existence of the firm?" http://business2.blogs.com . October 31, 2005.

Snowden, D.J. "Managing for Serendipity or why we should lay off 'best practice'." Ark Group's Knowledge Management Magazine 8. http://cognitive-edge.com/ uploads/articles/39_Managing_for_Serendipity_final.pdf. 2003.

Weinberger, David. Small Pieces Loosely Joined: A Unified Theory of the Web. New York: Basic

Books, 2002.

Weinberger, David. Everything is Miscellaneous: The Power of the New Digital Disorder. New

York: Times Books, 2007.

Zikopoulos, Paul C., Chris Eaton, Dirk deRoos, Thomas Deutsch, and George Lapis. Understanding Big Data. New York et al: McGraw-Hill, 2012.

About the Research Chair

The Institute for Media and Communications Management (MCM) at the University of St.Gallen was founded in 1998 with the support of the Bertelsmann Foundation and the Heinz-Nixdorf Foundation. It focuses on new media management. The institute's research activities center around media industry management, electronic commerce (business media), knowledge management (knowledge media), corporate communications and computational media.

For further information: http://www.mcm.unisg.ch

Summary

The data, search and browsing histories of Internet users give companies the ability to generate important information via crowdsourcing that will not only change the communication structure between customers and providers of services and products, but will also have a major impact on markets and on companies themselves, as customers acquire an external role as influencers and an internal role as participants in the decision-making process.

Each company can decide on the appropriate level of participation, emergent networking and transparency. However, these three factors can become liabilities to the success of a company that cannot keep pace with accelerating viral communication and continual restructuring in response to shifts in the customer base and consumer opinions, and cope with the open source-based exchange of information.

Customers run the risk of filtering out new possibilities outside their precisely defined comfort zone through the overcustomization of service and product offers generated by the detailed analysis of their preferences and desires. Simultaneously, data analysis with forecasting functionality is gradually narrowing the scope for management decisions. Consequently, companies will have to reintegrate the element of surprise and intuition ("serendipity") into their structures, products and services.

As customer data becomes increasingly transparent, the issue of privacy and data protection will also make steady gains, as customers can be expected to start resisting demands to disclose all of their data.

B2C

Business-to-Consumer

The Author

Rupert Stadler was born in 1963. After graduating in business administration, he started his career at Philips Communications Industrie AG in Nuremburg. Stadler joined AUDI AG in Ingolstadt in 1990, where he assumed various controlling tasks in sales and marketing. In 1994, Stadler assumed the role of commercial director for Volkswagen/Audi España SA, Barcelona. From 1997 onward, he served as the head of the board of management's office for the Volkswagen Group, and additionally as the head of group product planning in 2002. In 2003, Stadler became a member of the AUDI AG board of management. In 2007, he was appointed chairman of the board of management of AUDI AG and in this capacity joined the board of management of Volkswagen AG.

Customer and Product Relationships for the Individual Mobility of the Future

Rupert Stadler, AUDI AG

"Once upon a drive....." This is how the car industry began its meteoric rise more than 125 years ago. Today, the world's "car population" is estimated at more than one billion.[1] This figure could actually be tripled by 2030. Individual mobility – a cherished dream of mankind since the invention of the wheel – is now the foundation of our interactions in society, without which our lives would be inconceivable.

To ensure that individual mobility retains this role in the future and continues to develop intelligently, engineers are striving to refine high-tech solutions, from chassis materials and drivetrains to onboard electronics. It will be the customer who decides which ideas succeed in the global arena and take shape as innovations of choice. Whatever the outcome, the cars of the future will be even further removed than today's cars are from the horseless carriages of our great-grandparents' day. The outlook: Cars that use neither gasoline nor diesel fuel, but instead run on renewable energy from an electric outlet. Cars that can change color at the push of a button thanks to nanotechnology in the paint. Cars that know exactly when the next traffic light will turn red and where dangers lurk, because they communicate with other cars, thus almost completely eliminating accidents. Cars that drive themselves to the carwash or recharging station, and then look for a parking space – all without the driver being involved. And one day, perhaps, cars that independently drive their passengers around. That is what a journey to the future might show us.

Once we realize that continuous change is the engine behind the success of an industry, then we will understand that the key customer-manufacturer relationship is to be found in the "customer-product-manufacturer" triangle. Of course, it is crucial at first for the customer to find the product attractive. But if an industrial company fails to go one step further and connect with its customers, and is unwilling and unable to listen to and learn from them, success will remain elusive.

Taking that insight as a starting point, this article examines the effects of innovative customer and product relationships on the basis of the

---

1 German Association of the Automobile Industry, Facts and Figures 2011

changing automobile industry. That includes the relationships of customers to their cars and to other customers as well as the technical networks connecting cars with each other and the future exchange of data between cars and their manufacturers. These relationship systems are heavily intermeshed and can also be examined and evaluated on an individual basis.

Individualization: Changing Customer Needs in the Premium Segment

Those seeking to reinvent the car would be well advised to focus on future drivers and their desires and expectations. The customers of tomorrow – male and female alike – will want more selection without being overwhelmed by too many choices; they'll want eco-friendly, climate-friendly car travel without having to sacrifice a premium driving experience for the sake of "being green;" at the same time, they'll also want to enjoy more individual service and more personal comfort.

Customers will probably configure their own vehicles at home on a computer or as a three-dimensional projected image. Just like today, they will still be able to choose from a range of features, but will also certainly enjoy the experience of extreme individualization down to a lot size of n=1: That means that each car will be as unique and customized as a bespoke suit. It will actually be highly unlikely that exactly the same configuration will be ordered twice. Even nowadays, an Audi can be configured in millions of different ways. In 2020, when Audi delivers a new car every 16 seconds, there shall be even more potential for differentiation – because especially in the premium segment, most car buyers want to set themselves apart from the crowd and are looking for a high level of individuality.

Premium customers have a highly emotional connection with their vehicles. For them, the car is much more than just a means of getting from A to B. Design is the number-one factor determining the purchase decision. Excellence in automobile styling goes far beyond breathtaking shapes, glistening chrome and sweeping lines. It bridges the gap between functionality, safety, ergonomics and aesthetics. Nowadays, good design principles also include innovative design in vehicle lights as well as new colors. Years ago, Audi established white as a car color at a time when other car makers seemed unaware of anything but shades of silver and black. Today, the color innovations extend from "Samoa Orange" to "Shiraz Red," "Scuba Blue" and "Wasabi Green," which enhance the stand-out effect on the road by reflecting each car owner's individuality.

Many customers place great emphasis on performance. This is determined not only by a car's top speed, but also by its sporty road dynamics with excellent roadholding, braking and steering characteristics. For example, a ride in an Audi R8 GT Spyder will surely get anyone's pulse racing, and will inevitably bring to mind Audi's motor sport triumphs at the 24-hour races in Le Mans. And even if they rarely resort to the full 560 horsepower in everyday driving situations, every customer who chooses this kind of sports car is also buying a dose of sportiness.

Over the past century, the automobile industry has profited from the rapid rise in the need for mobility. The distances people cover in everyday life and at work have become much greater. Increased division of labor in our society has also led to changing demands on the flexibility and mobility of the working population. Higher household incomes and lower weekly working hours have made consumers much more demanding with regard to their leisure-time choices. Demographic changes are also affecting customer expectations. People are living longer and want to remain active and mobile for longer. At the same time, they are retiring later. Consequently, the debate on tighter restrictions for older drivers runs entirely counter to the needs of our time.

A premium car represents its driver's philosophy of life. In this regard, Audi is a signature brand with enormous appeal, because every car with four rings on the radiator grille bears the signature of its designer, its development engineers, and those who individualized it in the production process. As a result, it embodies the quality standards of some 72,000 people who support the brand every day to the utmost of their abilities. Every car contains sophisticated precision engineering machined to the kind of exacting standards that might be expected in a Patek Philippe watch. For example: An Audi A8 is a computer on wheels. It has the computing power of around 50 microprocessors that reliably control everything from driving dynamics and comfort to safety – wether you're driving through icy 25 degrees Celsius or a blistering heat of plus 50. A smartphone will give up the ghost when it's left lying around too long in the sun and will soon start beeping an "overheat" warning. It would be inconceivable for a car's operating system to crash as still routinely happens in computers. That's because, in a car's cockpit, higher standards understandably apply. Also underscoring the high quality standards are the materials used and the tight tolerances to which they are worked. These are the factors helping to ensure that premium customers are happy to spend more.

In rising markets such as Brazil, Russia, India and China, the automobile is very much a status symbol. In Western Europe, by contrast, a shift in values is now evident. With less emphasis being placed on "bigger, faster, more expensive," the customer of the future will expect premium products that are "more efficient, more intelligent, and offer more value." Premium cars, especially, will have to be eco-friendly and signal the responsible use of resources. In the future, customers will be even more concerned with fuel efficiency, emissions, sustainable production and the recycling of the vehicle, as well as its overall social acceptability.

Resource Efficiency: The Order of the Day

The impact of the phenomena summed up as *Limits to Growth*[2] by the Club of Rome in 1972, and in a more recent follow-up, *2052: A Global Forecast for the Next Forty Years*[3], is particularly evident in the mobility sector: the finite reserves of fossil fuels, capacity limits to the transportation infrastructure of large cities, and the effects of mobility on the environment and the climate. The industry faces big differences in the regulatory playing fields around the world in which policymakers are constantly redefining the rules.

But government intervention should be approached with due caution – as illustrated by the current controversy about the new laws mandating the switch from incandescent to energy-saving compact fluorescent light bulbs. Retailers and consumers had insufficient warning to prepare for the change. They then learned that the new bulbs had to be treated as hazardous waste because they contain mercury[4]. The automobile industry has to contend with the same issue with the energy-efficient Xenon lighting technology. Starting in 2007, Audi made the switch to mercury-free Xenon lights in its vehicles; meanwhile, the competition waited another five years, until a general ban was imposed on the use of environmentally damaging mercury in light bulbs.

"Objects in mirror are closer than they appear." The U.S. government requires car manufacturers to place that label on every wing mirror. Could you have guessed that a car model sold worldwide has to be equipped with dozens of different mirror variations?

It is not unusual in the car industry to run up against mutually contradictory regulations passed by the same lawmakers. Until now, all of the European exhaust emission standards and diesel particle filter regulations have actually had a negative impact on the amount of CO_2 emissions produced by cars. The planned EU directive on environmental noise also ignores climate protection. The example of car tires helps to

2 Dennis L. Meadows et al., The Limits to Growth.
3 Jorgen Randers, 2052: A Global Forecast for the Next 40 Years
4 SWR Wissenschaft aktuell. "Die (fast) quecksilberfreie Lampe."

illustrate the complexity: Criteria such as "rolling resistance" (and thus lower fuel consumption) and "rolling noise" are in direct conflict with one another. With badly coordinated political decisions, every manufacturer faces a tougher struggle to meet the worldwide fleet targets for CO_2 emissions.

Intelligent solutions are needed to keep the air clean, reduce traffic noise and protect the climate. The key goal in these efforts is to reduce emissions. Over the past decade alone, the car industry has cut nitric oxide (NOx) emissions by 47 percent[5] and CO_2 emissions by 16 percent[6] on Germany's roads, despite numerous new EU regulations that run counter to these targets.

Modern engines are no longer a significant contributor to air pollution. On the contrary: Studies show that engines running in densely populated areas such as Beijing actually clean the air they use. A simulation run by the IFEU Institute for Energy and Environmental Research in Heidelberg determined that between 1990 and 2030, we could see an overall reduction of 88 percent in particle emissions, around 50 percent in carbon monoxide emissions and 70 percent in nitric oxide emissions generated by motor vehicle traffic.[7] On the one hand, we have seen considerable improvements in conventional internal combustion engines. At the same time, electric drivetrain technology is looking increasingly viable for everyday use. Until battery-powered cars achieve adequate ranges, plug-in hybrids can offer the best of both worlds over the medium term. These are cars that are recharged from an electric outlet, and can continue running on gasoline or diesel fuel when the battery is empty. With the A6, A8 and Q5 hybrids, Audi now has the largest hybrid fleet in the premium segment. And with the new A3 e-tron model, Audi has combined the power of two heartbeats; this plug-in hybrid car offers a total range of up to 1,000 kilometers without having to stop at the gas station.

The transition from internal combustion engines to electric drive technology represents the biggest technological upheaval in the history of the automobile. It is comparable to the transition from the steam engine to the electric locomotive – but with a decisive difference: There are no overhead wires for cars. They have to carry their own power on board. But the scale of today's batteries does not allow anything close to the range needed for long-distance travel with reasonable size and weight. Over time, however, we will see an increase in ranges and a decline in prices. In 2008, lithium ion batteries still cost 1,000 euros per kilowatt hour of capacity. In the medium term, prices could fall to

5   Germany Federal Environmental Agency. Environmental Data for 2011.
6   German Association of the Automotive Industry, Information release from May 31, 2012.
7   IFEU: Institute for Energy and Environmental Research, Data and Calculation Model 1960-2030.

one tenth of that level. At the same time, the energy density of batteries could double by 2020, and afterwards will likely even increase fourfold in the 2020s through new technologies such as lithium sulfur and lithium-air batteries. This applies to both battery weight and space requirements.

"We want to extract five times as much wealth per kilowatt hour," says Ernst Ulrich von Weizsäcker, a scientist and the founding president of the Wuppertal Institute for Climate, Environment and Energy. He has used the term "econological economy" for an economy that deals appropriately with resources. He believes that MIPS – material input per service unit – can be improved through radical reengineering. We have to reinvent the world we now live in and try to achieve existing functions through new concepts. The result will be more wealth through less input from nature.[8] Audi ultra is one example of how we can consistently pursue the path of "less is more." Through the use of light-weight engineering, Audi has become the first manufacturer to reverse the spiral of increasing vehicle weights. With the A8 in the 1990s, Audi developed the world's first large-volume production car with a self-supporting aluminum body. It weighed just 245 kilograms. Until that moment, engineered components for comfort and safety were adding more and more weight to vehicles. The use of intelligent combinations of materials brought that trend to an end. The decisive factor is to reduce the weight of a car significantly without detrimentally affecting its handling characteristics or driving safety. Approaches leading the way, in addition to aluminum bodies, include glass fiber and carbon fiber composite materials. Entire component groups are taking on new functions, thus generating further weight savings. In the new Audi A3, for example, innovative lightweight construction has already helped to save up to 80 kilograms.

Growth can be deemed compatible with future needs or sustainable only if we bring about a manifold increase in resource productivity. The fact that this is achievable is illustrated by the development of fuel cells. Initially the size of a single-family home, they are steadily shrinking and are already not much bigger than a cooler you might take along for a weekend trip to the country. The clincher in von Weizsäcker's approach is that it boosts environmental protection and makes it compatible with the economic pursuit of prosperity. That is because car buyers are not looking for a car that makes them sacrifice a premium driving experience; on the contrary, they are relying above all on the innovative power of the German car industry. At the same time, there are limits on how much they are willing to pay for these innovations.

---

8   Ernst Ulrich von Weizsäcker et al., Faktor Fünf – Die Formel für nachhaltiges Wachstum.

At this point, the relationship level cutting across industrial sectors becomes important, because a fundamental technology shift can succeed at a price the market can bear only if manufacturers work on joint standards and a standardized infrastructure. The development of a recharging infrastructure for electric cars, suitable billing software for electric refueling, software interface standards and connector hardware are tasks of our time. We must also look at leasing models for batteries as a means of lowering barriers to entry.

Greenovation: Mobility in Balance with the Environment

From a sustainability standpoint, electric cars won't make sense until the required electric power is in fact supplied – fully – from renewable sources. Audi has set itself the long-term goal of achieving completely carbon-neutral mobility, and has consequently embarked on a unique path. The fact that the entire product cycle is taken into consideration – from development and manufacturing, through the utilization phase, and ending with recycling – is nothing new. What is new, however, is that a car manufacturer is also looking at the question of where energy for tomorrow's individual mobility will come from. This is why Audi began intensively studying the sustainable development of new fuels.

As a first step, engineers used wind to generate power. This can be used to recharge an entire fleet of electric vehicles. For the surplus power, the inventors had another idea: They used it to produce hydrogen as a means of storing green energy. The next challenge resulted not only from technical problems associated with the transport and efficient storage of hydrogen, such as the volatility of the gas and the energy required to cool it; it relates above all to the lack of a hydrogen infrastructure. In 2011, Germany had only 20 hydrogen refueling stations nationwide.

The solution: Combining hydrogen with CO_2 starts the process of methanization, i.e., the production of synthetic methane. With this concept, it is not only possible to charge plug-in cars such as the A3 e-tron with wind power at the generation site; the methane produced can also be pumped through existing gas lines to any desired location to fuel gas-powered cars such as the A3 g-tron with sustainably produced gas. Alternatively, the gas can later be converted to electricity to recharge electric cars. With this work, Audi has demonstrated that electric mobility can indeed be climate-friendly in the future if backed by a holistic concept. The process is ultimately sustainable not only due to the green power from wind energy; it actually provides relief to the climate by withdrawing methane from the atmosphere.[9]

Investments in energy efficiency are important for international competitiveness. "Greenovation" has recently become the general term describing intelligent combinations of efficient processes, eco-friendly materials and sustainable products in industrial production to ensure competitiveness.

Audi connect: A Seamless Connection to Your Surroundings

So what is a car maker doing at one of the world's biggest consumer electronics shows or computer fairs? Since 2011, Audi has given three opening keynote addresses at CES (Consumer Electronics Show) in Las Vegas. In 2012, we gave a keynote at CeBIT in Hanover – the world's largest computer expo, where we also had our own stand. The message we wanted to convey with our presence at both fairs? We brought the Internet inside the car; and now we are bringing the car into the Internet of things and services. And we proved: the "connected brain" of the car even allows piloted driving.

The innovative area we call "Audi connect" is fundamentally changing the relationship between customers and their cars. Assuming that in 2030, social distinctions will have less to do with material possessions than with intangibles such as time, self-actualization, relationships and sustainability, then the car of tomorrow will play a key role. In the future, customers will expect their professional and personal lives on and off four wheels to be mapped using seamless connectivity through a combination of "always on" technology (constant Internet links) and "data in the cloud" (constant data synchronization between multimedia end devices, including the car). Commuters in particular want the time they spend in their cars every day to be put to good use.

The car will transport information, create experiences and ensure that its passengers are networked. Consequently, *Audi connect* reflects the new fundamental need to be online anytime and anywhere, and thus to keep up to date and able to maintain relationship networks. The vision of a seamless transition also applies to entertainment. When you take a family vacation in the future, your daughter will stop the Harry Potter movie or Winnie the Pooh audio book on her way out the door, and, once she's safely belted into your Audi, will be able to pick up the movie right where she left off.

---

9 www.audi-balanced-mobility.com

Even today, car passengers can surf the Internet using an integrated hotspot. The first car with WLAN was an Audi A8. Up to eight end devices can be logged in. And why shouldn't the driver enjoy the same privilege and have e-mails read out loud for the sake of road safety? Naturally this would be done intelligently, summing up the key information – just like a good assistant or helpful passenger does. The car will become another tool for making everyday life easier. In the Audi App Center, our software developers are working on a whole range of mobile apps to be used in cars and on devices like smartphones. Offering innovative services like this will represent an important part of the way car makers create value for their customers.

Web 2.0: The Demand for Personal Information and the Power of Social Networks

The efficacy of traditional advertising has already suffered under the ever-increasing flood of information confronting consumers today. Companies that use customer relationship management (CRM) systems to communicate with customers without the appropriate fine tuning are taking the risk that totally different consumer segments – from the supermarket cashier to the university professor – will all be receiving the same message. And when manufacturers, importers, dealerships and service providers attempt to outdo one another by inundating the customer with almost-identical advertising through every available communication channel, it will most likely have the effect of scaring customers off. In the future, companies that use e-mail and conventional mail to reach potential customers are going to have to pay far more attention to the benefits for each individual recipient if they want their message to be heard. Does that mean the end of the letter in traditional form? Yes, it does. Customers are looking for added value. Customer relations of the future will have to become markedly more regionalized and personalized. Successful companies will become less anonymous. Instead, customers and others will experience them in a very personal sense through their employees.

However, the need for information isn't a one-way street. Customers of the future will play a much stronger role in informing other customers about their good and bad experiences with brands and models. The greater the popularity of social networks, the more customer-to-customer relationships will gain importance for shaping opinion, also online. Today, the advice of a friend or acquaintance already has more weight than the word of a sales representative, who always has a personal interest in making a sale. This effect is referred to as "word of mouth" or, on the Web, "word of mouse." It is amplified in online networks of relationships among people who know each other only through the Internet. Internet users see each other as neutral providers of unbiased information for potential buyers, ignoring advertising and media reports – at all times, across borders and unfiltered. Web 2.0 – which could be translated as "the Internet with a feedback channel" – offers the technological framework for this new need to share information, and has led to the democratization of publishing opportunities online.

Blogging, commenting, tweeting – today, every user can do these things. As a result, the classical distribution of roles as described in communications theory, with the mass media as transmitters and the populace as recipients, is no longer valid. For those sending out advertising content in the car industry, this means that the manufacturer no longer has a monopoly on information. Instead, we have a host of busy commentators on corporate and product news who can be faster and more critical than any journalist with their online postings.

And anyone who thinks they can deal with this phenomenon by trying to control it is in for a disappointment. The voice of the people is a firmly established and important instrument of freedom of opinion on the Internet. And more importantly: For buyers trying to make up their minds, it is becoming the main source of advice on the pros and cons of individual models. Those who dismiss blogs as a mere fad and close their minds to them, or who fail to make Web 2.0 players a part of the conversation, will find out very quickly: There is a relentless and uncontrolled flow of communication. However, instead of communicating with each other, the participants communicate about one another. Consequently, it is highly advisable for companies to get involved in social networks and to learn to deal objectively with criticism in the digital world – regardless of whether or not it is justified. Moreover, through social media, companies can extract information on what gets customers excited, what they don't like, and what can be improved without having to pay for elaborate reputation studies. They can even use this pool of information as a source of product ideas. Consequently, Audi tracks key blogs and Twitter feeds while maintaining its own social media presence – not just for customers, but also for journalists and other important trendsetters.

From a manufacturer's viewpoint, the Internet has opened up new channels of information on product innovations and business decisions that have much more credibility than advertising channels. In 2010, Audi became the first car manufacturer worldwide to stage a Web-only celebration of the launch of a new vehicle when the A1 compact was introduced as a modern city car. Quality online viral marketing is not carried out with manipulative intent. Instead, it takes aim at the impact of personal opinion and above all at the large-scale, uncontrolled and rapid spread of the message, similar to the spread of a virus.

Social networks even extend into the everyday lives of drivers: Drivers can check their Twitter feeds and Facebook messages on their cars' flatscreens using the Audi MultiMedia Interface (MMI). In a time when values are changing, virtual networking could lead to "eco contests" among drivers who would "race" the same routes at different times to see who can achieve the lowest fuel consumption. If they wanted, the top performers could have their names added to a top-scorers list. In addition, there could be a "Facebook page for the road," where participants could award plus and minus points for behavior in traffic, reach out to get to know someone after exchanging smiles at a traffic light, or even look for a life-long passenger.

While our competition is pursuing a "top-down" strategy when it comes to innovation and is thus serving the luxury-segment customer first, at Audi, issues of safety and infotainment aren't tied to tired old "class distinctions." And that is why younger target groups – "digital natives" who are at home with the Internet – will find the same package of leading-edge services in their Audi A1 and A3 models that the driver of an A8 sedan will enjoy. For us, this level of service goes without saying. When an Audi model gets a facelift, it also gets loaded with the latest features and services.

Audi mobility: New Services for Individual Mobility

New customer-to-customer relationships could also transform the quality of carsharing and carpooling schemes. People used to say, "Birds of a feather flock together." It is an undeniable fact that people identify most strongly with peer groups, i.e. those with the same socio-economic status or similar interests. A car manufacturer could provide the service of organizing such networks, including billing and insurance. In major cities, another trend is taking shape: It appears that, for many young people, owning their own car is no longer high on their list of priorities. As a result, innovative car utilization concepts will develop as alternatives to ownership as ways of meeting the need for diverse mobility solutions in different situations.

"Pay as you drive" is a concept by Audi. Users pay on the basis of the mileage covered. This makes mobility possible even in the most densely populated metropolitan areas. A field trial in Berlin with an A1 fleet was a big hit, especially with a large number of Generation Y participants. In this way, a pure car manufacturer becomes a premium supplier of individual mobility services that is expected to develop new business models for the temporary use of its cars – up to and including a "flat rate for mobility." The pleasure of having just one car as one's personal property is trumped by the charm of co-owning an entire fleet – a convertible for the weekend, a big sedan just for a change, and then an SUV for a ski trip. And of course, every car would come preset with its current driver's preferred seat, mirror and climate-control settings. The driver's individual destinations would be preset in the navigation system, and his or her regular music library and social network settings would be ready to hit the road too. Concepts like this are created under the name *Audi mobility*.

Mobility of the Future: Cars with Electronic Pilots

In the past, the only place where we saw self-piloted cars – or even flying cars – was in science fiction movies. Now, both of these technologies seem almost within reach. If the driver wants, an autopilot takes over the controls and guides the car to its destination with no human driver necessary. In 2012, Audi demonstrated how, even today, a self-piloted car can drive itself to the car wash and gas station and then find a spot for itself in the parking garage. Self-piloted cars would even help commuters win back a bit of time during their morning commute: When they don't feel like dealing with the traffic and driving themselves, they can hand over the controls to their car and spend the time reading the newspaper or watching the morning news.

The necessary technologies for these new forms of automotive mobility are already largely in place. Now it is up to lawmakers to establish the regulatory framework, above all in the areas of responsibility and liability for piloted driving.

When Will Smith took the wheel of a police car in the 2004 movie "I, Robot," set in 2035, to fight a robot rebellion in Chicago, he was driving the custom-designed Audi RSQ. It moved on spheres instead of wheels, which allowed it to be steered in all directions. This concept model showed how far ahead the Ingolstadt developers were with their first concepts for piloted driving and the sound design for an electric car.

A Life of their Own: Constant Contact between Products and Manufacturers

Today, a car has to go to a service shop for service or repairs. But it would certainly be more convenient for the customer if a mechanic or a mechatronics technician could drop by one day, hook up a tablet computer, identify the malfunction and then fix the problem on the spot. However, the future becomes fascinating when we take it one step further: The car would be able to use its error database to decide when service is needed and would transmit the information to the service shop, where technicians could then determine the level of urgency and arrange to have the necessary spare part on hand when the customer arrived. The driver, who may not even have noticed any problem with the car, would receive a friendly request to come to the workshop. After a prior check of the driver's calendar, the suggested appointment would be scheduled to keep waiting time to a minimum.

For software updates or simple system resets, it will not even be necessary to take the car into the shop in the future. Instead, the data will be transmitted automatically via satellite or by mobile telephone, keeping the control electronics updated over the entire life cycle. With the aid of client-server architecture, more and more customer applications in cars are hosted in data centers. This innovative product-manufacturer relationship allows the latest software to be uploaded to all model series overnight. On the hardware side, entertainment electronics have also been set free from the multi-year development cycles for cars.

With the 2012 Audi A3, Audi introduced the modular infotainment platform. It contains a powerful NVIDIA Tegra processor capable of real-time computation and display of 3-D graphics. It's no accident that we are cooperating closely with a manufacturer of graphic chips for the high-end computer game industry. At Audi, we want to have the most powerful processors available on board. But any chip, no matter how fast, will be obsolete within a few months. When the next one appears on the market, the hardware can be brought up to date quickly thanks to the modular design. To achieve this, the developers separated the Radio&Car Control Unit (RCC), which is built into the vehicle, from the multimedia module (MMX), allowing the MMX to be designed as a replaceable plug-in board. This ensures that the car and its electronics, services and content are all kept up to date – independently of one another.

Another scenario for an independent product relationship of the car with the outside world is eCall, the EU automatic emergency call system that will be standard equipment in all new cars as of 2015. In the case of a collision, it transmits the car's coordinates, the number of occupants and the type of collision to an emergency center and establishes a voice link.[10]

Swarm Intelligence: Increased Safety through Interactive Products

Car-to-car communication is the prime example of how road safety can be improved. Imagine electronic traffic controllers that are constantly calculating whether two cars are on a collision course, and can independently initiate an evasive maneuver. In the future, cars will exchange far more data: For example, they'll issue warnings of upcoming traffic jams, icy road conditions and obstacles on the road. For this purpose, the cars will create ad-hoc WLAN networks, resulting in "swarm intelligence."

The day will come when you will be warned automatically by another car when its sensors detect ice on the road or other hazards. On long trips, the swarm principle could be used for automated convoy driving on highways, creating a sort of "electronic drawbar."

Or imagine the following situation: You arrange a time and place to meet someone, but later on, this proves unrealistic for both parties. What if the navigation systems of the two cars were networked and could calculate the ideal meeting point and time? The computer would eliminate the need to make calls en route and would synchronize the arrival times of the two cars.

The next step is the integration of the traffic infrastructure such as traffic lights to optimize traffic flows. The activated car-spacing and speed-control systems will then be able to include data on phased traffic lights in trip planning, which will help to reduce fuel consumption. We call this type of product relationship "car-to-X communication." Audi has initiated a related project in Ingolstadt under the name Travolution, which combines "traffic" and "evolution." The aim is to improve traffic technology through evolutionary methods. By optimizing the timing of 46 sets of traffic lights in Ingolstadt's network of main roads, they are ideally synchronized to keep traffic flowing. In addition, this Audi project demonstrates how data can be transmitted to cars on the timing of traffic lights. Drivers can react by speeding up or slowing down to optimize fuel consumption and the flow of traffic. A driver who knows that the next traffic lights will change to red, any-

---

10 European Commission: "Support for an EU-wide e-Call Service."

way, in the next five seconds can just coast to an eco-friendly stop. An improved traffic flow and less stop-and-go traffic have led to lower fuel consumption and less air pollution in Ingolstadt. The results were measurable: savings of 700,000 liters of fuel and 1,700 tons of CO_2 per year. In recognition of these achievements, Ingolstadt was selected by the federal government and the German business community for one of the "Germany: Land of Ideas" innovation awards in 2009. Using the "Travolution principle," it is estimated that a major city like Tokyo could reduce its fuel use and emissions by up to 20 percent.

The intelligent networking of cars and infrastructure goes even further. Consider, for example, having to get out of your warm car at the gas station to face the wind and cold weather. That, too, could soon be a thing of the past if the payment process can be dealt with conveniently on the screen in your car. And how will electric car drivers find the next place to "fill up?" Your navigation system will find the recharging stations closest to your destination and display the prices. For touchless recharging, the vehicle is positioned right above the induction coil and asks for confirmation for a wireless transaction with the service provider.

Buying a Car: Virtual Reality in the Living Room

If customers had been asked what they wanted before the car was invented, they would probably have answered, "Faster coaches" (to paraphrase Henry Ford). As arrogant as this may sound: To be a trendsetter, you can't just ask your customers what they want today; you've got to develop an intuition for what they might want tomorrow. Steve Jobs, one of Apples founders, made this a central credo in his work.

As a brand that stands for "Vorsprung durch Technik," or "Truth in Engineering," we can of course try out new ideas through market research and customer surveys. But what will keep us a step ahead is our own relentless innovation work.

This is equally applicable to our sales and marketing concepts for the future. Will car dealerships look the same in 20 or 30 years? Or will people also be looking for more of an experience when buying a car? The members of Generation Y – the first group of people to grow up fully embedded in a digital environment with computers, PlayStations and smartphones – already differ completely in their approach to shopping from those who spent their earlier years with fewer electronic devices. As 3-D technology increasingly spreads to home use as well, it is quite conceivable that the car showroom will move from the dealership to the living room. The car of the future could then be configured in real time as a full-scale 3-D image right before the customer's eyes. Customers who use this technology to narrow down their selection at home can then store their chosen configuration and take it to the dealership. In the medium term, we will probably see two customer groups emerge:

- Those who know exactly what they want and prefer to use new media to make their purchase when and where they want, possibly with the help of a friendly avatar, i.e., a virtual person shown as a graphic animation on the screen. Bargain hunting and ease of comparison are just two reasons for the appeal of online shopping. Another is the desire for flexibility and the convenience of doing business from home. The arrival of the Internet age for car sales was already proclaimed – perhaps a bit prematurely – at the turn of the millennium. The surveyed customers were initially motivated above all by the desire to narrow down the offerings to find the best buy as near as possible to their home.[11]

- On the other hand, there will be the customers who we could call a brand's biggest fans, who will always see the intensive face-to-face consultation as an essential part of the buying experience. Despite widespread reports of its demise, this approach to buying cars still has plenty of life left in it. And finally: Although a test drive is possible in a simulator, it's not half as much fun.

Even now, augmented and virtual reality are being adopted by dealerships to present the sheer variety of products as more and more options and versions become available. The images are realistically enhanced using computer simulations on a 46-inch screen.

But there are more changes ahead for premium car sales that will serve to increase customer satisfaction. If you consider the fact that a test drive influences up to 75 percent of the decision to buy a new car, then the third undercover online study on test drives conducted by Bearing-Point in 2012 must have raised the alarm for many car makers. The researchers submitted 2,200 requests for test drives. Half of these requests had still met with no response 14 days later. Even in Germany, the ultimate automobile nation, every third person was still waiting in vain for a test drive date two weeks later.[12] So, how can we improve the test-drive process and make it faster and more customer friendly? This is another area presenting countless opportunities to implement Audi's piloted driving project described above.

---

11 Dietmar H.Lamparter, Zeit Online, "Der Preis ist heiß – Deutsche Autohersteller sind im Internet zweitklassig."
12 news.de, "Autobauer lassen Online-Kunden links liegen."

Until recently, after-sales service covered accessories, tires and car-care products. But in the future, a permanent relationship between the driver and manufacturer of a car could mean that the *user* of the car – and not necessarily the *owner* – would pay a fee to activate certain vehicle functions for a period of months, weeks or days. As ever more functions in today's cars are largely software-based, this is technologically quite feasible. In this way, cars could be continually updated over the product lifecycle, much like the updates to the operating system and apps on a smart phone. In 2002, Audi was the first carmaker that gave drivers the option of letting their cars automatically and electronically set the driving mode (Dynamic Ride). In the future, customers could even download an app – for a small additional fee – that would offer them a wider range of driving settings to choose from according to their needs and individual driving style. For example, things like engine tuning, steering or braking response characteristics would be adjusted automatically depending on which mode the driver preferred: sporty and dynamic, maximum comfort, or even more fuel efficient.

And if the user of a company car wants features not covered in the list price or lease agreement signed by the employer, he or she could decide whether to pay for the features at their own expense.

How we sell new cars to customers isn't the only thing that is going to change. The used-car market will also be affected. I remember being at a standard car auction in the U.S. a few years back. It was agonizing to see the condition of some of the used cars being sold at prices far below their actual value. It gave me the idea of creating a "Certified Pre-Owned Cars" (CPO) program in the States. The program leaves it to our dealers to professionally spruce up and repair used cars prior to putting them back up for sale. These CPO cars not only sell for a higher price, but they also generally retain more of their residual value, too – and in the U.S. market, Audi has since become the brand with the best residual value.

The Internet is playing an increasingly important role in the used car market. The first car-search apps are already on the market with functionality to enable iPhone users to look for cars with a given combination of price range and features available for sale within a certain radius. And in the customer-mobility provider relationship, some customers would certainly be open to the idea of the provider automatically finding a buyer at a pre-arranged interval, perhaps every two years. The customer would then choose a new car. This would stand the sales process on its head: Instead of the seller, the buyer would take the initiative. He or she could check the car's mileage online – naturally in anonymized form with no personal information about the current user. The owner would then see a message on the dashboard display indicating the price someone is willing to offer for the vehicle.

Missed Opportunities: When a Company Forgets its Customers

Never before in history have human beings and their needs changed as rapidly as in the period since the Industrial Revolution. And in the digitized world of the 21st century, the pace of this dynamic is rapidly increasing. Once-successful companies that failed to see the writing on the wall have been left behind:

- Kodak, famed for its roll films and industrially manufactured cameras for the past 125 years, slid into bankruptcy because the company was too reliant on analog technology and was pounded by losses as sales of analog film collapsed. Kodak stopped making film cameras in 2004, and the next year ceased production of black-and-white photo paper. Did the efforts to adapt to the market come too late? In mid-2012, Kodak finally had to stop making cameras entirely. The company was finished.[13]

- Sony achieved global fame back in the 1980s with the Walkman, with 335 million units sold in the 25-year period starting on July 1, 1979. Sony was also the originator of the first portable color TV, the 3.5-inch floppy disk and the CD. But in 2011, Sony had to lay off tens of thousands of employees. What happened? According to analysts, a number of mistakes can be blamed for the Japanese company's reversals. For example, Sony's fears of illegal copying prompted the use of copy protection on CDs and DVDs that initially rendered them unplayable.[14] In addition, Sony's decision not to set up its own online music download platform left the field wide open for Apple, which achieved an impressive 25 billion downloads worldwide through iTunes between 2003 and 2012 and hit the historic mark of 50 billion downloads in May 2013. Apple has also sold 250 million iPods, iPhones and iPads in just one decade.[15] Sony had failed to listen to its customers.

- And it was also Apple's success, but in the mobile phone market, that proved to be Nokia's undoing. In the view of analysts, the Finnish phone maker simply failed to keep up. In 2006, Nokia still had a one-third share of the market for web-enabled "intelligent mobile

13 Christoph Schlautmann, Handelsblatt, "Kodak droht der Untergang."
14 Rief et. al., Die Presse, "Sony kämpft um Comeback."
15 Brandon Griggs, "Apple's App Store hits 50 billion downloads."

phones"[16], then still in their infancy. But at Apple, the floodgates opened; when a smartphone became the "must-have" phone and customers started spending more money on mobile telephones than ever before, the Finns simply got left behind. Instead, they tried switching tactics and started producing "economy" mobile phones. Between 2007 and 2012, Nokia's shares plummeted and lost three-quarters of their value.[17] In the first quarter of 2012, the company had losses of almost a billion euros.[18]

- But not even Apple can rest on its iPhone laurels: In just a year and a half, we've seen the market share for smartphones running Android – a competing operating system – grow from 25 percent[19] to almost 60 percent.[20] In April 2013, Google – a principal member of the Open Handset Alliance – announced that every single day, some 1.5 million new smartphones with Android were being activated.[21]

- After its takeover of TWA at the turn of the century, American Airlines became the largest airline in the world based on passenger numbers.[22] But because the airline's fleet was old and the cost of fuel gobbled up half of total revenues, American Airlines was unable to offer its customers lower fares, and was overtaken by the competition.[23] In November of 2011, AA filed for bankruptcy under Chapter 11.[24] The company is now hopeful that a new fleet of Airbus aircraft that uses 30 percent less fuel will get it back off the ground.[25] In Europe, we're seeing the opposite trend: Now a subsidiary of Lufthansa, once-independent German low-cost carrier, Germanwings, will have to start offering its customers premium services in the future. This is part of Lufthansa's strategy to improve its market position and fight competition from airlines from the Gulf region.[26]

- In 2000, IBM had to call a complete halt to the manufacturing and sale of PCs. One of the main reasons was the business model of its competitor, Dell, which let customers configure their computers online – thus enabling its plants to carry out just-in-time production without inventories and with a direct sales model. While IBM looked on, the computer world had undergone a radical transformation, and was now a more flexible, low-cost business.[27]

---

16 Yasmin El-Sharif, (Spiegel Online), ""Smartphone problems – Nokia in search of a new boss"
17 Angela Göpfert, ARD Börse, "Mobile Wachstumphantasien."
18 Göpfert (Handelsblatt): "Nokia und NSN schockieren mit Millardenverlust."
19 heise.de, "Android überholt Symbian, Apple verliert Marktanteile."
20 Matthias Parbel,(heise.de), "Android und iOS beherrschen die Smartphone-Welt."
21 Eric Zeman, (informationweek.com), "Google Reports 1.5 Million Android Activations Per Day"
22 Research and Innovative Technology Administration, "Passengers, All Carriers, All Airports."
23 focus.de, "American Airlines hofft nach Pleite auf Neustart."
24 FAZ.net, "American Airlines ist insolvent."
25 focus.de, Ibid.
26 Ulf Brychcy, (Financial Times Deutschland), "Lufthansa zählt Germanwings an."
27 focus.de, "IBM 5150 Personal Computer. Der PC feiert seinen 30.Geburtstag."

With needs constantly changing, only those willing to subject their own business model to continuous reevaluation will survive in the long term. To stay with the last example for a moment: When IBM launched its 5150 model on the market on August 12, 1981, the first personal computer had arrived. Its price in Germany was 3,540 deutschmarks. The most exciting development with PCs over the 30 years since then has not been the fall in prices by more than half, but rather the immense increase in performance. For 800 euros, today's computer buyer gets a thousand times faster processing speed (5 GHz today versus 4.7 MHz back then) and more than a 100,000 times more memory (2 gigabytes now versus 16 kilobytes in 1981).[28]

For most well-established market participants, it is a challenge to shake off any complacency from past successes, to keep improving the efficiency of production processes and above all, on the product side, to keep making good things even better. Anyone who stands still is actually moving backwards. The major players in the car industry face the same struggle for survival as manufacturers of consumer electronics.

Twenty years ago, three researchers at MIT in Boston held up a mirror to Western car industry representatives. They were referring to the Japanese leadership in the development of lean production systems for cars, described by Womack, Jones and Roos in their book, *The Machine That Changed the World: The Story of Lean Production*. Since then, continuous improvement processes, value-stream mapping and production management based on key performance indicators[29] have become firmly established all over the world, and not only with car manufacturers.

Through this study, lean management has become a guiding principle for many other industries as well. The challenge posed by Japan at that time could come from China in 10 years: a threat that European car manufacturers should take seriously, believes Goldman Sachs. In 2020, they could experience what the solar energy sector and manufacturers of high-speed trains are now going through: high-tech products at extremely low prices, made possible by China's enormous economic development programs.

At Audi, we've never viewed the Far East as a threat, but rather have always seen it as an opportunity. Our early entry into the Asian market – well ahead of all the other premium brands – has proven to be the right decision. In 2011, China became Audi's largest single market. Audi created the world's very first touchpad screen that recognizes

28 focus.de, Ibid.
29 Womack et al., The Machine That Changed the World : The Story of Lean Production, (New York, 1991).

Chinese characters. Naturally, our Chinese customers find this very useful. But it is also a symbol of our esteem for their culture.

Being identified by customers with the image embodied by "Vorsprung durch Technik" does not happen overnight. Around the world, the brand has become renowned through its innovations and efficient production processes. The foundation was laid by a number of inventions, from a space-saving front-wheel drive solution under the old Auto-Union brand in the 1930s, to the quattro drivetrain in 1980. With the Procon-ten technology, Audi took the lead among all carmakers in providing drivers with effective protection against head injuries from the steering wheel. In the event of a front-end collision, the steering column is automatically pulled away from the driver by steel cables attached to the engine block – and the driver's seatbelt automatically tightens and locks. In TV ads, we used a box of matches to demonstrate the mechanical principles involved. Before the arrival of sensor-activated air-bags, the Procon-ten technology saved thousands of lives.

In 1981, Prof. Dr. Ferdinand K. Piëch – then the member of the board of management responsible for technical development – gave the go-ahead for the use of aluminum in lightweight car construction. The idea for using this material came to him when he was on a tour of a beer-can production plant in Denver, Colorado. Even back then, aluminum cans were being collected and recycled all over the USA. Piëch realized that the material would also be ideal for the construction of lightweight car parts because of its additional advantage of making cars easier to recycle. The idea resulted in the development of a new manufacturing system – a process that took more than a decade. Audi is still benefiting from this pioneering effort. For engineering excellence, we are at least one model generation ahead of the competition.

In 1999, Audi sent the first prototype with a self-supporting carbon-fiber chassis to the starting line at the Le Mans 24-hour race – blazing the trail for more Audi successes with ultra-lightweight construction. The fight to eliminate every gram of weight continues, in pursuit of our goal of seeing four rings on the lightest model in every segment.

The highly efficient fuel injection system that powered Audi to two victories at Le Mans was also originally designed for motorsports. In 2001, Audi won the race with the TFSI gasoline engine, and five years later with the TDI diesel engine. The next big innovation arrived on the track in 2012: Audi's R18 e-tron quattro became the first hybrid car to take the checkered flag at the 24-hour race. Motorsports yielded more than a dozen innovations for that model series – from the advanced steering wheel-mounted gear shifter to the tire pressure control system through to the downsizing of engines to improve gas mileage with no noticeable loss of performance.

Not all of these technology transfers were planned from the outset. But it is always a priority for developers to strive at all times to turn their ideas into real customer benefits.

To network even the most diverse of disciplines, we are launching *InnoBook* at Audi – a sort of "Facebook for experts and innovations." It gives our employees a virtual arena where they can work together to generate new ideas. It's fast, innovative and entirely free of hierarchies.

New technology cannot be called innovation unless it can be successfully launched on the market. Audi has been able to go into series production with nearly three quarters of its concept cars – more than any other car manufacturer. This can be seen as further proof of Audi's success in hearing what its customers are saying. After all, the best impetus for improvement is still the customer. In the medium to long term, a company that sets the goal of systematically eliminating every source of dissatisfaction will steadily improve its products and services – to the delight and satisfaction of its customers. One way Audi is putting this strategy into practice: We have established a sort of "customer roundtable" for cross-divisional discussion of letters and emails from customers, feedback from our dealers and market research data. We first envisioned using the "roundtable" as an instrument in promoting a more customer and quality-oriented style of management. But after its initial successes at the regional level, it was adopted in 2012 by Audi and all of its dealerships worldwide.

Company Credo: Credibility in Customer Relationships through a Value-oriented Approach

In the future, basic authenticity will be far more important to companies than any clever customer communications or loyalty program. It's only then that a company can survive the judgments of online communities, which are anyway very effective at making it clear what is good or bad – at least in the opinion of the outside world. Those who try to fool their customers with smoke and mirrors will soon find themselves on the road to nowhere. The only way to look authentic is to be authentic, by establishing sustainable corporate policies in harmony with economic, ecological and social criteria, and then to live by these policies without exception.

Audi has a global online fan base numbering more than 21 million – from Facebook alone. We engage them in a dialog on such issues as mobility in the future as it is impacted by increasing urbanization. Experts believe that the world's population will reach nine billion by 2050[30], with two thirds of that number living in cities. The number of large metropolises will double. What this will mean for road traffic is almost unimaginable by today's standards. In 2010, Audi created the Urban Future Award to gather ideas for the future of megacities. The many exciting proposals received from all over the world inspired the company to take the next step in 2011 and develop the Audi Urban Future Initiative, a think tank serving as a platform for cooperation among architects, urban planners, sociologists, futurologists, policy-makers and citizens. The results of their work will have a direct influence on the society of tomorrow and its living environment.[31]

By engaging in a dialog with a broad spectrum of groups in society to shape the issues and challenges of the future, a company also secures a foundation for its business activities in the coming decades. Corporate social responsibility calls for sustainable solutions that go beyond the actual product and its benefits to customers. New customer and product relationships will also change the company of the future because these relationships will transform the basis for doing business with them: An automobile manufacturer becomes a provider of mobility, software and information – not to mention an urban planner. "The future is already here — it's just not very evenly distributed." These thought-provoking words are from the bestselling book *Neuromancer* (1984) by the science fiction author William Gibson, who already envisaged the concept of cyberspace.

If so much is changing, are there relationship systems that will endure in this new business environment? I'm convinced that only a return to core values will stabilize the free interplay of forces in our everyday life. With this, I am talking about trust and responsibility – the basis for any good relationship. That's because an active role in shaping society is available only to those who are on the playing field, and not the ones who watch from the sidelines. We need people with courage and a moral compass who are willing to assume responsibility and think in the long term. In the 21st century, these entrepreneurial types will be needed at every hierarchical level. Consequently, corporate leadership in step with the times will foster the participation of employees and customers and encourage all stakeholders to play a formative role. The basis is provided by cooperative approaches to work, active knowledge management, transparent decision-making processes and open com-

30 United Nations, "World Population Prospects: The 2010 Revision."
31 www.audi-urban-future-initiative.com

munication. This boosts employee motivation and customer loyalty. And finally, an appropriate share in corporate profits by employees and shareholders serves as a reward for their commitment and an expression of esteem, and also increases the sense of identification with the company.

Particularly in a digital world, the ability to maintain real social relationships alongside the virtual social networks will always remain a sought-after skill. Consequently, it is now more important than ever for our young people to learn social competencies.

In my view, there is an unfortunately widespread inability to distinguish between value-oriented and values-oriented management. However, in any discussion about our future, it is vital to talk about fundamental values such as trust, openness and honesty. Ultimately, a consensus on values decisively shapes the relationships between customers, employees, the industry, suppliers, neighbors, shareholders and the environment.

Of course, it was a magical moment for everyone working at Audi when we delivered more than a million cars to customers for the first time in our history in 2008. The board of management will be similarly moved in 2020, when the sales reports show that deliveries have topped the two-million-a-year mark. But it's not just the daily share price, the weekly sales reports, the monthly financial forecast or the quarterly figures that count in the end. First and foremost, in my view, among the decisive factors for real (or as we now call it, "sustainable") business success is our ability to assume social responsibility and create value for everyone.

When we recall the words of the founding fathers of the car industry, the relentless pioneering spirit of that era and the drive for perfection comes through loud and clear: "The best – or nothing!" is the much-quoted, never-say-die motto of Gottlieb Daimler. August Horch was somewhat more modest: He once proudly told his apprentice, Edgar Friedrich, "I've developed a pretty good car." But, after a pause, he murmured to himself: "But still bad enough to leave room for improvement!" There was probably relief in his voice, because he had found something else to tinker with. And it's this spirit of the founder of Audi that lives on today in our employees, who do their utmost to make the cars with the four rings on the radiator grille even better.

Individual mobility will always have a place in our society. And it will be our job to determine what that place will look like.

Bibliography

Brychcy, Ulf. "Lufthansa zählt Germanwings an." http://www.ftd.de/unter- nehmen/industrie/:billig-airline-lufthansa-zaehlt-germanwings-an/70049959.html. Financial Times Deutschland. June 13, 2012.

http://www.bloomberg.com/news/2010-07-20/nokia-rallies-on-journal-report-phone-maker-trying-to-replace-ceo-kallasvuo.html.

European Commission. Commission Recommendation on September 8, 2011, calling for support of a European Union-wide e-Call Service. From the Official Journal of the European Union, No. L 303, November 22, 2011. Brussels.

CNNMoney. "American Airlines files for bankruptcy." http://money.cnn.com/2011/11/29/news/companies/american_airlines_bankruptcy/. November 29, 2011.

Focus Online. "American Airlines hofft nach Pleite auf Neustart." http://www.focus. de/finanzen/news/luftverkehr-american-airlines-hofft-nach-pleite-auf-neustart_aid_688948.html. November 29, 2011.

Focus Online. "IBM 5150 Personal Computer. Der PC feiert seinen 30. Geburtstag." August 12, 2011. http://www.focus.de/digital/computer/computergeschichte /ibm-5150-personal-computer-der-pc-feiert-seinen-30-geburtstag_aid_654589.html.

Gera, Stefan. "Alles Auto, oder was?" Der Standard, June 2, 2009. http://derstandard.at/1242317264023/ Kommentar-der-anderen-Alles-Auto-oder-was.

Germany's Federal Environmental Agency (Umweltbundesamt). "Daten zur Umwelt 2011 – Stickstoffoxid (NOx) Emissionen." May 31, 2012. http://www.umweltbundesamt-daten-zur-umwelt.de/umweltdaten/public/theme. do?nodeIdent=3573.

Göpfert, Angela. "Mobile Wachstumsfantasien." ARD Börse. February 27, 2012. http://boerse.ard.de/con- tent.jsp?key=dokument_595308.

Göpfert, Angela. "Quartalszahlen – Nokia und NSN schockieren mit Milliardenverlust." Handelsblatt. April 19, 2012. http://www.handelsblatt.com/unternehmen/it-medien/quartalszahlen-massi- ve-verluste-auch-bei-nokia-siemens/6529780-2.html.

Heise.de. "Smartphones: Android überholt Symbian, Apple verliert Marktanteile." January 31, 2012. http://www.heise.de/open/meldung/Smartphones-Android-ueberholt-Symbian-Apple-verliert-Marktanteile-1180547.html.

IFEU – Institute for Energy and Environmental Research, Heidelberg. "Aktualisierung Daten- und Rechenmodell: Energieverbrauch und Schadstoffemissionen des motorisierten Verkehrs in Deutschland 1960-2030." (TREMOD, Version 5.2) für die Emissions Report 2012 (Reporting period from 1990-2010). Heidelberg, 2011.

Lamparter, Dietmar H. "Der Preis ist heiß – Deutsche Autohersteller sind im Internet zweit-klassig." Zeit Online. November 25, 1999. http://www.zeit.de/1999/48/199948.info-fuss_.xml.

Meadows, Dennis, and Donella H. Meadows. The Limits to Growth, a report by the Club of Rome on the state of humankind. Stuttgart, 1972.

Griggs, Brandon. "Apple's App Store hits 50 billion downloads." CNN online. May 15, 2013. http://edition.cnn.com/2013/05/14/tech/web/itunes-50-billion/.

news.de / dpa. "Studie – Autobauer lassen Online-Kunden links liegen."

http:// www.news.de/auto/855295842/studie-autobauer-lassen-online-kunden-links-liegen/1. April 12, 2012.

Parbel, Matthias. "Android und iOS beherrschen die Smartphone-Welt." http://www.heise.de/resale/meldung/Android-und-iOS-beherrschen-die-Smartphone-Welt-1584381.html. Heise.de May 25, 2012.

Randers, Jorgen. 2052 – A Global Forecast for the Next Forty Years., 2012.

Research and Innovative Technology Administration – Bureau of Transportation. "Passengers, All Carriers, All Airports." June 8, 2012. http://www.transtats.bts.gov/Data_Elements.aspx?Data=1.

Rief, Norbert, and Stern, Nicole." Sony kämpft um Comeback." http://diepresse. com/home/techscience/hightech/749381/Sony-kaempft-um-Comeback. Die Presse. April 14, 2012.

Schlautmann, Christoph. "Fotoindustrie – Kodak droht der Untergang." Abgerufen von: http://www.handelsblatt.com/unternehmen/ industrie/fotoindustrie-kodak-droht-der-untergang/6021928.html, Handelsblatt (05.01.2012).

SWR Wissenschaft aktuell. "Die (fast) quecksilberfreie Energiesparlampe." May 12, 2012http://www.swr.de/ blog/wissenschaftaktuell/2012/05/03/stromsparen-ohne-sonder-mull.

United Nations: World Population Prospects – The 2010 Revision. New York, 2011.

Verband der Automobilindustrie, e.V. (German Association of the Automobile Industry). Tatsachen und Zahlen – 75. Folge 2011. Berlin, 2011.

Verband der Automobilindustrie e. V. (German Association of the Automobile Industry), Department of Statistics, Analysis and Forecasts. May 31, 2012.

von Weizsäcker, Ernst Ulrich, Karlson Hargroves, and Michael Smith. Faktor Fünf – Die Formel für nachhaltiges Wachstum. Munich, 2010.

Womack, James P., Daniel T. Jones, and Daniel Roos. The Machine That Changed the World: The Story of Lean Production. 1991.

Zeman, Eric. "Google Reports 1.5 Million Android Activations Per Day", http://www.informationweek.com/mobile/mobile-devices/google-reports-15-million-android-activations-per-day/d/d-id/1109568?. Information Week. April 16, 2013.

The Company

August Horch wrote the first chapter in Audi history when he founded the company in Zwickau in 1909. In 1932, four car makers – Audi, DKW, Horch and Wanderer – merged to form Auto Union. The company's trademark was four interlocking rings: one for each company. After the end of WWII, the company was reestablished as Auto Union GmbH. Between 1964 and 1966, the company was taken over by Volkswagen AG. Today, Audi has production plants in Ingolstadt and Neckarsulm (Germany), Györ (Hungary), Changchun and Foshan (China) and Brussels (Belgium). In 2015, Audi will start production in Brazil. In 2016, a new Audi plant will go into operation in Mexico. The Audi Group is present in more than 100 markets world-wide. The company's 100% subsidiaries include AUDI HUNGARIA MOTOR Kft. (Györ, Hungary), Automobili Lamborghini S.p.A. (Sant'Agata Bolognese, Italy), AUDI BRUSSELS S.A./N.V. (Brussels, Belgium), quattro GmbH (Neckarsulm, Germany) and Ducati Motor Holding S.p.A. (Bologna, Italy). Audi currently employs more than 70,000 people worldwide, 50,000 of whom are employed in Germany.

For further information: http://en.wikipedia.org/wiki/Audi, www.audi.com and http://www.audi.com/com/brand/en/company/production_plants.html

Summary

The customer's new level of power: In the "customer-product-brand" triangle, the focus is on the customer. The company no longer holds a monopoly on information, and customer-customer relationships on the Internet are becoming increasingly important. Social networks and blogs have become the places people go for product advice, and have much greater credibility than classical advertising.

Taking advantage of online trends and ideas: On the Internet, there's no single entity that controls popular opinion. Thus, even critical feedback needs to be dealt with objectively and constructively. In the future, a company will use social networks (even internal ones) to filter and gather information on what its customers like, where there's room for improvement and even to come up with new product ideas. This discussion will be fast-paced, free of hierarchies and highly innovative.

The intelligent car: In the future, products will network with other products. In Web 3.0, the web of things and services, we will see the emergence of added value – above all in the areas of safety and comfort – through the exchange of information between cars and their environment and surrounding infrastructure. Furthermore, a service environment in which the car is networked with the manufacturer will allow for fully automated software updates and maintenance requests, which will make life easier for drivers. The Internet has also fundamentally changed the way cars are sold: from the individual configuration of new cars to how the online used-car market operates. But the Web will never be able to replace the thrill of a real test drive.

The need for new business models: Companies that attempt to ignore or circumvent the changing realities and opportunities created by new technology will fall by the wayside. Even a multinational corporation can go bankrupt if it ignores the signs of the times. But companies that make their employees and customers part of the dialog about future issues will build a solid foundation for the coming decades and benefit from the social revolution of the 21st century.

The Author

René Obermann was born in 1963. After completing secondary school, he began his career with a business traineeship at BMW AG in Munich. In 1986, he set up his own company, ABC Telekom in Münster, Germany. The company was bought by the Hong-Kong conglomerate Hutchison Whampoa in 1991. René Obermann was Managing Partner of the resulting company Hutchison Mobilfunk GmbH from 1991 onwards and chief executive officer from 1993 to 1998. He joined Deutsche Telekom AG in 1998 as Director of Sales and Member of the board of management at T-Mobile Deutschland GmbH. In 2000, he was appointed CEO of T-Mobile Deutschland GmbH. From 2002 until 2006, Obermann was the CEO of T-Mobile International AG & Co. KG and member of the board of management of Deutsche Telekom AG. In 2006, he assumed the role of CEO of Deutsche Telekom AG. In addition, Obermann has been the Vice President of the German Federal Association for Information Technology, Telecommunications and New Media (BITKOM) since 2007, and was appointed to the Supervisory Board of E.ON AG in May 2011. At the end of 2013, René Obermann stepped down as CEO of Deutsche Telekom AG and became CEO of Dutch cable operator Ziggo on January 1, 2014.

"Like" or "Fail"? – Customer Relations with the Facebook Generation

René Obermann, Deutsche Telekom AG*

The online shop "spreadshirt.de" lets customers design and print shirts with slogans and designs of their own choosing. They decide on the color, size and pattern at the click of a button via computer, smartphone or tablet. At "mi adidas", athletes can create their own soccer, running or lifestyle shoes from scratch. "DaWanda" connects thousands of small fashion and jewelry designers with shoppers who are looking for something individual and unique. And if they want to, customers can even order products based on their own designs or specifications.

These are just three examples of the enormous changes in the relationship between customers and the products they buy, seen in recent years. We have come far since Henry Ford's edict, "any customer can have a car painted any color that he wants so long as it is black". Customers nowadays are much more confident and vocal about their individual needs. They expect from companies to incorporate these requirements, as can be seen in the modern automotive industry.

The Internet, but also computer-aided development, production and logistics enable this high level of customer participation in brand and product development. Tim Berners-Lee, the father of the World Wide Web, did not see his invention as a "technical toy", but rather viewed it as a social invention that would support cooperation among people – something which also gave it the potential to revolutionize communication between providers and users.

His invention has enjoyed gigantic success. Even 20 years later, its growth and expansion remains unstoppable. In 2011, Deutsche Telekom alone saw data usage of 400,000 terabytes per month – the equivalent of 200 billion pages of typewriter-generated text. The Internet has penetrated all walks of life – and it is no longer limited to our PCs. Now it is becoming increasingly mobile. Currently, more than 60 percent of all the mobile phones that we sell in Germany are web-enabled smartphones. One of the key factors driving this is the spread of social networks. Today, around three-quarters of all Internet users in Germany are members of at least one online social network (see

* René Obermann was chief executive officer of Deutsche Telekom AG from November 2006 to December 2013.

BITKOM, "Soziale Netzwerke II," December 2011). Above all, it is young people who wish to remain connected to their circle of family and friends – at all times and wherever they go.

The Rise of a New Kind of Customer Power

This constant social networking also changes the relationship between companies and their customers. Customers can contact companies more directly and express their expectations more easily, and quite rightly expect a response. However, many companies appear clumsy as they try to adopt the use of networks like Facebook or Google+, and tend to see them more as threats than as opportunities. Ultimately, customer reactions can be quite unpredictable – high praise for a company or product can go hand in hand with brutal, open criticism. But one thing is for sure: refusing to use these channels of communication is not an option. People will keep talking about us, whether we like it or not.

And there is also a positive side to this: online recommendations and service and product ratings are now more important than ever. According to a global survey by the Nielsen Company in 2012, 92 percent of consumers with Internet access were already basing their purchasing decisions on the online recommendations of friends and acquaintances. Customer reviews and comments have become more relevant than traditional advertising. For companies, this implies: They can no longer rely solely on classical marketing. They need to encourage positive customer ratings – and ensure that these ratings are seen – and they must also learn how to be more effective in counteracting the impact of negative reviews. This will decide whether a brand or product gets millions of "likes" on Facebook – or whether it will lead to a "shitstorm" and subsequent failure.

This shift poses a major challenge to all of us – and perhaps especially to Deutsche Telekom – since communication is the core of our business. Our networks provide the basis for this new communication and consumer culture. On top of that, it is very difficult to use pricing to challenge our competitors (particularly in a regulated market and as a formerly state-owned entity). Our competitive edge lies in the products, services and brand experience we have to offer. A good and trusting relationship with our customers is, indeed, one of our most important competitive advantages.

Which raises three questions:

1. How can we offer tailor-made products for an increasingly heterogeneous market?

2. How can our customers become part of our brand, thus strengthening it?

3. And what should our customer service look like in the day and age of Facebook, Twitter and other social media platforms?

Customer-Oriented Product Development

Many companies have long come to the conclusion that customers are more than just consumers, a source of data or a research topic. Customers are now involved in the product development process – which is something we practice at Telekom, too. We call this process "co-creation". The "Creation Center" at Telekom Innovation Laboratories tracks the day-to-day lives of the most heterogeneous possible customer group, to determine what kinds of demands and expectations they have for new products.

"Co-creation" is a vital component of our product development. But that is not enough. To quote Henry Ford again: "If I had asked people what they wanted, they would have said faster horses." Or in other words: Customers do not always know today what we will need and want tomorrow. When the first UMTS licenses were auctioned back in 2000, there were only a few people who could even imagine what to do with them. Today, the mobile Internet has become an integral part of everyday life that we cannot do without – and this explains why it is a market worth billions.

Turning the Brand into an Experience

Having great products is one thing, but the need to market them is another. With this in mind, the Internet can be seen as both: a challenge and an opportunity. While we still communicate with customers via traditional TV and print advertising, we are also combining these communication efforts with an invitation to the customer to actively contribute to our marketing activities. At Telekom, we have already revamped some areas of our marketing communications to reflect this new approach. One example of this type of participatory marketing was our ad campaign, "A Million Voices – The Network that Makes Everything Possible". To a great extent, this campaign was created with user-generated content. We provided the stage and the space, but the creation of the content was left up to our customers.

The question we asked ourselves at the beginning of this campaign was: How can we get customers in Germany excited about our products, even though we are selling something quite abstract, namely mobile and landline phone services? And that is what proved to be our biggest challenge, because one can neither see, nor emotionally experience things like "greater network quality". So our idea was to get as many customers as possible to collaborate on something together via the Internet that would, in turn, be seen by a lot more people. With the support of the German musician Thomas D, users were asked to record themselves singing the chorus or lead vocals of the hit song "7 Seconds". These audio or video files could then be uploaded via a smartphone app or through the website created for the project. Platforms such as Facebook, YouTube and Twitter were used to spread the word about the campaign and to answer any questions or comments the users had. The campaign was a huge success: Users sent in more than 10,000 files. The smartphone app was downloaded 24,500 times and, during the campaign alone, we counted around half a million visits on the various social media platforms and over 15,500 new Facebook fans.

"A Million Voices" was completely new territory for us and nobody could predict whether as many people as we hoped would actually take part. In retrospect, we can definitely say: The risk was worth it.

Rethinking Service

What is true for product development and marketing is of course even more applicable to customer service. The decisive factor is the ability to utilize the potential of the Internet to offer good service that is extremely fast, tailored to individual needs, and yet still cost-effective. At the same time, a premium provider like Deutsche Telekom must create emotionally appealing services and shopping experiences with quality features to clearly differentiate us from competitors – among other reasons, to win over new customer groups. Examples of this approach are seen in our "4010" and "MyZeil" store concepts. The "4010" retail stores simultaneously function as a retail experience concept and as event platforms. They primarily target young people and aim to improve their impression of our conventional Telekom shops. Their lounge character and trendy beats make them club and store in one.

We have also started offering customers a completely new kind of shopping experience with our very first flagship store "MyZeil" in Frankfurt, Germany. This store features a mix of individual consultation, product presentation and a multifaceted service palette. Services include on-the-spot support for PC and mobile phones, digitization of photos, slides, rolls of film and video cassettes, and furthermore, individual and group seminars on smartphones, netbooks, tablets and the Internet. For us, the new store is a "future lab" which gives us a lot of new insights into how to optimize our customer care and develop additional services. We plan to transfer some of these elements to our other stores across Germany in the future. In the process, customers turn from consumers to co-creators. Offering them an outstanding experience is of utmost importance here, too.

Taking our cues from the services we offer on the Internet, we are focusing on "automated self-care". With this tool, we give our customers quick and convenient access to information that enables them to solve their problems themselves – 24 hours a day, 7 days a week, independent of store hours. Among others, we offer a smartphone app and a video center that contains helpful troubleshooting videos. Besides giving our customers more flexibility and faster access to assistance, this feature has another decisive advantage: It saves money.

The use of social media platforms such as Facebook and Twitter provides further ways of setting ourselves apart from competition. We have been using these platforms since May 2010. Our "Telekom-hilft" (Telekom Helps) service for example, offers customers real-time online communication. The objective is to provide service whenever our customers need it – no matter where they are. They can report problems and contact our service team directly.

One thing applies especially for our Twitter channel: It isn't always easy to provide good service in 140 characters. On Twitter, the actual language and style used is completely different to the way we communicate on other channels. But the main thing is the success we enjoy with this medium. The channel is very popular among users and provides us the chance to get in contact with new – mainly younger – customer segments. Currently, "Telekom-hilft" has almost 27,000 followers on Twitter and more than 43,000 Facebook fans (as of August 2013).

The main success factors are authenticity, personal service and, above all, taking our customers seriously. And we seem to be doing something right in this regard: among other honors, we were recognized for having the best innovative approach in the area of "Service Desk Innovation" in the "Service Desk Award 2010" – and "for making innovative strides into new territory with a completely different set of expectations and conditions", according to the Service Desk Forum jury.

Based on this positive feedback, we have expanded the "Telekom-hilft" team. We have also established a "Community Platform" that lets users communicate directly with members of our service team – and vice versa. This has made "Telekom-hilft" an indispensable addition to our more traditional customer-service channels which complements our overall service portfolio.

Conclusion

We are seeing a fundamental shift in the relationship between customers and manufacturers. Consumers are becoming "prosumers" (a combination of "producer" and "consumer") who increasingly want to get involved and who expect their ideas, needs and wants to be acted upon. Both the Internet and the rapid spread of social networks strengthen and encourage this development.

For companies, this implies: In certain areas, they will have to relearn how to deal with customers. "Communication between equals" is something that takes on a whole new meaning when millions of people can watch and react immediately. We need to make sure that our customers know that their opinion matters and that we are listening to both: their suggestions for improvement and their criticism. But it is not just listening – we also need to take action accordingly.

For us, this represents a massive transformation in our way of doing business, our processes and, above all, our corporate culture. This transformation can only happen if we make our customers and their needs and feedback the focal point of our business. We will be successful if we are able to get our customers involved in a meaningful way at all levels of the value chain, from product development through to marketing and customer services.

The Company

Deutsche Telekom AG was formed at the beginning of 1995 in the course of the "second postal reform" in Germany through the re-incorporation of the state-owned Deutsche Bundespost Telekom as a stock company at the end of 1994. The company went public in 1996. Today, Deutsche Telekom AG is one of the leading integrated telecommunications companies worldwide. With 230,000 employees in around 50 countries, the company earned revenues of more than 58 billion in 2012.

For further information: http://www.telekom.com/company

Summary

We now live in a state of constant social networking. This has completely changed the relationship between companies and their customers. Online shopping recommendations and ratings for products and services play an increasingly important role in our decisions on whether to purchase a product or use a service – or not. And it is no longer enough to try and set ourselves apart from the competition via pricing – customers today expect "the whole package", including the product, service and brand experience.

Customers have become more than just buyers, sources of data or research objects – they are becoming a part of the product development phase, too. In a collaborative process called "co-creation", companies are involving their customers directly in product and service creation.

The Internet offers people new forms of brand experience that go above and beyond what classical advertising can do: a good social-media campaign that gets customers involved (participatory marketing) can do a great deal to increase both a company's public recognition and overall popularity.

Through the use of innovative design that gives customers an emotional connection to the service and shopping experience, the "point of sale" in the form of concept stores will continue to be an important way to engage and excite customers about a brand, a product or a company. Additionally, customers nowadays expect quick access to information and assistance – everywhere and ideally 24/7 – independent of store opening hours. Twitter, Facebook and other social media sites give companies the opportunity to communicate in real time with their customers.

The Author

Herbert Hainer was born in 1954 and studied business administration in Landshut. From 1979 until 1987, he worked as a sales manager for Germany with Procter & Gamble GmbH. He joined adidas in 1987 and served as sales director for hardware (bags, rackets, balls), and as the sales director field (footwear, apparel, hardware) from 1989 until 1991, before filling the role of national sales director with adidas Germany from 1991 until 1993. He became the managing director (sales and logistics) in 1993, and in 1996 assumed the role of senior vice president for Europe, Africa and the Middle East with adidas AG. In 1997, he joined the executive board of adidas AG. He acted as the deputy chairman of the executive board of adidas-Salomon AG from January 2000 until March 2001, and since March 2001 he has been the chief executive officer of adidas AG.

Facing up to Big Data and Coming Out on Top – The Digital Communication Revolution

Herbert Hainer, adidas AG

When the FIFA World Cup starts on June 12, 2014, in São Paulo, the world will experience yet another revolution in digital communication. adidas will thrill the fans and place itself right at the center of the spotlight – not only in the stadium and the outdoor viewing areas, but also online.

Am I exaggerating? The Internet stands for consumption and communication on a gigantic scale. It is the key medium for our core target group, the 14- to 19-year-olds. It is the world where young people want to be, and where they get their ideas, and the time they spend there is constantly increasing. And we're there too, where they are networking, making friends, shopping, finding information and sending out messages. This is where we communicate with them, and it's also where we get our campaigns started.

That is no exaggeration. We're in the network and entwined in it. Our brand – as I write these words – has more than 65 million Facebook fans and, by the time you read them, will presumably have gained some more. In any case, we have one of the biggest digital fan followings in the world. Our video clips get millions of views on YouTube. And the traffic on adidas.com has increased by 26 percent over the past year.

adidas has always been a global marketing trendsetter, but it was never as exciting as now, in the age of digitization, to be a trailblazer. The networked world makes any notion of distance, inapproachability or limitations purely relative. We analyzed this development at an early stage and did not hesitate for a moment before utilizing the new reality of the Internet. There is no question: The Internet speeds up learning processes and multiplies options. The challenges for brand management are increasing at a drastic rate.

Between "then" and "now," there is a whole era: Many things were simpler, clearer and more structured 30 years ago – starting first with our communication with consumers. In those days there were only two TV channels in the Federal Republic of Germany. With a TV ad on ZDF or

ARD, we reached 98 percent of our target group and many viewers in the former German Democratic Republic, the GDR, as well. It was also easier to evaluate the attitudes and buying patterns of consumers.

The Internet as a Cultural Artifact

And what about today? The atmosphere in the networked world reveals a tumult of impressions, insights and opinions. It pervades all social hierarchies – poor, rich, educated; the usual sociodemographic classifications no longer apply. All of us, at home or at work, are at the controls in the multi-communications system cockpit. We can choose from 300 television stations, and the full freedom of the Internet is coinciding with people who are growing up with this new freedom. In the schoolyard, the school bus, in the café, while visiting friends – the Internet is just there, and is now taken for granted just like the telephone, radio and television. The time when it was a luxury is long past. It is now a cultural artifact and, for some, actually a necessity of life. We are amazed at the technological revelations of the Internet and stunned to witness the ingenuity of the 21st century. The freedom of the World Wide Web correlates with a society that is in the process of shedding its old skin. People are better informed, more attentive and individualistic; they want to change and try out new things. They want to place their own emotions, their own experiences and their own wishes more in the foreground.

Consequently, today's more individualized society and the fragmentation of the market are resulting in a level of complexity and a dynamic never experienced before. Everything is changing and getting jumbled up together. Those who misinterpret these changes or ignore them will have no chance of achieving their goals.

The logic of this development: no marketing aimed at all advertising media; instead, a tight focus on the Internet. During the 2010 soccer World Cup in South Africa, we had already cut back on classic television, radio and print advertising in favor of Facebook, Twitter and YouTube. Two years later we optimized this strategy for the Olympic Games in London and the UEFA EURO 2012 in Poland and Ukraine.

Optimization: Where can it take us? More and more people around the world are getting Internet access, and are experiencing almost incidentally the relentless forward momentum of a technology that can hardly be put into words.

The Internet imposes a new rhythm on our concept of time. What's new now becomes old almost instantly. Are we actually overtaking ourselves? Anyone walking out of a store with a new mobile phone is actually holding an outdated mobile phone. This idea may seem absurd, but it is actually impossible to turn new knowledge into products as fast as it is being created.

Modern – But not Modernist

When we think about the impossible today, we are already very close to our goals. There are more than 1,000 IT specialists working at adidas who think about how we can position our brand in technological terms and network it with people. The sheer scale of the possibilities entices our marketing people with entirely new tools for communication and building customer loyalty:

- adidas Neo: With this young, fashionable and networked brand, we are experimenting with new paths. We want to know what is possible and then to transfer this knowledge to adidas. In the Neo shops, a special mirror takes a picture of the customer who is trying on an outfit and, if desired, sends it to Facebook or Twitter. Friends see it and answer by clicking the "Like" button or by saying, perhaps, "Why not combine that with something else?" Neo is always online. Our shop employees are always linked to a special Twitter feed that helps them to react very quickly to changing trends and order new inventory.

- F50 miCoach: In the fall of 2011, we launched a soccer boot that uses a sensor to track and log every move the player makes on the pitch. With these data, the coach gets a detailed overview of his or her team. How many kilometers did each player run? How many sprints did the right winger do? How fast was the left defender? Players can analyze their own strengths and weaknesses and make adjustments to their training. And, above all, they can exchange their data with friends and compare themselves not only with teammates, but also with superstars like Lionel Messi and Lukas Podolski.

- "miCoach": Via smartphone, runners receive precise performance and cardio data, ad hoc input ("pulse high, slow down"), and can use this information to adapt their training plan in real time.

- 3-D mapping technology: Fans who would like to wear the adidas jersey alongside the stars of the German national team like Philipp Lahm get their chance with this virtual reality software – at least in a computer game.

Technical gadgetry? No. It's simply what is modern in our time. Modern – but not "modernist." We're not promoting an exaggerated belief in progress. But we are using every available technology to heighten the interaction between people and our brand and take it to the level where it is useful for athletes and speaks to the emotions of our customers.

Creating Unique Worlds of Experience

It quickly became clear to us that we would have to change the way we reach out to position ourselves in the world of experience where the digital generation is at home. We have always been proud of our innovative achievements, and have been brief and to the point in communicating about them. Now we're doing it differently. With our new "adidas is all in" brand campaign, we are raising our brand to a new level: The campaign showcases the unique presence of adidas in a diverse range of sports, cultures and lifestyles, and creates an arc spanning sports, music and fashion in a credible manner. The campaign features appearances by more than two dozen brand ambassadors, including the soccer stars Lionel Messi and David Beckham, Derrick Rose of the NBA, the pop icon Katy Perry, the adidas skateboard team, designer Jeremy Scott and many more.

This is not just any campaign. It is the biggest in our company's history. One might expect that it would be the CEO who would contact the global workforce of 47,000 employees to set the tone for this campaign, but the global soccer star Lionel Messi took on that task on my behalf. He wrote an e-mail to the employees saying how happy he was to be one of the key figures in the new global campaign. With this message, he communicates emotions and creates fresh moods and new interest that spread to the Internet and energize our fan base. The Internet links people, and we must network our thoughts and ideas to achieve our maximum potential visibility with the 14- to 19-year-old age group. To do that, a soccer star is a better choice than a CEO.

When we were thinking up and developing this campaign, we already had the "aha" feeling that we were onto something great. And we were right: The ads for this campaign are a huge hit with our young target group all over the world. We estimate that 1.25 billion consumers will see the campaign during its three-year run, above all through the rapidly growing digital channels. That means that we will reach 80 percent of our target group, made up of the world's teenagers.

Pushing Us to Get Better

It's not hard to imagine how agile we have to be with this differentiated marketing approach, as trends become increasingly diverse, short-lived and complex. The tried-and-true recipes of yesteryear are about as modern as stone tools.

Just a reminder: The customer is the most powerful participant in the economy. But customers do not play the role of referee; they always act unilaterally and force suppliers to do their utmost to win them over. This pressure results in permanent change. Those who can't match this pace are unproductive; those who can are productive. But the one that sets the pace is the market leader.

Our core target group is completely renewed every five years. During this five-year period we must stay on top of all the trends, and at the same time keep our finger on the pulse of the core group growing up behind them and their special characteristics and communication habits. How demanding it is to keep up is demonstrated by our age of fundamental innovations.

Just 15 years ago, no teenager had a mobile phone, and 10 years ago we started to see the first ones with their own mobiles. Just five years later, every teenager had one. Nowadays, the conventional mobile phone is "out." Everyone wants or already has a smartphone. And as for Facebook, today's teens take it for granted as if it had always been there. Just six years after its launch, the massive social network is now poised to welcome its one-billionth user. And I am convinced that we will soon see the emergence of other new digital communication channels that we can use.

Powerful Momentum

The digitized world is helping us to make stronger gains in market share than our competitors, and is speeding up our growth. At the same time, the Internet forces us to get it right when we evaluate users' fascinations. We like to show our enthusiasm, but are also very conscious of what we are getting into. The Internet is not only a fast-moving medium, but also highly unfocused, running the gamut from smart emotions to chaotic creativity through to embarrassing revelations.

With this density and blinding speed, it's easy to get carried away with knee-jerk reactions and end up blindly following every passing fad. The fact that the Internet makes everything possible is what makes trust so important. Trust means buying a certain product that one can rely on, or following a certain idea. Trust means security. It gives the customer the positive feeling of having made the right choice. Trust is a way of making life easier and enriching it.

Speed Without Coercion

Mistrust means stress, because the risk of being shortchanged lurks around every corner. Mistrust is exhausting, because it forces us to be constantly on guard. We can look at the word "trust" from any angle – we will always end up back at the starting point. It's always about making up for a lack of knowledge or orientation through trust. When a brand gets to that point, it is ensconced in the consumer pantheon in the upper echelon of the most valuable brands.

We have found our sense of scale and our pace. We cannot let the Internet control us; nor can the zeitgeist dictate our strategy. It is compulsory for us to be in a position to protect what is true in our brand and to remain authentic. That's why we keep asking ourselves: Is this still our brand, or are we crossing a threshold? We have to be careful. If we dilute our brand because we want to be all things to all people, there will be people somewhere in the world who don't like that, and trigger an uncontrollable avalanche. That's why direct access to the customer via the Internet is not only a productive blessing, but also a fateful curse. It is a logical axiom: The more renowned and popular a company becomes, the bigger a target it presents. Otherwise, criticism would fizzle out. The danger that Internet users will use social networks as a forum for reputation-damaging criticism is also a reality.

Just post one's opinion – unseen, emotional, untrue, insulting and uninformed. Whatever has gone out, is in. And whatever is in, stays in. It creates its own reality. A shapeless reality, a "not-hung-up-on-facts" reality, an "I-don't-care" reality; a reality that does not serve truth, or search for it, but rather has no aim beyond the desire to do some kind of damage.

This form of opinion-making control coalesces into an actual threat when it turns into what the online world calls a "shitstorm." Within just an hour, a blast of outrage can take shape through blogs, Twitter feeds and Facebook postings. Because the Internet neither has opening hours nor sticks to regular working times, a company has to be ready to react.

Consequently, we take a pragmatically forward-looking approach to the Internet, based on the fundamental values and insights of the adidas Group.

First: Transparency and Self-Confidence

Those who can't cope with the transparency of the Internet have no chance of survival in that medium. We definitely have the advantage of being well accustomed to publicity. Whenever an athlete is exposed for doping, the International Olympic Committee, the IOC, announces the next city to host the Olympics, or the German parliament passes new sports-related legislation, journalists expect us to comment.

adidas means sports. Sports mean attention, and attention means publicity. That is the logic driving our actions. We couldn't hide even if we wanted to, because sports are our passion – and there's no hiding passion.

Second: Constructive Dialog

Because the Internet is wide open to everyone, we make sure that we are seen and heard. We do not hide. In our official corporate blog (http://blog.adidas-group.com) we provide insights into the adidas Group. Our bloggers are our employees from 50 different countries. They write about their experiences and specific topics, about China or Australia, about their work at world championships or on a new product, or an encounter with a star athlete, about environmental issues and working conditions at Asian suppliers. There is no shortage of topics. And behind these topics there are people who are committed to the adidas Group. The reason for stating this so emphatically is that the passion for our brands is always rooted in people, and not in an abstract structure. If we are always open and honest in dealing with this passion, we will have credibility.

A good image requires having credibility at all times. And this credibility not only ensures respect when business is booming and everything is going well, but also gains us sympathy during times of crisis when things take a turn for the worse. A good image is like a mysterious force that ties people in. It is an enormous challenge for our public relations people to manage our reputation to ensure that we do not lose this force.

Consequently, by personalizing our company and our brands with our blog and giving them many different faces, our communication of values such as respect, identification and trust gains authenticity. Our message: I don't want to dominate you as a consumer; I want to be your best friend. And I hope that you will invite me to be your friend.

Third: Social Acceptability

We create value by creating jobs, paying taxes and earning profits. It is important to us to be a good member of society. People's ideas, their concerns and wishes, their likes and dislikes give a moral dimension to our work. People want things to be fair. When ethics and ideals change, but companies keep acting in accordance with other value standards, sooner or later there will be disagreements. A company that wants to remain successful and profitable must be acceptable in the eyes of society and also act to preserve the environment and the climate, i.e. must be sustainable in its activities. There's no getting past that realization.

Fourth: Tradition as a Way of Staying Modern

As markets become digitized, we shouldn't delude ourselves that people have become so modern and bedazzled by the latest fads that they no longer have any sense of history or of tradition as it is lived and understood. Because the Internet is a wonderful invention that enriches our modernity, it makes our tradition even more valuable. Tradition does not stand opposed to modernity. For us, tradition means that we are proud of our company. But tradition also means a responsibility for the future. Without this responsibility, tradition would be meaningless. Tradition doesn't mean preserving values, but rather nurturing and growing values so that they mean something to people.

Our founder, Adi Dassler, was an impressive figure. When he stitched together his first sports shoes in the 1920s and went on to build the world's largest sports company in the decades that followed, he was more than just a businessman. First and foremost, he was an inventor and a friend of the athletes – such as Muhammad Ali, Jesse Owens, the great boxer Max Schmeling and soccer legends Uwe Seeler and Sepp Herberger, to name just a few. Of course all of that is history, but this history lives on and shapes who we are.

No matter how much we professionalize our business, we know exactly where we come from and what we're made of. Companies with a history behind them are simply wired differently from those that have no idea what history means. History means identity, a sense of security, and sometimes it even gives you goose bumps. In our very own "Walk of Fame" at adidas, on permanent display at our headquarters, we present great athletes with our products. Another way that we maintain and underscore the values and traditions of our company is the history book that we have put together for our employees.

Fifth: Quality Comes at a High Price

Sometimes the Internet is little more than a bargain counter. Search engines track down products and compare them with other products and prices. We have a brand that communicates – and has – value. A consequence of this fact is that, with our brand, we communicate a value that we will not sell cheaply using the digital bargain counter. So online shoppers hoping to pick up goods on the cheap would be well advised to avoid us.

Any company that lets its customers draw it into a price war will not only see its margins shrink in the long term, but also its reputation. Penny-pinching consumers will perhaps show gratitude for a discount by making a purchase, but they have no interest in customer loyalty. All that remains is the ruined shell of a brand that has been haggled to death. And that's dangerous. Companies that put up with that kind of customer are always on the defensive. They are constantly putting their products on sale to try to build customer loyalty, and end up harming themselves.

By putting these five points forward, we may stir up some hostility here and there, but by and large they should guarantee us a fair dialog, praise and valuable suggestions. Above all, however, we are making clear that we are getting involved in the Internet in the best way – not just as a "sales machine" but rather as a "cultural machine." Consumption and dialog are not parallel worlds; they constantly overlap and find common ground.

Strong brands have the power to become even stronger and more powerful if they access and utilize their possibilities realistically. That will give them the opportunity to continue to boost the company's value and enable the company to have a profitable future. In my view, that is a fantastic outlook.

What's more, Big Data is now closing in on the 2014 FIFA World Cup. If we recall for a moment that Twitter recorded up to 3,000 tweets per second during the last soccer World Cup in South Africa, then it is clear that, during the World Cup in Brazil, we can expect an astronomical number. But another fact will also ensure that the next World Cup generates superlatives: When the global market leader for soccer takes the stage in the country with five World Cup wins to its name, the world will experience "adidas is all in" and at the top of its game. I'm already looking forward to this World Cup and our communications with millions of fans around the world.

The Company

The company was established in 1949 by Adolf (Adi) Dassler: hence the name "adidas." The relentless rise of the brand with three stripes started with the soccer World Cup victory in 1954, when the entire German national soccer team wore adidas shoes with interchangeable cleats. Today, adidas offers an extensive range of sports shoes and apparel for training, competition and an active lifestyle. In 1989, adidas was transformed into a stock company, and in 1995 the company went public. Since 1998 it has been included in the DAX index. The Group includes the core brands adidas, Reebok and TaylorMade-adidas Golf. In 2012, the adidas Group had 46,306 employees and total sales of approximately 14.9 billion euros.

For more information: www.adidas-group.com

Summary

Social networks such as Twitter and Facebook are excellent tools for creating customer loyalty, especially for lifestyle products. They can be used for campaigns individually tailored to the target group that get users involved. This achieves an enormous reach and builds trust.

As advertising platforms, Facebook, Twitter and YouTube have already overtaken the conventional media of television, radio and print. Customers can share or rate content directly. Conversely, through social media monitoring, companies can spot emerging trends as well as positive or negative feedback in the community and react promptly. Advertising campaigns can be linked to individuals or institutions, and not just products. This increases their reach and can help to attract new customers.

In the future, the networking of companies, consumers and products will also give rise to entirely new business models. Instead of selling just a product, companies will offer an entire concept and lifestyle. It will be important, however, to be versatile and consider the needs of target groups based on age and gender.

Participation in and use of social media involves skills that companies must learn. Half-hearted, poorly designed efforts are worthless. Address your customers' needs and listen to them. Surprise them – as in the recent case, with the offer of free downloads of the complete song used in an advertising campaign. It usually only takes a small expense to be rewarded with a strong response, so that both sides have something to show for it.

The Author

Dr. Johannes Teyssen was born in 1959. After studying economics and law in Freiburg and Göttingen, he received a post-graduate scholarship to study in Boston in 1984. He then worked as a research assistant at the University of Göttingen and held a legal clerkship at the Celle Higher Regional Court before completing his doctorate. He joined PreussenElektra AG in 1989, where he remained until 1998 and ultimately rose to the position of head of the Legal Affairs and Distribution Companies division. From 1998 until 1999, he was a member of the board of management of HASTRA AG, Hanover, and from 1999 until 2001 served as the chairman of the board of management of AVACON AG in Helmstedt. In 2001, he joined the board of management of E.ON Energie AG, Munich, and acted as chairman from 2003 to 2007. Since 2004 he has been a member of the board of management of E.ON AG, and has served as its chairman since May 2010.

Intelligent Networking in the Home of the Future – The Fundamental Transformation of the Roles of Consumers and Companies through the Refurbished Energy System

Johannes Teyssen, E.ON AG

Introduction

The energy turnaround in Germany has become a social and political reality within a very short time. It is still unclear, however, whether this transformation can be achieved as smoothly as some planners' blueprints suggest. But, in the absence of any real alternative to this path, E.ON is also determined to face this challenge head-on.

The discussions about greenhouse gases and the efforts to reduce them have been with us since the 1990s. For many years, E.ON and other companies have been researching, developing and investing in highly diverse technologies aimed at bringing about a sustainable energy supply. Nevertheless, since the energy policy decisions made in the wake of the Fukushima reactor disaster in March 2011, the transformation of the energy sector has gathered unprecedented momentum, particularly in Germany. Initially, the spotlight was aimed squarely at the large-scale energy world, with massive investments in new distribution networks, wind farms and power stations. It was only gradually that the focus shifted to the customer. There, too, a transformation is taking shape that will fundamentally redefine the roles of consumers and energy producers over the coming years and decades.

This article will discuss these developments and their consequences for the energy supply in greater detail. Section 2 will examine the Internet-driven intensification of competition and the challenges of everyday business. Section 3 offers a brief glimpse into a very real workshop for the emerging future of our energy supply. In Section 4, we look at the most important trends in the future world of energy. This is followed by Section 5, which presents a vision of the future in which the energy supply relationship takes the form of an "energy experience." Section 6 then summarizes the key insights.

The Everyday Competition to Win Customers

Since the energy market was liberalized, more than 26 percent of all German households have changed their electricity supplier, and 14 percent now have a new gas supplier. In 2011 alone, more than 3 million consumers chose to buy their electricity elsewhere, while the number opting for a different gas supplier exceeded 1 million. This greater willingness to switch has intensified competition and heightened the price pressures. The industry body BDEW (the German Federal Association for the Energy and Water Supply Industry) reports that on average, consumers can choose from among 102 power suppliers and 37 gas suppliers. So far, however, these companies, with the electric power and gas they provide, are offering largely identical products, i.e., commodities.

The main criteria with which the energy companies seek to set themselves apart are their rates, services, customer support and the "greenness" of the energy generation process. Most energy providers offer up to 15 different power and gas products geared to various customer needs: basic supply tariffs, discount rates or green products, and time-based or technology-based tariffs, for example for customers using smart meters or heat pumps. Some companies offer additional services such as free energy consultation or special efficiency measures. Through the climate debate and the resulting rise in public awareness, coupled with higher prices, saving energy has become very important to the majority of the population. The key drivers for realizing further gains in efficiency are consumer behavior and new technological solutions. Energy companies have been quick to respond with product offerings to address both of these factors.

Without a doubt, one of the major forces driving the intensifying competition in the energy market is the Internet. Constantly online, even when on the go with laptops, tablets and smartphones, customers can communicate and retrieve information at all times. Within minutes they can compare products, services and prices and then switch suppliers with a single click. Online pricing portals create a level of transparency never seen before and also generate greater media coverage. Hardly a month goes by without new press releases from the portals, reporting on the latest price changes or new rankings, which are eagerly seized upon by all kinds of media outlets.

Companies must adapt their offerings to meet customer expectations. Online shopping is king, and of course that trend is now firmly established in the power and gas markets. For E.ON, too, it has become equally commonplace for customers to take out power contracts online as it is to access the service portal to manage and update contract details using customer self-care functionality. However, conventional telephone-based service continues to play a very important role. At E. ON, a workforce totaling nearly 2,000 employees at the various service companies take care of the power and gas customers in Germany, covering the entire range of services – from customer care and energy data management to billing and accounts receivable. Every year our employees handle several million customer inquiries.

However, E.ON wants to do more than just provide energy and good service. It also wants to learn from its customers how it can improve. For this reason, it has been relying for several years on a customer-loyalty tool known as the Net Promoter Score (NPS). Every year up to 400,000 E.ON customers respond to a detailed survey either online or by telephone. The key question used in the NPS method is: "Would you recommend E.ON as an energy provider to a friend or colleague?" Customers can indicate their agreement on a scale of zero to 10. This method was developed by the consulting firm Bain & Company, which has implemented it in more than 100 companies around the world, including several global players. E.ON assesses all responses in detail. Along with concrete ideas to remedy specific problems, the results of the NPS survey generate approaches for a systematic process of improvement. E.ON has used the responses to date to make changes to forms and customer correspondence, optimize the formalities when customers relocate, and improve its web portals, among other changes.

In the meantime, some 76 percent of all Germans are registered in a social network. The number of German Facebook users has now reached 20 million. Companies have control over their own websites and online advertising, but social media platforms are beyond their reach. Blogs, online reviews and price portals provide customers with information on products, services, prices, opinions and experiences of other customers and enable users to communicate with one another. The energy industry is anything but a trailblazer when it comes to social media. Nevertheless, many companies – including E.ON – are now active on various platforms, maintain their own Facebook pages, post YouTube videos and send out news to Twitter followers. Taking into account the enormous need for discussion as the energy supply system is revamped, E.ON has deliberately anchored its new image campaign in a dialog format – and not merely in the form of staged dialogs in TV commercials or on posters, but rather as a genuine invitation to the public to join in a discussion via dedicated feedback pages and online chat functions.

Although the Internet and social networks have heightened the level of competition in the energy market, the decisive challenge for the energy industry in the coming years still lies ahead. Rebuilding the energy system will not only call for new technologies and huge investments; it will also mean changes for the traditional role of energy consumers and suppliers.

Exploring the Future in Stuhr and Weyhe

New technologies are still at an early stage, and require testing in pilot projects. Ideas that are being tried out and tweaked today can make life easier in the future for millions of people, while helping to provide long-term solutions to the problems of climate change and facilitating an affordable energy supply that conserves resources. E.ON has set up a unique, nation-wide model project in Germany to explore how a secure electric power supply could operate in the future with intelligent networking and controls: the "e-Home Energy Project 2020" in Stuhr and Weyhe in the state of Lower Saxony.

In these two communities to the southwest of Bremen, E.ON is now setting up a laboratory to study the future energy supply. After conducting an extensive energy assessment of 40 single-family homes, including a check of the outer envelope and the heating equipment, realistic power saving concepts are developed. In addition, E.ON supports the homeowners with investments in such forward-looking technologies as solar panels and efficient air conditioning equipment. Another incentive for participating households is the offer of subsidies for electric cars. These elements of the project are already yielding revealing insights into how a sustainable energy supply could look. But there is one more decisive component: intelligent networking.

In each of the 40 houses in the project, E.ON technicians have installed a smart meter that measures and stores the timing and quantity of energy consumption. The smart meter automatically uploads this data at regular intervals to the energy distribution network. Customers can log in via an online portal at any time to view their consumption data. This makes it easier for them to analyze their energy use and identify additional potential savings. The smart meter also records the quantity of energy produced by the household itself and fed back into the grid. The key pieces of technology in the pilot project are the prototypes of controllable local grid transformers installed outside each house. They are needed for automatic identification and balancing of fluctuations in the grid current resulting from the local feed-in of power or increased energy consumption.

The decisive factor for the "e-Home Energy Project 2020" is above all a regular flow of information on power generation and consumption in the household. The data analysis is carried out by the Lower Saxony Energy Research Center (EFZN), a research institute located in Goslar and affiliated with the Clausthal University of Applied Sciences, and by E.ON. Over a three-year period, solid hands-on experience will be gathered for a realistic supply and grid set-up of the kind expected to take shape over the next 10 years. Consequently, the project in Stuhr and Weyhe will play an important role in planning an energy supply that remains stable and secure in the future. Many of the trends and technologies have already moved beyond the testing phase and are now exerting a decisive impact on the development of the energy sector.

Components of the Future Energy Supply

The question may sound simple, but the answer is complex: How can you network a wind farm in the North Sea with a single-family home in Bavaria, far away in the south of Germany, so that each is always aware of what the other is doing in energy terms? For this – put simply – is what is needed if we are to offer customers flexible, time-linked power pricing based on current feed-in levels from renewable sources. Customers could then recharge their electric car battery at times when cheap wind power is on offer. Our current networks are not set up to meet needs of this kind, as they have primarily served to distribute power from centralized power stations to the most remote corners of the country. But this paradigm has already been shaken up considerably in recent years. The impetus for this development has come from German homes and the changing needs of their inhabitants. Consumer behavior has evolved. For many people it is no longer enough just to save energy or obtain it from renewable sources. Increasingly, they want to generate energy themselves and feed it back into the grid. These consumers who are also producers are referred to as prosumers. Their emergence will mean a more varied and less centralized energy supply in the future.

Decentralized energy generation will account for a greater share of total energy production in the future. Customers want to be less dependent on power utilities and are installing their own power generation equipment, in the hope that they can earn returns on their investment while doing their part in steering a new course towards a sustainable and resource-conserving energy future. In the meantime, solar energy is being generated by hundreds of thousands of solar power installations on the roofs of German homes as well as solar energy farms.

In the future, highly efficient, power-generating heating systems will be installed in the basements of many single-family and semi-detached dwellings. For example, gas-fired micro-CHP (combined heat and power) systems can heat a home while generating power, achieving optimal efficiency rates of 90 percent and more.

A key component of the future energy world will be decentralized storage equipment such as batteries and heat pumps. The storage function of these relatively new technologies is not always immediately grasped. But electric cars, for example, can do more than just make transportation more climate-friendly. The batteries of large numbers of these vehicles could one day jointly comprise a large non-centralized storage reservoir serving as a buffer for the fluctuating, weather-dependent power supply from renewable sources. Heat pumps can also perform a storage function by using times when the power supply is plentiful to fill the hot water tank. Small, decentralized storage resources can thus contribute to the integration of renewable energies in the future in the same way as large pumped-storage hydroelectric power stations.

Networking and control systems will also play a key role in the energy world of tomorrow. Consequently, smart meters and networks represent a sort of basic technology for many of the developments described above. The objective is to link the world of large-scale energy production with the small-scale world of prosumers at home, to optimize energy flows and ensure the necessary transparency in consumption and costs. This has given rise to the term "smart energy." Smart meters in particular will be a vital component, as they are essential to the implementation of time-dependent variable pricing and delivering the data needed for efficient energy use.

Despite these dynamic changes, the customer is only seeing a very gradual emergence of the new energy world. We will have to wait for the coming decade before we see fully integrated energy management with smart technologies ensuring the constant balancing of centralized and decentralized components as well as generation and consumption. Many components of the new energy world are already on the market today, however, such as decentralized energy solutions, smart meters and electric cars. For example, E.ON. has invested heavily in the development of micro-CHP technology and set up its own subsidy program for the market launch. Other offers include complete starter packages for electric transportation and smart meter solutions with proprietary analysis tools.

And the changes are still coming. Product packages will become more widespread. For example, a smart meter and a time-dependent green power rate will be bundled with the charging device for an electric car.

This will create a strong incentive to recharge the battery at certain times. Household appliances such as washing machines can also be combined with smart home appliances. This will allow consumers to manage their household utilities and appliances online and benefit from lower rates.

The Energy Experience

But the prospects go much further. Driven by the growing consumer awareness of sustainability issues and their desire for more transparency and individuality, a new vision of the future is taking shape in which the energy supply is conceived as an energy experience. To sketch some of the possible paths this development could follow, it is worth starting with a glance beyond the boundaries of the energy sector.

A look at must-have products that have become an integral part of people's lives around the world, such as the iPod, iPad, etc. by Apple, reveals the success criteria for the world of experience their designers attempt to create. While the strong brand identity of some technology companies has faded over time, making them interchangeable with their competitors, Apple has succeeded in positioning itself as a global brand. With excellent, appealingly designed products complemented by intelligent services such as the AppStore or the iTunes music platform, Apple created a highly desirable world of experience for its customers.

Complementary, experience-based benefits are also part of the strategy for the Oregon-based sporting goods manufacturer Nike. In addition to its basic product, namely running shoes, the company offers special running sessions for its customers. Nike has also teamed up with Apple to launch a runners' information system. A microchip attached to the shoe transmits a runner's data to an iPhone, which uses an app to produce graphic output for comparison with other training sessions. Additional analysis tools are available through an online portal. For example, athletes can check their own results against those of other runners. These two examples show that lifestyle-based companies have moved on from the days when they merely sold individual products, and now offer comprehensive solutions. They could serve as a model for energy companies seeking to create their own "energy experience" for customers.

An initial concept for a world of experience in the energy sector is designed to meet customers' need for more transparency while giving them access to communication platforms where they can discuss their experiences. Smart meters collect the required data, with appealing visualizations and further analysis then produced using apps and web-based tools. An example already offered on the market is the E.ON EnergieNavi. This resource is available online or as a smart phone app, and uses smart meter input to give users a clear picture of their power consumption as well as other services. For example, it supports the retrieval of information on energy consumption or allows comparisons with past usage.

Portal solutions present another way of offering additional services, for example through the central recording and visualization of the performance data of heat pumps or micro-CHP systems. In the future, apps could provide customers with regular feedback on their consumption habits. They would then gain insights into their electric power usage and could decide when to switch networked equipment on or off. Environmentally conscious customers could check the carbon intensity of their current power mix and look at comparisons with other technologies. This could prompt changes in behavior, for example if customers wait for cheaper, off-peak power rates before switching on their washing machines.

These services can also be combined with popular social media formats to create a sense of community and a world to be experienced. The data could be presented in a sort of "energy Facebook" as a springboard for discussion or as the basis for competitions to see who can generate or save the most energy. This "energy experience" is still largely limited mainly to the transparent presentation of data, possibly complemented by comparative tools or dialog options. However, it may serve as an important step towards greater sensitivity and a shift in the perception of energy issues among consumers. Energy is no longer a boring, standardized product of which consumers are only dimly aware. Instead it is increasingly getting attention as a vital future issue that can be directly experienced right now.

Smart Home, the second energy experience, starts with the above scenario and goes much further. It proposes an answer to the question of how we intend to live and spend time in our homes in the future, and what role energy and technology can play. The key word here is networking. In the house of the future, the heating system, lights and ventilation will communicate via interfaces along with home appliances, entertainment systems and household technologies such as windows and awnings. When the sun is shining, the blinds will close automatically, and when a plentiful supply of wind power or solar energy results in low rates, the freezer will lower the temperature by a couple of degrees. Smart washing machines will be linked to the smart meter and will switch themselves on when the power supply is plentiful – so that rates are low.

In addition to the core tasks of energy and load management, Smart Home applications can be extended to other aspects of life, which may open up new business segments for energy companies. For example, under the heading "assisted living," devices monitor and record the vital signs of occupants of a home and transmit them to nursing care providers. For greater convenience, intelligent systems will be in place to coordinate delivery services, and programmable devices will water and fertilize gardens. It is also possible to set up central control of all aspects of burglary prevention, from outdoor motion sensors to the detection of glass breakage in doors and windows. If a fire breaks out, the sprinkler system starts automatically. When the inhabitants are all away from home, the televisions stop wasting power in standby mode because all unneeded circuits will be shut down – with the exception of the refrigerator and alarm system. No matter where they are, the homeowners will be able to control the heating system and lights or check to make sure that the stove is switched off.

For this second type of "energy experience," it will also be crucial to achieve the greatest possible simplicity and transparency to produce a concept that the consumer can experience directly. Perhaps customers will eventually have access to an energy solution cockpit and other services covering all aspects of home living. However, the technology must be understandable to the average person and provide appropriate visual output. Many of the applications described above can be integrated into existing media such as Google, Facebook or in-house closed circuit TV channels.

E.ON sees the entire range of smart home technologies and services as a highly promising business segment for the future, and we have therefore made them a focal point of our innovation activities. It is one of our biggest challenges to utilize the vast range of potential offerings and develop intelligent products geared towards solving problems and creating experiences. Innovative smart home concepts not only require expertise in the energy sector, but also wide-ranging skills in IT and communication technology. Areas of particular concern: the tricky issues of data protection and security measures to ward off hackers. Legislators and utilities will have to rise to the challenges posed by the risks stemming from the rapid expansion of home networking and intelligent networks.

Conclusion

The energy market has faced entirely new challenges in recent years, primarily through the increasing importance of the Internet and new customer demands. Companies are confronted with a tougher competitive environment in the private household market and are reacting with appropriate offers and services such as special online rates and customer self-care portals. Closely tracking the needs of customers and being willing to learn from them are among the most urgent tasks for professional customer management.

However, the biggest challenge for future product and customer relationships stems from the transformation of the energy sector which has acquired unprecedented momentum in Germany, especially in the wake of the Fukushima nuclear accident. A transformation is taking shape that will fundamentally redefine the future business model in the private customer segment and redefine the roles of consumers and energy producers over the coming years. As "prosumers," customers will no longer merely consume energy. Increasingly, they will be generating and storing it themselves and feeding it back into the grid. Energy efficiency, decentralized generation and storage, electric mobility and the intelligent networking and management of households are the key themes for this trend, which has reached market readiness in many areas.

But the prospects go much further. Driven by heightened consumer awareness of sustainability issues, the objective limits of resource consumption, the demands of climate protection and the desire for greater transparency and individuality, the future energy supply concept can increasingly be seen as an "energy experience." With the rise of value-added services in connection with smart home applications, the core of the energy business will be expanded to include other areas of home living such as safety, security and support services. But to keep customers interested in the long term, these services will have to be packaged as an energy experience and presented in a visually appealing way. Social media formats and channels are an ideal platform for making energy into something real for customers and enabling them to share their experiences with others.

All of these ideas, the major investments and the many research projects started by E.ON, such as the pilot project in Stuhr und Weyhe, add up to a very promising perspective as the company makes the transition from today's energy utility to tomorrow's innovative energy manager and service provider. We're already well underway.

Literature

Federal Association for the Energy and Water Supply Industry (BDEW) Customer Focus: Households (in German). Berlin, 2012.

Kolks, Uwe, and Jens Kallrath. "Zufriedene und loyale Kunden.""Satisfied and loyal Net Promoter Score bei E.ON." Call Center Profi 8/2010: 32-34.

Kolks, Uwe, Alexander Pippert, and Jan Meyer. "Energie erlebbar machen. Mit innovativen Angeboten Kunden gewinnen," in the book by authors / editors Servatius, Hans-Gerd, Uwe Schneidewind, and Dirk Rohlfing. Smart Energy. Wandel zu einem nachhaltigen Energie-system. Berlin, Heidelberg: SpringerVerlag, 2012, 81–100.

Vogg, Stefan. "Langer Atem notwendig." Frankfurter Allgemeine Zeitung (November 28, 2011), B1.

The Company

E.ON AG was formed in 2000 through the merger of the energy groups VEBA and VIAG. The company is listed in the DAX index and is one of the world's largest private-sector power and gas companies. The company's approximately 79,000 employees working at locations in Europe, Russia and North America generate annual sales of nearly 113 billion euros.

For further information: www.eon.com

Summary

Today's portals for comparing gas and power companies are currently only a simple tool helping customers to identify the cheapest energy suppliers. In the future of the energy supply sector, however, networks will be able to do much more.

The intelligent networking of consumers and the energy supply system via Internet and smart grids will be instrumental in bringing about the energy turnaround and promoting the use of renewable energy sources.

The spread of intelligent and networked devices offers greater convenience for consumers, for instance by allowing them to control their lights or heating system when away from home. And the use of networked end devices will lead to improved energy efficiency, and thus to energy savings.

Smart meters make it possible for consumers to exercise more control over energy use over the course of the day. The Internet and the related advance of networked electrical appliances in households will lead to improved transparency in energy consumption. The use of the supply of wind and solar power, which tends to fluctuate, can be optimized through intelligently networked end devices. The resulting "energy Internet" would then represent a vital contribution to making the energy turnaround a reality.

The Author

Dr. Markus Hofmann was born in 1965. He studied chemistry at the University of Ulm and completed his doctorate at ETH Zurich. From 1995 to 1999, he headed the "Insurance Risk Management Department" and the "Risk Adjusted Capital" project at Hoechst AG/ Hoechst Versicherungs-AG in Frankfurt. From 1999 to 2001 he served as the corporate risk manager with VA Technologie AG in Linz, Austria, while working for the industrial insurance broker IVM, Linz, and as the managing director of that company's London-based subsidiary. In 2001 he was appointed to the management board of AXA Versicherung AG and in 2002 his board mandate was extended to include the AXA Konzern AG. Dr. Hofmann was until 2012 responsible for the entire property and casualty insurance business in AXA Germany as well as the claims department and reinsurance. In addition, he was a member of the Global P&C Board of the AXA Group worldwide. Since 2013 he is responsible for the Commercial / SME Business in the Allianz Versicherungs-AG.

Dr. Dominik Reinartz, in his position as head of strategic marketing with the AXA Konzern AG, supported Dr. Hofmann as a co-author in the preparation of this article.

Dr. Reinartz now works in corporate development for Allianz SE Global Automotive.

Is the Hybrid Customer for Real? The Customer in the Insurance Industry of the Future

Markus Hofmann, AXA Group*

Insurance Products as Classical Push Products

Long lines of enthusiastic customers waiting outside stores to watch the unveiling of new smartphones and tablet computers have become a familiar sight. A similar phenomenon at presentations of new insurance products is inconceivable however, these products cover financial risks that could seriously jeopardize individuals livelihoods if the insured event occurs, as in the case of major property or liability damages or permanent disability. The reasons for the lack of strong ties between customers and insurance are mainly due to the nature of the products. Insurance is a service, and thus – unlike many "pull products" in the consumer goods industry – it is not something customers can hold in their hands physically. In addition, many insurance products are complex and difficult to understand for the average costumer. Customers must take into account numerous facts and criteria to arrive at a rational purchase decision. A specific analysis and evaluation of the customer's current risk situation is needed along with the level of insurance coverage and the price. In addition, customers usually need intensive advice and consultation, not only with regard to products, but also taking into account their overall needs in the context of their individual living situation. Consequently, the insurance industry products can be seen as push products.

The Hybrid Customer in the Digital World

The pervasive influence of the digital world is already evident today in customers points of contact with an insurance company, an agent, or an insurance broker.

The digital age has actually dawned much earlier than many observers expected. Digital media is now playing an ever increasing role in everyday life. The constant use of the Internet, and especially its intensifying use in mobile applications, is now part of the everyday routine for many people.

*Markus Hofmann was member of the Global P&C Board of the AXA Group worldwide from June 2002 to September 2012.

More than 74 percent of Germans are already online.[1] Major indicators show the drastic and rapid change of the digital of the digital age population, particularly in the trailblazing area of social media. The ranks of Facebook users in Germany have swelled from 16 million to 23 million over the past 12 months, and worldwide Google+ membership has reached 170 million users since July 2011.[2] The total number of Twitter followers of the four pop stars Lady Gaga, Justin Bieber, Katy Perry and Britney Spears actually exceeds the entire population of France.[3] Mobile utilization of the Internet on smartphones and tablet computers is also on the rise. One indicator of this trend is the explosion in worldwide downloads of mobile applications. In Germany alone, total sales of apps increased from 94 million euros in 2010 to 210 million euros in 2011[4]. At the same time, smartphone sales in Germany rose 31 percent from just under 9 million units to 11.8 million units. As a result, a survey conducted on behalf of BITKOM by the market research institute ARIS showed that one German in three now owns a smartphone.

In the now solidly multimedia present, it is the communication channels above all that are steadily becoming more numerous and flexible. Natural communication boundaries can largely be overcome through unlimited interactivity options. In the insurance business, however, with its intensive advisory needs, personal contact remains indispensable for many customers. In contrast to the past, when customers dealt almost exclusively with the agent, new possibilities are now available to policy buyers to support the process of finding information, finalizing the policy and obtaining service.

During the first phase – seeking information and obtaining advice – the hybrid customer utilizes a broad spectrum of conventional information channels. They include the personal visit to the agent's or brokers office, examination of advertising materials, TV ads and also searches of digital media. In addition, prospective buyers are increasingly turning to online resources for information such as the agent's, broker's or insurance company's website. There is also a trend towards greater reliance on independent information through comparative portals. Other sources of information are blogs, forums and social networks. Already today, 40 percent of customers conduct online research before taking out a policy, mainly for products involving relatively little consultation

---

1 (N)online Atlas 2011, "Eine Topographie des digitalen Grabens in Deutschland."www.initiatived21.de/wp-content/uploads/2011/07/NOnliner2011.pdf. 2011.
2 Statista, Nutzer von Facebook in Deutschland 2012. http://de.statista.com/statistik/daten/studie/70189/umfrage/nutzer-von-facebook-in-deutschland-seit-2009; Statista, Weltweite Nutzerzahlen von Google+ bis April 2012. http://de.statista.com/statistik/daten/studie/215589/umfrage/prognose-zu-den-weltweiten-nutzerzahlen-von-google-plus).
3 Statista, "Frankreich zählt derzeit circa 63 Millionen Einwohner." http://de.statista.com/statistik/faktenbuch/364/a/laender/frankreich/bevoelkerung-in-frankreich
4 BITKOM (Germany's Federal Association for Information Technology, Telecommunications and New Media), In Germany alone, total sales of mobile apps in 2011 amounted to 210 million euros (based on data from research2guidance, a marketing research institute).

such as risk life insurance, private motor insurance, or private liability insurance.[5] During the past five years, online searches for such products have tripled.[6] These figures are indicative of a general trend toward preliminary web searches, with 97 percent of Internet users seeking online information prior to purchasing products, and 50 percent of online buyers initially consulting online reviews from other users.[7]

In the second phase – the contract signing phase – customers now in many cases have the choice of finalizing the purchase through their agent, broker or directly online. In addition, customers have opportunities to take out policies through so-called aggregators, i.e. special platforms offering insurance products. Nevertheless, compared with actual customer behavior, the significance of direct online buying of insurance products is frequently overestimated. Only one in four insurance customers who look for information online (or about 10 percent of all insured individuals) decide to take out a policy online within an average time of four weeks.[8] In the long term, however, it is obvious that online purchases of policies will increase for products requiring relatively little advice such as car insurance or medical coverage for foreign travel. This is also evident in the small business segment. In the U.K., for instance, these customers – such as florists, bakers and even hairdressers with limited inventories and easily calculable risks – can now purchase standardized small-business policies quickly and easily online.

In the third phase – in case of questions on the policy, changes, complaints or a claim – the customer turns to the agent, broker or the insurance company. In the case of the "hybrid customer," this contact can take place either offline or online. Alongside conventional channels such as the telephone or regular mail, customers can submit questions or complaints to the agent or insurer via Skype or social networking platforms. They can arrange for changes to policies via the hotline, for instance, and also make them directly themselves by accessing the insurance company's portal. The day the insurance customer has to file a claim then becomes the proverbial moment of truth. In contrast to the banking sector, in which customer contact is quite frequent, this situation is singular and thus a decisive moment for evaluating the

---

5 "Allianz Studie: Online informieren – offline kaufen," Versicherungsmagazin, 2010; Versicherungsjournal online, "Was Kunden vergeblich von Versicherern erwarten," www.versicherungsjournal.de/vertrieb-und-marketing/was-kunden-vergeblich-von-versicherern-erwarten-106513.php, 2010 (German language sources)
6 Fleischman-Hillard and Harris, The digital influence index study, 2010.
7 Arbeitsgemeinschaft Online Forschung, "AGOF Internet facts 2010-III: 97 Prozent der Onliner bereiten ihren Einkauf im Netz vor," www.agof.de/index.1029.de, 2010; Hofmann, Katrin, Bitkom and Scout24 studies on online research. "Foren, Weblogs und Social-Media-Plattformen beeinflussen Kaufentscheidung," IT-Business, www.it-business.de/news/management/pos-gestaltung/werbung-marketing/articles/254414, 2010.
8 Arbeitsgemeinschaft Online Forschung, AGOF Internet facts 2010-III: 97 Prozent der Onliner bereiten ihren Einkauf im Netz vor," www.agof.de/index.1029.de, 2010; Hofmann, Katrin, Bitkom and Scout24 studies on online research. "Foren, Weblogs und Social-Media-Plattformen beeinflussen Kaufentscheidung," IT-Business, www.it-business.de/news/management/pos-gestaltung/werbung-marketing/articles/254414, 2010; "Allianz Studie: Online informieren – offline kaufen," Versicherungsmagazin, 2010.

insurance company and its services. In this case, new media can help customers – many of whom will be feeling uncertain – to obtain quick and uncomplicated support. Today, claims are no longer reported via the insurer's website, but rather using mobile smartphone applications. In addition, customers can use these tools to track the status of their claim. This high level of transparency bolsters the customer's trust in the agent and the insurer. Consequently, we can state:

> *Web-based forms of self service for insurance customers are not yet fully developed. In the future, web-savvy users will increasingly be able to resolve issues themselves online.*

This is the reason why the hybrid customer selects a mix of available online and offline alternatives for contact as the occasion requires. But who are these hybrid customers, and what do they expect?

The Digital Natives: Conformist Generation Y in Search of Security

The hybrid customer can be found in all segments of society and age groups, so that these criteria cannot be used here for customer segmentation purposes. Instead, the degree of utilization and familiarity with digital media appears to be more to the point. Using these criteria, we can distinguish among three customer profiles. First, there are the occasional users in the 50-plus age class, who represent a substantial portion of insurers' overall customer base. Approximately 53 percent of people in this age group use the Internet. The second group, the functional users, range in age from 30 to 49. In Germany, 90 percent of these people are already online, mainly for work-related purposes. When using the Internet in their personal lives, they primarily write e-mails or occasionally do some online shopping. The third group, made up of people under the age of 30[9], is comprised of the so-called digital natives, 97 percent of whom are online. Although this group represents a relatively small portion of insurers' overall customer base, it already plays a special role. Most of them were born after 1980 and have grown up in surroundings in which the new technologies play an integral role.[10] At the same time, a defining feature of this generation of young adults is that, while being fully comfortable with the new media, they have very conservative values and approaches to life as well as a strong desire for security. For this reason, in psychological studies of contemporary culture, they are sometimes called the

---

9 (N)online Atlas 2011, "Eine Topographie des digitalen Grabens in Deutschland," www.initiatived21.de/wp-content/uploads/2011/07/NOnliner2011.pdf, 2011.
10 Prensky, Marc, "Digital Natives, Digital Immigrants," www.marcprensky.com/writing/prensky%20-%20digital%20natives,%20digital%20immigrants%20-%20part1.pdf, 2001

"Biedermeier generation" in honor of the Biedermeier era, with its conservative, bourgeois sensibilities.

A defining characteristic of these young people are their anxieties, such as the fear of failure in the career world. As a protective mechanism, they are developing a set of rules to provide guidance. They also display a strong sense of order.[11]

Insurance products are a perfect match for this generation, fraught with uncertainty and fond of order and structure. To meet the needs of these modern conservatives, products and agents must support and guide the customer without seeming to adopt a nanny role. Key characteristics of the products are flexibility, transparency and economic value. In addition, the Biedermeier generation, as a group of digital natives, has a special set of expectations defined in large part by social media. As explained below, these needs not only present new challenges, but also offer enormous opportunities for insurance companies. Success in leveraging these opportunities will depend above all on whether insurers succeed in the balancing act between avoiding the appearance of conventionality while enhancing customers' sense of worth and positive self-image when buying insurance.

"I 'Like' It": Challenges and Opportunities through Social Media

The continuing development of the digital world is not only resulting in a steady rise in mobility, both physical and temporal, but also to new forms of interaction. Through social media, the communication of companies with their customers is undergoing a paradigm shift. It is no longer taking the form of one-way, one-to-many communication. Instead it is increasingly shifting in favor of the consumer toward a many-to-many form, in which senders and receivers of communications are on equal footing. So far, insurance companies, as compared with the consumer goods sectors such as the fashion industry, have taken a relatively cautious approach to social media. It is becoming more evident all the time, however, that customer expectations and the rise of market transparency are making it obligatory to become active in this area. Consequently, insurers are not facing the question of whether they should adopt this new form of communication, but rather how, where and to what extent. It is important to bear in mind that it is not only about maintaining customer contact. Instead, the priority must be a dynamic interaction.[12]

11 Rheingold (editor), Psychologische Analyse der aktuellen Lebenskultur junger Erwachsener. 2010, 2011.
12 Albers, Carola, Der Einsatz von Social Media zur Steigerung der Wettbewerbsfähigkeit von Unternehmen. 2010.

Opportunities to build a customer relationship arise not only when purchasing decisions are made but also by presenting the company. Word-of-mouth marketing will become more important, as seen in the use of such tools as the "Like" button on Facebook, which allow users to record positive ratings of companies, events or products. They are a decisive parameter for customers when evaluating a product or company, as – unlike conventional advertising – they enjoy the perception of greater credibility with other users. Opinions and status updates on social networks can also help the insurer and the agent to identify customer needs and to tailor their communications more specifically and individually to them. This can be used in a targeted manner to develop and maintain the insurer's image. For example, with the right blend of news, entertaining content covering a wide range of themes, well-designed advertising and direct responses to customer queries, it is possible for an insurer's online presence to significantly enhance an insurer's image. With the "Ready for take-off" Facebook page, AXA addresses the needs of the digital natives, for example by offering job application tips.

While the invitation to a discussion, as described above, represents a major opportunity for insurance companies, this aspect also poses a challenge. After all, social network platforms can offer users a forum for commenting publicly and, quite possibly, inaccurately about the insurance company and its products. For this reason, many insurers are cautious about their involvement in social networks due to fears of irreparable harm to their image in an online world that never forgets. A further challenge is to provide sufficient resources to avoid being seen as merely "going through the motions" with a superficial online presence. Full exploitation of this medium is possible only by continually maintaining the website and engaging in a real dialog with customers, and by keeping pace with emerging technologies. As a result of these observations, we can anticipate that:

> In the future, social media will offer customers the opportunity to make direct online purchases of policies requiring relatively little consultation and to report claims in an uncomplicated manner, as is already possible today using apps.

Oasis in the Service Desert: Customer Loyalty Through Innovative Services

Mobile smartphone and tablet applications are steadily gaining in importance. In addition to making phone calls, smartphone owners are using their devices above all for short online sessions for specific purposes. This amounts to a sort of multimedia break – to check information, do online banking, compare prices or make mobile payments, for instance. As a result, smartphones are increasingly gaining the status of mobile all-around devices – a sort of "office in a cigarette case."[13] This is opening up opportunities for companies, especially in the service sector. However, their use for the sale of complex insurance products is limited, as they are unsuitable for the intensive advice and consultation required. The exceptions are the products mentioned above for which buyers require little advice and that are purchased quickly, regionally and on the move, such as medical coverage for foreign travel. Many other ideas are also under consideration. It is quite conceivable that customers will use their smartphones in the future to purchase insurance products that do not exist today. One possible example would be a short-term, one-day accident insurance policy purchased and paid for online, right at the ski lift, by scanning a QR code. However, the plans for app-based mobile services are not limited to the sale of products; they are also intended, when a claim arises – the "moment of truth" – to produce happy customers through quick and uncomplicated claim settlements, and with unexpected services when customers are on the move.

However the use of apps also involves risks. Ultimately, they reduce customer contact, which is such an essential aspect of the insurance business, by letting customers deal with their own needs externally. Mobile applications may even lead to a significantly reduced presence on the part of the insurer, culminating in a loss of brand recognition. An example of this – of which the iOutBank app is one instance – is offered by the experience of some banks, which surrendered their independent profile through cross-bank applications, and thus failed to develop a face of their own with customers.

For the insurance industry it is therefore important to use modern technology to its advantage. Simpler customer contacts, efficient and lean processes and product solutions with real value are necessary to enhance an insurer's competitive profile, gain the trust of customers and reduce costs. Even today, insurers are attempting to position themselves as comprehensive service partners by offering assistance services. At present, these services are still primarily aimed at private customers, and in some cases are offered by insurers in combination with their insurance products. There is a wide range of possible services, including travel assistance, which may, for instance, include hotel accommodation and the booking of another flight when a customer's flight is delayed. Other services, such as help finding a locksmith or other tradesmen, home care services in case of illness or household help, are offered as required. With these offers, customers have access to compre-

13 Tuma, Thomas, "iPhone, also bin ich," Der Spiegel, 27/2012

hensive support from their insurer. Assistance services will become important in the future to meet increasing needs of private individuals as well as business customers. Smartphones and tablets are the ideal platform for making these services conveniently accessible to customers on a mobile basis and making them available both at home and abroad.[14]

As a result:

> Assistance services will become important criteria for customers when purchasing insurance, and will thus become a key distinguishing feature of insurers. Product-oriented strategies will be expanded to include services available via smartphone or tablet.

The Hybrid Customer is for Real

In the insurance industry of the future, service applications will play an even greater role in the customer relationship as a result of increasing mobility and flexibility. When the concept of the hybrid customer first arose, there was little but hype behind it. But now the hybrid customer is for real, and will play a decisive role in shaping the future. Due to the defining characteristics of many insurance products, however, close customer contact for personal advice consultation will remain a defining feature alongside the many self-service possibilities. What is important is the reaffirmation and continued reinforcement of trust, which is a fundamentally important factor for the industry, through transparency in interactions with the agent. Consultation will consist of solution-oriented communication between the customer and the agent, with both on equal footing, taking place in the form of an immediate and direct dialog with the aid of new media.

Consequently, it will be crucial to adapt to customer expectations in the insurance industry through services, transparency and added value. But that does not mean chasing every fad that comes along. Instead, insurers should be trying to anticipate the key trends before they happen. In a constantly and rapidly changing insurance world, we must therefore continue to take a comprehensive and proactive approach to identify changing customer needs. Only then is it possible to provide prospective insurance customers with comprehensive service and to continue developing as an all-around service partner, true to the words of Ovid, "Times change and we change with them."

---

14 Wehr, Stefan, "Kundenservice per Smartphone," Performance, 2011.

Bibliography

Albers, Carola. Der Einsatz von Social Media zur Steigerung der Wettbewerbsfähigkeit von Unternehmen. 2010.

Arbeitsgemeinschaft Online Forschung (AGOF). "AGOF internet facts 2010-III: 97 Prozent der Onliner bereiten ihren Einkauf im Netz vor." www.agof.de/index.1029.de. 2010.

BITKOM (Germany's Federal Association for Information Technology, Telecommunications and New Media). "Allein in Deutschland wurden 2011 mit mobilen Apps 210 Millionen Euro umgesetzt," based on data from the market research institute, research2guidance. 2012.

BITKOM (Germany's Federal Association for Information Technology, Telecommunications and New Media). "Jeder Dritter hat ein Smartphone," based on data from the market research institute, ARIS. 2012.

Fleischman-Hillard; Harris Interactive. The digital influence index study. 2010.

Hofmann, Katrin. Utilizing studies by BITKOM and Scout24 for information research. "Foren, Weblogs und Social-Media-Plattformen beeinflussen Kaufentscheidung." IT-BUSINESS, 3/2010. www.it-business.de/news/management/pos-gestaltung/wer-bung-marketing/articles/254414/. August 20, 2012.

Initiative D21. (N)online Atlas 2011. "Eine Topographie des digitalen Grabens in Deutschland." www.initiatived21.de/wp-content/uploads/2011/07/NOnliner2011.pdf. 2011.

Prensky, Marc. "Digital Natives, Digital Immigrants." On the Horizon (2001), Vol. 9. Nr. 5: 1-6.

Rheingold (editor). Psychologische Analyse der aktuellen Lebenskultur junger Erwachsener. 2010. 2011.

Tuma, Thomas. "iPhone, also bin ich." Der Spiegel, Nr. 27/2012.

Versicherungs-Magazin. "Allianz Studie zeigt: Online informieren – offline kaufen." 2010.

Versicherungsjournal. "Was Kunden vergeblich von Versicherern erwarten." 2010.

Wehr, Stefan. "Kundenservice per Smartphone." Performance. 2011.

The Company

Today's AXA Group can trace its roots back to 1839, with the formation of Kölnische Feuer-Versicherungs-Gesellschaft, also known as Colonia. In 1991 a holding company structure was put in place, headed by Colonia Konzern AG. A majority stake was acquired in 1993 by the French insurer, Union des Assurances de Paris (UAP). With the acquisition of UAP by the AXA Group in 1997, Colonia became part of the world's largest insurance and financial services company. The AXA Group has operations in 57 countries and serves approximately 101 million customers with a global workforce of 163,000 employees. In 2011, the company had total sales of 86.1 billion euros. In Germany, the AXA Group is among the largest providers, with 10.6 billion euros in premium income.

For further information: www.axa.de/servlet/PB/menu/1077251/index.html

Summary

The insurance industry is only just beginning to utilize the possibilities of Web 2.0. Through active involvement in social networks, insurance companies can obtain a wide range of useful information about their customers, their desires and their preferences. They can also utilize this information in a more targeted manner. In addition, this will bring about a more active engagement with the digital natives.

In the future, social media will offer customers the opportunity to make direct online purchases of policies requiring relatively little consultation and to report claims in an uncomplicated manner, as is already possible today using apps. The customer will gather information and examine the pros and cons of the products offered by various providers. Consequently, a transparent website and comprehensive service could prove decisive.

Assistance services will be a decisive purchasing factor for insurance buyers in the future, and will thus become a decisive feature for setting insurers apart from their competitors. Product-oriented strategies will be expanded to include services available via smartphone or tablet.

The Author

Roland Boekhout was born in 1963. After studying business administration at Erasmus University in Rotterdam, he graduated from the CEDEP General Management Program at INSEAD in Fontainebleau. He joined the ING Group after working with Unilever from 1988 until 1991. He held various management positions with the ING Group, including stints in the USA, Poland and Mexico, among other locations. Since October 1, 2010, Roland Boekhout has held the position of chairman of the management board of ING-DiBA. He is also the chief executive officer of ING Germany and a member of the ING Group Banking Management Team. In addition, he belongs to the Leadership Council, a body made up of the ING Group's top 20 managers.

Follow the Orange Lion – How a Bank Succeeds at Being Different and the Challenges it Must Face to Do So

Roland Boekhout, ING-DiBa AG

Different – And Successfully So

In a famous scene in the film "The Matrix" (1999, Andy Wachowski), the hero, Neo, must choose between continuing to live in an illusory world or setting out in search of reality. To embark on the search, he must follow signs. This first is a white rabbit in the form of a tattoo: "Follow the white rabbit!" Now, it's not hard to imagine that, for many customers, the financial sector could look a bit like the matrix in that film. What is real, and what is just a distraction, an alluring illusion or even a deliberate deception? However, this notion is not lifted from a Hollywood film. It's part of our everyday world – as we learn again and again in studies and reports on the financial industry. Wouldn't it be a good thing if there were enough signposts to help customers to discover reality? They wouldn't need white rabbits. An orange lion will do just fine.

ING-DiBa is Germany's third-largest retail bank. From the Frankfurt headquarters and offices in Hanover, Nuremberg and Vienna, a workforce of approximately 2,900 employees serve more than 7.5 million customers. The bank has no branches, which means that the service is provided mainly by telephone and online. The business rests on five pillars: savings, with the "Extra-Konto" daily interest savings account and the term deposit products; the current account business; real estate finance; consumer credit; and the securities business. These successful segments are based on a business model with two special features. First, there is the fundamental principle of turning the cost benefits of direct banking into customer benefits. All products and services are governed by this principle. Second, for many years ING-DiBa has been demonstrating that banking transactions do not have to be a commission-driven "black box." The orange lion stands for transparency, fairness and openness.

Figure 1: The beer-coaster strategy

With its philosophy of affordable, uncomplicated and fair direct banking, the bank's offer was perfectly timed to match the needs and lifestyles of a large number of people. It has been winning honors and awards for years, especially from consumer and customer groups. The share of new customers gained through recommendations is well above average.

The "bank with a difference" places emphasis on a rather untypical corporate culture characterized by flat hierarchies, open communication and a strong orientation towards the needs of customers and staff and the continual improvement of products and services. For ING-DiBa, this corporate culture is an indispensable, unmistakable and inimitable factor that comprises a fundamental pillar of the bank's philosophy and ultimately represents a competitive edge. "Successfully different" – ING intends to make that motto its recipe for success in the future as well. It is clear, of course, that past successes are no guarantee for strong future performance. How "different" we want the bank to be in the future – and how different it has to be – that is the decisive question.

Trust 2.0

The banking business, especially the retail side, is nowadays a mature and experienced industry. The challenges are no longer posed mainly by the development of new products, but rather in how best to provide financial services for the customer and ensure a smooth interplay of a small number of basic products.

Since the financial crisis, the industry has faced increased pressures to improve efficiency and reduce costs, while dealing with a loss of trust. Banks now face customers who have greater autonomy and flexibility, and who expect more in terms of credibility, services, and the staff who provide those services, who must now function as multichannel agents.

But an even bigger challenge to the industry falls under the heading of what would once have been called "soft skills": After two international banking crises within just a few years, a steady stream of headlines on serious cases of improper advice to bank customers, and confusing or hidden fees, trust in the industry taken a beating as never before. Consequently, the most important task in the coming years will be to regain the trust in the banking industry. The factor of trust has now changed from a soft skill to a factor crucial to our existence: It is no more and no less than a license for banks to operate.

ING-DiBa can certainly state that it did not disappoint its customers during the financial crises, and that it is generally doing a great deal to help establish a new kind of banking characterized by transparency and a customer-oriented approach. Nevertheless, ING-DiBa is a part of its industry: It is perceived as a German bank – and, as a result, must address the challenges of this crisis of trust just as much as any other bank. Morality and ethics in banking are taking on a new dimension.

Efforts to visualize the factor of trust generally rely on customer feedback data. Customers' willingness to recommend a bank and their reported satisfaction score are not only signs of trust, but can also act as early warning signs that help us to take action in a timely and targeted manner. ING-DiBa sees this as a key starting point. We are especially interested in boosting the already high percentage of customers willing to recommend us, for example by

- making our existing customers even more aware of us,
- expanding our customer recommendation programs,
- ongoing communication, for example through social projects,
- increasing the number of categories for referral incentives,
- stronger focus on target groups.

A lot more can be done in that area. A good example in this regard is the Bank of America, which tells its customers about its corporate responsibility (CR) activities through its cash dispensers. In general, CR is a very promising avenue for contacting customers in a new way to establish trust. Sustainability and trust are related concepts that can be combined in a credible manner. This applies in particular to long-term business relationships. Banks must find a way to get from the old transaction-based marketing philosophy to the new relationship-based marketing. The goal is to win over the customer in the long term. However, this calls for a dialog-based approach, geared not so much to the selling of products as to the building of loyalty.

A study by Bain & Company showed that the loyalty leaders in an industry can achieve significantly stronger sales growth than their competitors. Consequently, customer loyalty will become more important as a competitive factor in the future. And a company's reputation – and not least of all its online reputation – will increasingly act as a driving force. It is also a key factor for recommendations in virtual communities today – because the web never forgets. Therefore, it is crucial for companies to take a forward-looking approach to reputation management. But there are no simple recipes for success in planning and managing one's online reputation. Instead, there is plenty of experimentation: Social banking, crowd funding, the peer-to-peer principle, alternative payment channels such as PayPal, Google Checkout and Facebook Credits are indicative of the scope of the methods currently being tried out. One thing is certain: Like society as a whole, the financial industry is subject to the digital transformation, as seen in the example of online banking. It is still uncertain where the journey is heading. Nevertheless, it appears certain that the possibilities of digitization can and must be used to reach the desired goals and remain competitive.

Net Promoter Score Benchmarking

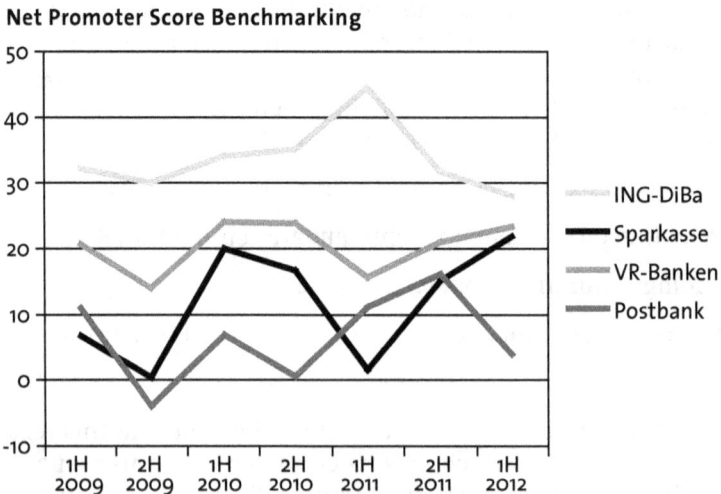

Figure 2: Net Promoter Score

The interaction between customers and the bank is therefore the main challenge. A shift is taking place from a product orientation to one that revolves around customers and service. How do I establish a long-term interaction, characterized by trust, between customers and the bank. What does Trust 2.0 look like? In this regard, ING-DiBa has a clear philosophy that it has been communicating for years. In some cases, however, the specific instruments and processes for implementing it still have prototype status.

The Paradigm Shift

We are seeing big changes in customer relationships. Purchasing and consumption habits are becoming increasingly unpredictable, and customers now expect services to be available at all times. They want to decide when and where they will use a service. This puts ING-DiBa at a clear advantage. We are available 24 hours a day, 365 days a year with free access to all cash dispensers worldwide, and have an award-winning online banking platform. The share of consumers across all age groups who prefer to make purchasing decisions online has already reached 63 percent according to recent studies by the University of Bonn and the Gottlieb Duttweiler Institute in Switzerland. With 300,000 customers logging in every day, online interactions also account for the majority of customer interactions for ING-DiBa.

In addition, customers have always preferred to act on the recommendations of other customers or friends and family. The difference today is that they now have access to this kind of help for almost any product – and at all times. Communication is becoming more individualized and fragmented all the time. It's getting harder to group people in "clusters," and their behavior is more difficult to predict. For many companies, this shift in power is initially experienced as a loss of control. But in fact, it represents a cultural challenge that opens up new opportunities. Social media is paving the way to a new customer philosophy while raising the question of which consequences follow from customer autonomy.

Over the years, ING-DiBa has used all kinds of media: letters, the telephone, regular mail, the Internet, mobile devices and now social media. That is because more and more communication is taking place via social networks, communities, blogs, forums and wikis. They are becoming networked. Today, people are no longer willing to live without them. The communication culture has undergone permanent changes while taking on a new dimension: Communication now takes place between the masses and in public.

In this new world, banks and customers often come together on different levels: Neither the banks' offerings nor the customers' habits show real uniformity. Some clear trends are evident, however. Customers in the Netherlands and the Scandinavian countries have been the quickest to embrace self-banking. A study has shown that some 50 percent of bank customers in the Netherlands report not having entered a bank branch within the past year. The corresponding figures for France, the U.K. and Germany ranged between 15 and 20 percent. In other words: This trend will rapidly gain momentum in Germany during the coming years. Networking will intensify, and spontaneous activity will increase. As it becomes easier for mass movements to arise spontaneously through the creation of resonance in social networks, there will be a fundamental shift in power from the supply side to the demand side. This naturally raises the question: How can I deal with this?

It was only recently that ING-DiBa had its first experience with spontaneous mass activity on the Internet. On the company's Facebook page, a dispute arose between vegetarians and their opponents. It was triggered by a TV ad. The basketball star Dirk Nowitzki, who endorses ING-DiBa, is offered a slice of sausage meat in his favorite butcher shop, so that he'll "grow up big and strong." The fact that the butcher gave Nowitzki a piece of meat, and not a vegetarian product, unleashed a rapidly escalating debate that soon became known as the "sausage war." At first glance, the intensity of the response seems impressive. But what should a company do in a situation like this? The bank merely moderated of the discussion and urged the adversaries to express themselves in a civilized tone. It did not otherwise intervene. The Facebook community respected that approach and the so-called "flame war" – or, as some social media fans would have it, "shitstorm" – soon died down. Naturally, this does not amount to a recipe for handling every incident that will come along. But it was an interesting initial experience. But experience is exactly what the company needs to get to the point where it can react professionally and make customer communication in Web 2.0 an integral part of its conventional PR activities.

Figure 3: The sausage war

Now, what does this paradigm shift actually amount to? No one doubts that it is taking place, but interpretations vary. Some see the essential shift in real-time communication. It poses unprecedented demands on communication, but also on the management: When do I have to intervene, what do I need to know, and what tools am I permitted – and not permitted – to use?

Companies have always turned to narratives and storytelling, and to the realization and retelling of success stories. But how does "storylistening" work, i.e. the way customers take in and understand these narratives? Because, when faced with autonomous and extremely well-informed customers who may even act in groups, there is one thing, above all, that a company must know how to do: listen. What solution should I offer to the customer for which problem? What will the customer of the future need? Where is my potential for change? Am I still up to date?

"Socially Driven Services"

One of the main criteria by which people judge companies today is how companies treat them. Socially driven services represent a new service channel with their own laws, possibilities and standards. They are utilized to launch services linked to Internet use and social media technologies that help customers to help themselves or each other. It would thus be fair to call them a new way of helping people to help themselves. When implementing them, the company's service image and reputation must be improved, and the "wisdom of crowds" must be utilized – key tasks for a company. Classical marketing instruments have reached their limits: Inflexible strategies are reaching fewer people. The new channels do not replace the conventional ones, but complement them effectively in consumer relationship management. Social media must be integrated into the multichannel mix, and even be seen as part of the business model.

Just one example: "Plain vanilla" telephone contact, an important communication channel for the bank, can become "multiflavored" through video functionality, chat options, real-time information, advice hotlines or virtual service advisors. The possibilities are wide-ranging. Online channels that let customers "join in the action" present many different options. The trick is to pick the right method and skillfully allocate resources. Herbert Hainer, the CEO of adidas, says that 30 years ago, a TV ad that ran on ARD and ZDF, Germany's biggest TV networks, reached 98 percent of the target group. Similar statements apply to the banking industry. How do I achieve 98 percent coverage today?

Virtual communities bring together people who frequently have the same interests, regardless of location, non-verbally, and without face-to-face contact. Nevertheless, they create a certain sense of belonging. Consequently, we must ask: How can we take the feelings created through ties to these communities – confidence, permanence, stability – and extend them to the customer's ties to the company? How – in the special case of our bank – can we engender a "DiBa" feeling?

1,000 times 1,000

The campaign "DiBaDu und Dein Verein" marks the first time that ING-DiBa has ventured into Web 2.0. This initiative has extended the scope of the internal corporate volunteering program "We Care" to the general public. For seven years now, with this program, the bank has encouraged its employees to get involved in their communities. Through intensive internal publicity, the company promotes the idea of social responsibility, and employees who take action receive support, both through financial incentives and through the company infrastructure (e.g. through working time credits). The program is firmly anchored in the corporate culture and has had a long-term impact on the mentality of our workforce, with one in three employees now making some form of social commitment. It was therefore our goal to transfer this internal program to the general public. This idea aligned with the bank's new advertising campaign "ING-DiBa – Die Bank und Du" launched in 2011.

With this campaign, the bank is visibly carrying out a strategic change. After a period of intensive growth and with a market identity based on the best possible terms and conditions, we are shifting our focus to an identity as an established, broad-based retail bank that wants to engage in a dialog with its customers and the public. For ING-DiBa, taking this natural development process to a new level of customer loyalty is a key challenge for the future. But what specific form can this dialog take?

Social networks present a very promising territory. Like most companies, the bank is only taking its first steps towards the professional use of social media, on a par with its past use of conventional corporate communication tools.

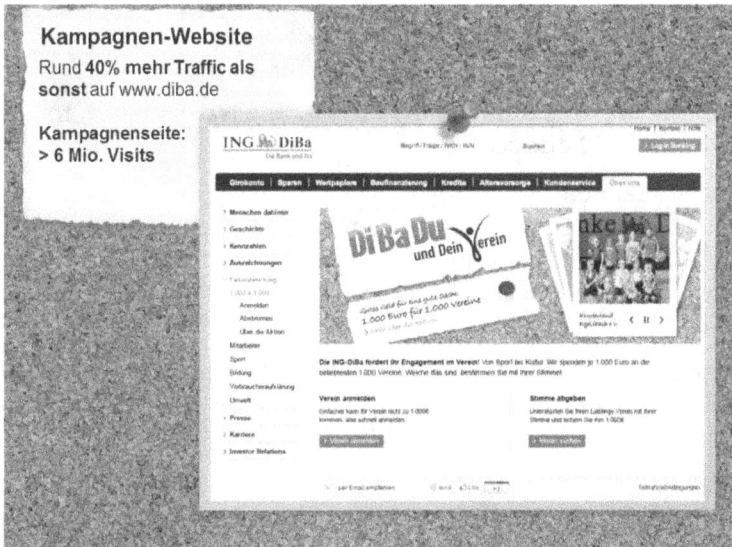

Figure 4: ING-DiBa"you" (DiBaDu in German) and Your Club

The main target group of the "DiBaDu und Dein Verein" was comprised of non-profit associations in Germany. To gain a detailed overview of the phenomenon of volunteerism, which is the bedrock of German club culture, the bank conducted a study prior to the campaign. It was carried out in cooperation with betterplace.org, Germany's largest fundraising platform, with headquarters in Berlin: The study, entitled "That was fun – volunteering in Germany," showed that more than 23 million people engage in volunteer activities in Germany. The total potential for such commitments, namely the 24 million people willing to donate their time, is relatively high in Germany. How this potential can be activated is an issue that relates both to corporate responsibility (CR) and the issue of how to attract and retain customers. According to the study, promising channels include social networks such as Facebook, Google Plus and Twitter. Clubs and social networks both play the role of marketplaces for social contacts. The study shows that people have an equally strong desire to get in contact with others and to volunteer (60 percent) – although the form of voluntary commitments sometimes differs substantially. For example, the results showed that involvement through social media may take the form of "sporadic online involvement and micro-commitments by people sitting at their computers at home, at work, or even on the go."

ING-DiBa saw these findings as a good basis for a campaign (in the period from October 4 to November 15, 2011), in which different voluntary (club-based) activities could get together with the social media world. The campaign had three components:

1. **Sponsoring**: One million euros in funding was provided, to be donated to 1,000 different clubs.

2. **User-generated process**: The campaign took place entirely on the Internet, with the bank only defining the process and the rules and providing the registration platform; the selection process for the clubs to be eligible for a 1,000 euro donation was left to the energy and commitment of the participants themselves.

3. **Marketing/communication**: A key factor for the success of the campaign was the complete absence of sales-based activities, conventional advertising or product-related communication.

The campaign was not linked to secondary motives at any time, and was driven entirely by participants' voting activities. As a result, there was complete credibility in classifying and advertising "DiBaDu und Dein Verein" as a CR project. Due to this strategic purism, the campaign was extraordinarily effective in enhancing the image and esteem of our bank. Success in a purely business-related sense was never the aim of the campaign; nor was it achieved. By contrast, the improvements in our reputation and brand recognition as well as the experience acquired in what is, for us, still a new sphere of customer communication represented an inestimable gain. Moreover, the German word "du" – the familiar form of address for "you" used in the campaign ("ING-DiBa – Die Bank und *Du*") – was specifically linked with a target group for the first time and received a good response.

A focal point of the campaign – the portal of which was positioned as a frame on the ING-DiBa home page – was achieving the greatest possible publicity through advertising and media channels. For this purpose we used all of the normal customer communication tools such as print mailings, e-mail, print advertisements (in club magazines, for instance), web banners, flyers (for example when mailing out current account statements), the publication of a study on volunteerism, press releases, PR releases, media cooperation, for example with *Focus Money* and *Radio Energy*, and of course all of the bank's internal communication resources. One avenue that proved very labor intensive, but nevertheless had a lasting impact, was the intensive contact with the clubs that were applying for donations and voting. First, the project team had to perform its task of ensuring that the clubs were officially recognized as non-profit organizations. Second, communications with them often revolved around the credibility of the campaign itself. As the weeks passed, however, the web community increasingly helped to reduce this part of the workload with their clear recognition and acknowledgement of the campaign's seriousness. And, without doubt, this enhanced the bank's reputation.

The response was extraordinary. During the campaign – and afterwards – ING-DiBa became the talk of the town. Registrations came from a total of 19,329 clubs from all over Germany, most involved in sports or in activities for children and youth. First place, with 18,064 votes, went to the Zebrakids from Duisburg. An astonishing 17.5 million votes were cast. The investment paid off just with the enormous traffic on the bank's site, which was sometimes up by 40 percent. Definitely a factor in this huge response was the leverage effect of social networks. On Facebook alone, 55,000 people clicked the "Like" button, and Google search results yielded similarly strong numbers. First and foremost, however, the design, overall tone and concept of the campaign matched the philosophy and outlook of the Web 2.0 community. The bank's role was only as the initiator and donor; all aspects of the actual campaign – the voting by the clubs – were governed by the community. This was a decisive factor behind the outstanding 97 percent of the participants giving a positive or neutral rating to the campaign.

There was another effect that, although it was not a strategic priority, strongly impacted the project with its sheer momentum. The bank succeeded in creating a transparent and exciting process that prompted many clubs to spread the word about themselves and the work they do:

a communicative snowball effect that was evident in the media coverage. There was a sharp rise in media reporting on the bank during the six-week period, with almost half of the coverage dedicated to the campaign. This was mainly due to initiatives undertaken by the clubs themselves. They advertised, mainly in regional media, on their own behalf, and thus for ING-DiBa as well. This illustrates that the worlds of clubs and social media are not only similar in many respects; in fact they complement one another in their impact. Whether it happens at a weekly pub night or through online postings, viral marketing (i.e. word-of-mouth advertising) works brilliantly. But the campaign, with Germany's Minister of Family Affairs, Kristina Schröder, acting as honorary patron, owed its success to another factor as well: credibility. Initially, many participants suspected that it might be nothing but a sales campaign in disguise. And the more it became obvious over time that "DiBaDu und Dein Verein" was operating under a social responsibility agenda, the more positive the response, and the more participants were willing to pass the word to others and say good things.

What remains is the question: How can I tie this highly sensitive social media community to ING-DiBa in the long term without frightening them away with advertising? The fact that, to some extent, our bank's readiness to face the future and our business success will depend on the answers to this and similar questions is a key insight from this project.

Follow the Orange Lion

The example of the DiBaDu campaign shows that time-tested communication instruments and, even more so, time-tested themes, can be carried over into the new Web 2.0 world. As a result, the bank may even have found an effective strategy for the future. Classical communication offerings are reformatted as social media services and – with their basic substance intact – gain a new efficiency level. One example is the dialog with consumer-protection advocates, which is a special focus of ING-DiBa's communication activities. At a very early stage, the bank adopted a policy of constructive dialog instead of the confrontational approach customary in the industry. This has paid off. For example, the highly respected Helmut Schmidt Journalism Award is a strong force for enhancing our reputation, and also stands for excellent networking. The consumer portal www.finanzversteher.de sets new standards for transparency. As an alternative to (fee-based) banking advice, it already offers independent-minded customers the help they need to help themselves in the form of numerous interactive tools. The idea is to start a "financially literate community" through a product-neutral, interactive portal, very much in line with the "wisdom of crowds" concept. But these are only a few examples of the bank's strategy of being "successfully different."

Figure 5: Financial literacy

The final examples mentioned above mainly relate to ING-DiBa's core competencies and follow the thematic priorities where we have enjoyed success. And that will remain so. Coming to grips with social media does not necessarily mean reinventing ourselves. ING-DiBa is "successfully different" because it lives a form of banking that is still out of step with these times: transparency, fairness and a consumer-oriented approach. It refuses to be "part of the matrix" – part of an industry that still clings to non-transparency and self-interest. By contrast, ING-DiBa wants to be a trailblazer, pointing the way forward to a different kind of banking: Follow the orange lion.

The Company

Today's ING-DiBa AG can trace its roots back to BSV Bank für Sparanlagen und Vermögensbildung AG, established in Frankfurt in 1965. It was reincorporated as Allgemeine Deutsche Direktbank in 1994. In 1998, 49 percent of the shares were acquired by the ING Groep in the Netherlands, which increased its stake to 100 percent by 2003. In 2004 the new name, ING-DiBa, was introduced. ING-DiBa welcomed its five-millionth customer in 2005. In the spring of 2012, ING-DiBa was voted Germany's favorite bank for the sixth consecutive year. Today, with approximately 7.5 million customers, ING-DiBa is the third-largest retail bank in Germany.

For more information: www.ing-diba.de/ueber-uns/geschichte/ and
http://de.wikipedia.org/wiki/ING-DiBa

Summary

Banks must now deal with a much more critical customer base – and not just since the time of the financial market crisis. This is especially true for the retail banking business. Customers are asking far more questions than before. They are more sure of themselves, better informed and more critical, a change that can almost certainly be attributed in large part to the Internet and social networks and the wealth of knowledge that can be accessed and shared through them.

This is a challenge that all banks must face. What will be crucial for the future customer relationship, however, will be whether banks see their dealings with critical customers as a bothersome chore, or whether they treat such customers as equals.

In this regard, ING-DiBa is "successfully different." Unlike many other banks, it has a business model that is actually geared to customers who ask critical questions, are curious, and don't just take the answers at face value – because those who ask questions are interested and will arrive at their own decision. Initiatives such as the consumer portal www.finanzversteher.de and the "DiBaDu und Dein Verein" campaign are emblematic of this conviction.

With these new communication concepts, the bank is also gaining experience with the combination of classical communication instruments with the possibilities of Web 2.0. The priority is taking the customer seriously as a partner in a true dialog. It is no accident that, for ING-DiBa, one aspect of innovation in the banking business, among others, is the significant reduction in the lack of transparency. And that is where Web 2.0 and the bank's business models come together.

The Author

Dr. Michael Frenzel was born in 1947. He studied law at Ruhr University in Bochum and successfully completed his doctorate whilst working at the University as a scientific assistant. Frenzel joined the Westdeutsche Landesbank(WestLB), Düsseldorf in 1981, where he was promoted to various managerial positions. In 1988, he became a member of the Preussag AG executive board and in January 1994, he was promoted to chairman of the executive board. Under his leadership, the multi-business conglomerate Preussag was repositioned into Europe's leading tourism Group within only a few years. One of the main milestones was the acquisition of a stake in Hapag-Lloyd, which was followed by the acquisition of leading tourism companies such as TUI/Hanover, Thomson Travel/London, and Nouvelles Frontières/Paris. In 2002, the annual general meeting passed a resolution to change the name of Preussag AG to TUI AG. In 2013, he resigned as chairman and chief executive officer of TUI AG, but will remain linked to the group as chairman of TUI Deutschland and TUIfly.

Furthermore, he represents the interests of the tourism sector within important associations by being president of BTW (Federal Association of the German Tourism Industry) and Chairman of WTTC (World Travel & Tourism Council).

How the Tourism Industry can Utilize the New Social Networks

Michael Frenzel, TUI AG*

Customer Communications Before the Advent of YouTube, Facebook and Twitter

The digital revolution has increased the bandwidth of relationships between the tourism industry and its customers. This has, in turn, had far-reaching effects on our business models. Just 20 years ago, customer communication between tourists buying travel services from tourism companies operated through clearly defined channels. People's travel patterns were also very predictable: Germans, for example, liked to take two weeks of vacation in the summer – preferably to Italy, Spain or some other Mediterranean destination. And often, they would return to the same hotel every year where they knew the hotel manager, the other guests and the surrounding area. Customers generally had a travel agency nearby where they could go for advice and assistance with planning and booking their trip – especially if they wanted to visit a new excursion destination. The owner and employees at the neighborhood travel agency got to know their customers over a period of years, and were implicitly trusted by them. For customers, the agency was the communication link to or the face of tourism operators. In addition, the travel catalog – full of informative and attractive material on the available packages – played a vital role. Over the winter, people planning holidays could leaf through the catalogs at leisure with their families to compare prices and destinations. Classical advertising also played a role in this kind of customer communication when the industry wanted to promote specific destinations or offers. Over time, the classical sales channels, with proprietary travel agencies and agency partnerships, was complemented through the use of call centers and direct sales through cooperation partners. Gradually, tourism operators began presenting their travel packages on the Internet. Initially, however, websites were intended mainly to help prospective customers search for information, and generally did not allow online bookings. A multi-channel management based on the sturdy and reliable foundation provided by travel agencies was seen as the formula for successful marketing and sales management. If something went wrong

* Michael Frenzel was chairman and chief executive officer of Preussag AG (renamed TUI AG in 2002) from January 1994 to February 2013.

during a vacation, the situation could be remedied through a flexible complaint management system. Justified complaints were handled through direct customer contact and a joint back-up service system, allowing for quick compensation. For many years, the relationship between travel operators, sales partners and tourists rested mainly on these pillars. This is the way it was, incidentally, all over Europe, although travel habits differed.

The style of customer communications described above continues to play a key role in the tourism industry today. Here in Germany, the bulk of package holidays are still booked at travel agencies. But nevertheless, the arrival of the Internet in customers' lives beginning in the mid-1990s led to a fundamental change in the travel industry. The advent of the digital age caused a massive upheaval in our lifestyles and in the way we research and book our trips. New and hitherto unknown aspects and forms of communication arose between tour operators and customers.

As a result of this web revolution, there is not a single destination, airline or resort – and hardly even a decent restaurant – without its own website. This has made it easy for any tourist to use a search engine to find their dream destinations and take a virtual tour with their computer to find out all they want to know. Most people can now, from the comfort of their own home, use their own computer or, increasingly, their smartphone, to be their own tour operator. They can research every imaginable detail of their trip, plan individual components, and finally complete the booking. Which means that travel agencies and tour operators have lost their monopoly on the information we need to plan the nicest days of our year. We now have the highest possible level of transparency and interaction. All of the information relevant to planning a trip is just a few clicks away. Tour operators are seeing their former dominance shifting from tour catalogs to the Internet – where customers can book holidays with just one mouse click.

The Emergence of Online Business Models

In this initial phase, as customers became increasingly receptive to the improved technological possibilities, we saw the emergence of new online business models, for example Expedia and Booking.com. Expedia, originally a Microsoft spin-off arriving from the USA as a so-called online travel agency, gradually established itself in various markets across Europe, and today is also present in new markets such as China.

But classical tour operators, charter airlines and other tourism service providers caught on quickly and have integrated Internet-based channels (e-mail, Internet and also, increasingly, mobile access) into their respective business models. As a result, the online channel has become a mainstay in TUI's multi-channel strategy. Customers can visit Fritidsresor.se or Thompson.co.uk, for example, to learn about or book the most popular products we offer as Europe's largest travel operator. In some of our markets, for example in the U.K., our travel sites lead the market. In the meantime, Internet sales represent 23 percent of our total global revenues at TUI – and as Internet penetration continues to increase in these markets, we expect that share to grow accordingly.

But has this shift influenced communications between travel companies and travelers? For one thing, nowadays it's not just travel agent personnel who interact with customers – websites are also doing a lot of the "talking" on behalf of their organizations. As a result, a good website is just as critical a factor for success as service and customer relations for a traditional travel agency. And the significance of online management will only increase in the future.

Social Media as a New Platform for Interaction and Communication

Since the beginning of the 21st century, another Internet development set off a second wave of transformation: The rise of social media networks redefined all aspects of travel-related communications. Now it's no longer just tour operators, airlines or hotels extending offers to potential customers; instead, travelers are using Facebook, YouTube, Twitter and various blogging platforms to talk about what they've seen, done and experienced. They're writing their own travel stories, posting photo travelogues and raves and rants about their trips. Which hotel is really good? Which bar serves the best drinks? Which airline offers the best service? An almost endless, unfiltered stream of travel and vacation recommendations, information and tips floods through social networking channels for unfiltered consumption by interested users. Countless communities joined by common interests have sprung up to discuss vacation and travel. In early 2012, a Google search for "Urlaub" ("vacation" in German) generated 6.6 million hits for German-language Facebook pages alone. "Vacation" is a product with a strong emotional resonance, and is thus ideally suited for social media interaction.

The Internet has become a sort of "multiplication machine" on a vast scale, making it possible to create interactive platforms in many different areas – including, or especially, the tourism industry. Users can communicate with companies, but also with each other. Next to the product information presented by travel operators, a virtual world has sprung up, equal in status, where customers or users communicate their real vacation experiences. What was once "one-to-one" communication is now "one-to-many" communication.

Classical communication between enterprises and their customers is steadily being expanded and complemented by asynchronous online communications among users via e-mail, blogs, online rankings, chats and personal travelogues with videos and photos. With social networks, in place of conventional linear communication, we are experiencing communication "among equals" among ever-expanding, diversifying and often specialized communities. All of this is happening of its own accord without any input from tourism companies. We've also seen the emergence of travel forums and vacation blogs with no profit motive. The communication on the new platforms is primarily driven by peoples' passion for travel and the sheer fun of it, as well as their desire to share their experiences with others. This is turning special travel experiences of customers into a sort of conversational social currency.

At the same time, these new forms of communication are having a massive impact on the entire travel industry. Travel trends are being created online, resulting in indirect advertising for destinations or hotels. The opportunities for travel providers to create travel offers and services based on interactive conversations with their customers online are impressive. When it works the potential payoff is huge. On the flip side, negative customer feedback can be very bad for business.

For example: When the guitar belonging to musician David Carroll got destroyed during a United Airlines flight, he posted a song to YouTube that has since become an online legend: "United Breaks Guitars." Carroll's musical parody about his bad experience and the airline's poor customer service went viral, and has so far been viewed 12 million times and attracted thousands of user comments. It was a PR nightmare for the airline. Once a story gets traction on the Internet, there's no way of putting a lid on it.

Consequently, the entire tourism industry must face the challenge of how to deal intelligently with the new forms of communication offered by social networks and the role of customers as potential multipliers. The Internet is more than just another sales channel. The key question is: How can social media be used as a modern marketing tool to maintain a dialog with customers and create customer loyalty? How can we use social networks to turn our customers themselves into authentic brand ambassadors? And: How can a genuine dialog take place between travelers and travel companies in social networks?

The Influence of Rating Portals

The first big development for tourism in social media was the rise of rating portals. On platforms such as TripAdvisor (worldwide), Holiday-Check in Germany, DaoDao in China, and Tourout in Russia, travelers can write up their holiday experiences and post them in discussion forums where anyone can read them. This form of free expression has become a powerful force, because more and more holidaymakers getting ready to book trips are referring to and being influenced by the experiences of others. On TripAdvisor alone, there are 60 million customer reviews. Consequently, tourism brands simply cannot afford to ignore these online ratings. It is now a standard practice for companies in the industry to include customer ratings on their own websites. The comments and opinions are generated for the most part through online surveys of travelers after they return home from their holidays. Experience shows that the conversion rates, i.e. the percentage of site visitors who actually book a trip, increases substantially, in some cases by 100 percent, when the site includes customer ratings. Recent surveys show that 86 percent of travelers who book online consider ratings of this kind to be "extremely important" or "very important." And 78 percent of those who visit a tour operator's website for information about a planned vacation spend at least 10 minutes reading customer reviews, which means that they study them in some detail.

On the Web, the viewpoints and opinions expressed by customers on social networks are considered to be neutral, and therefore reliable and trustworthy. In the virtual world with no personal contact to companies, people place their trust in those who are communicating their real-life experiences. Back in 2005, TUI's brands in the U.K. market were way ahead of the competition, and scored points with customers when they were the first in the market to include independent guest ratings on their websites. The Thomson site openly responded to customer criticisms on the site and used them to make improvements, for example in the choice of hotels, product design and marketing, and also in the overall quality and price strategy. The TUI-branded websites now have more than two million customer ratings. This enhances our credibility. But it's not just about quantity. It's also important for customers to be able to read ratings by travelers with similar needs, wants and hobbies.

For companies in the tourism industry, customer ratings are also significant in another way: We can learn from them! The information in social networks provides extremely helpful input for our product-development teams about what our guests really want. By utilizing this information, we are then able to improve our existing products and develop entirely new travel offers and packages. In the future, the focus in the travel industry will be less on standardized travel packages made for the masses. Instead, we will see a shift towards flexible, differentiated offers, complemented by high-margin, specialized travel tailored to the unique needs and wishes of target groups. Consequently, social networks will be an indispensable source of information and tool for us in identifying and recognizing exactly what our customers want.

Facebook and YouTube

Facebook has become the key medium for tourism companies that want to actively connect with their customers. In China, where Facebook isn't available, companies use the similar Sina Weibo, which is extremely popular there. The Russian equivalent of Facebook is Vkontakte. At the beginning of 2012, TUI had 1.5 million Facebook fans worldwide – fans who regularly visit our pages to post their own vacation and travel stories, pictures and videos, who come there to arrange to meet others for vacations, who post comments, and even fans who have set up their own sub-communities around a specific brand. Our travel brands use Facebook's "Open Graph" to provide their fans a wide range of collaborative functions, for example invitations to group tour bookings or status updates for their families and friends from their current adventures. Our videos are also gaining in popularity on YouTube: In total, more than 30 million people watched TUI videos on our websites and on online channels such as YouTube or Vimeo in 2011.

Social & Mobile

In the social media world, the mobile phone is also playing an ever-increasing role as a lifestyle-oriented medium for customers. Today, more people in the U.K. are now accessing Facebook from their smartphones than they are from their home computers.

The meteoric rise of the smartphone has also opened up whole new areas of opportunity for tourism companies to communicate with their customers: Connecting the two areas – social and mobile – has great potential. Travelers can use their mobile phones to take pictures or videos and then upload them straight to the Internet – without waiting until they get back to their hotel room later in the day or return home from their holiday. And your smartphone knows your exact location, too, when you're on vacation: something that is especially helpful when traveling in foreign countries for finding your way around and finding special tours or other local offers. These technical capabilities are paving the way for new and valuable tourism smartphone apps for our customers.

On top of all of this, the smartphone is ideal for status updates and customer service when schedules, itineraries or contact information changes in the course of a trip. Let's recall for a moment the events of April 2010, when the volcanic eruption in Iceland covered Europe with an ash cloud that seriously impacted air traffic for weeks. TUI was able to reach its customers more quickly via Twitter and Facebook to inform them of cancellations and delays than via classical media such as TV, radio and newspapers – and in some cases our customers were even updating each other. Twitter was also instrumental in helping TUI keep its customers abreast of the latest news during the swine flu outbreak in Mexico a few years back. Among all of the social media channels on offer, Twitter is the mobile communications format that is best suited for distributing vital information in short messages – in contrast to Facebook, where people are more likely to exchange their thoughts and opinions, or share videos and photos, and where the focus is generally more on discussion. Twitter can be used to get quick and timely answers to questions: What's happening in my immediate vicinity at the moment? Where can I find a certain store or get a taxi? Where can I pick up some beach towels before I go to the pool? Twitter makes an ideal concierge – always available to help travelers solve problems. In the meantime, TUI and its brands boast more than 100,000 Twitter followers who use our Twitter feeds to keep up to date and informed in real time during their travels.

Case Studies: Examples of Key TUI Social Media Activities

The following examples serve to illustrate various dimensions and aspects of the interplay between tourism companies and social networks.

Listening and Getting Involved: First Choice

The British TUI brand, First Choice, is firmly anchored in the all-inclusive, family package tour segment, with a focus on developing expertise in responding to social media info requests about traveling with children. How do I keep my young children occupied and happy during a flight? Are there any stores that sell baby food around here? Answers to questions like these can be found on specialized sites such as Mumsnet.com and Babyexpert.com. The First Choice team started by listening to comments and postings before developing a strategy for deciding which topics to address and also when, how, and with whom to address them. Only then did First Choice enter into a dialog with the users of those portals. This gave us – and continues to give us – the ability not only to take advantage of the knowledge being shared on these sites by users, but to also position ourselves as experts. (www.firstchoice.co.uk)

Social Media Integration Across the Corporate Structure: TUI Germany

Just as the First Choice team geared its social media communications to the specific travel needs of families with children, TUI Germany has created an online resource that offers expert knowledge on every aspect of the travel experience. Our website aggregates the knowledge of on-site sales teams, travel package developers, local destination experts and other travel professionals and makes it accessible to customers. Even before our customers depart for vacation, they can get all of the exclusive, insider travel tips and "secrets" about their destination.

Ideally, the entire company should be involved in making our wealth of expert knowledge accessible to customers. Here, too, the goal is to offer added value to tourists, who receive advance information and expert knowledge prior to their travels and share in the experiences of others. Then, supplied with all the information they need, they can design their own exclusive travel experience. (www.tui.com).

Fan Pages on Facebook: Marmara & Club Robinson

The French TUI club brand, Marmara, runs a popular Facebook fan page featuring an animated avatar named Matt. He is a hit with our French Marmara guests – especially with children. Guests upload content to Matt's world, mainly articles they write themselves as well as photos and videos they post on the bulletin board. This Facebook fan page now has approximately 200,000 fans. Often, long dialog threads materialize with no input from the Marmara team. It is a prime example of a fan page taking on a life of its own. Naturally this contributes to a high level of brand trust and customer loyalty. Customers feel a true connection to this page and to Marmara (www.marmara.com).

Germany's Club Robinson brand also has its own Facebook page. In keeping with the "club" spirit, it has become a very popular community page. It is used by all those who feel that they belong to the club community. In contrast to the Marmara page, which is first and foremost about entertaining fans and giving them a place to exchange stories about their travel experiences, the Club Robinson page is a forum where fans exchange club-specific information, including organizational tips. It is quite often other club guests who answer questions posted on the page, and not the Robinson social media team. The focus is thus on added value as well as the networking of people with similar interests.

Club Robinson also uses this vehicle for marketing purposes. But that works only because of the overall user-friendliness of the page – and its popularity. The Robinson Facebook page is thus a good example of how individuals who want to talk about a great vacation experience can become brand ambassadors when they enthusiastically tell others about their trip. The page is also used by people looking for company on their holiday – "I'm traveling to the Mallorca club in May – who wants to join me?" (www.robinson.com)

Facebook Open Graph Integration: Trek America

The Trek America website is a well-designed and sophisticated application that offers a prime example of how we can utilize Facebook for intensive interaction between tour operators and travelers – throughout the whole vacation cycle. Trek America's customers are mostly young British travelers who book extensive tours of the USA lasting several weeks. The first Facebook contact with these guests is at their initiative. In this target group, 98 percent are already active on Facebook, and 60 percent of them sign up for the private Facebook community page after they book their trip. They compare the interests and preferences of other travelers registered on the page – and if it's a good match, they arrange to meet and travel together. Five weeks before their scheduled departure, the young British travelers are invited to join the Trek America Facebook group. Families and friends back home can use Facebook to follow the trip online and can view photos, videos, and travelogue updates and keep track of the traveler's current location. There is a constant exchange of travel tips on each destination stop along the tour. Where can you get a reasonably priced good meal in Las Vegas? What is a must-see when I'm in San Francisco? Where can I meet up with other young people in Los Angeles?

Some travelers who have already done their own tour of the USA stay in the group to share their experiences and give tips to others. The Trek America page, which was launched in July 2010, has been honored with a "Best Use of Social Media" award. The cross-selling revenues generated by the page quickly surpassed the initial cost of creating and operating the platform – further proof of its popularity with customers. Everyone who plans a trip with Trek America via Facebook and then documents and shares it with friends and family back home will always have a very unique and durable connection to the tour operator. (www.trekamericalive.com).

The Integration of Social & Mobile: TUI.com's Rainy-Day Game

In 2011, TUI Germany developed a game called Donnerwetter.Jetter (in English, someone who jets around in thunderstorms) as a marketing campaign. It centers around the subject of bad weather conditions and how to make the most of it. What's innovative about this game is the combination of a mobile app with the TUI Facebook page: Players can download a smartphone app that identifies their location and the current weather conditions there, and uploads this information to the TUI Facebook page. The worse the weather, the more points a player can earn during a specific period of time. The player with the highest score – i.e., the player who has seen the worst weather – wins a trip to the Dominican Republic, where they're sure to have sunshine. The verdict of many users of this entertaining blend of location, weather, content and an app: "cool." So cool, in fact, that Donnerwetter.Jetter won a bronze medal in the annual Art Director's Club competition in the "digital/mobile" category.

Social Commerce: Laterooms

Laterooms is TUI's own English-language hotel portal, similar to HRS in Germany. The Laterooms Facebook page is set up so that, in addition to hotels, users can look for cultural and sporting events and other entertainment happening during their stay. Users can also book tickets to the attractive events listed on the portal. Moreover, Laterooms can help people with planning their own events, such as weddings, for example by sending invitations to their Facebook friends via the Laterooms fan page. Naturally the invitees will also receive information about accommodation options.

These examples represent just a small sample of the online and social media activities of the more than 200 brands that make up the TUI world. We have massively expanded our use of social media over the past few years and will continue to do so. These efforts will be rooted in the three fundamental trends in the tourism industry – increasing demand for non-standard product experiences, the emergence of digital networking capabilities between customers and tour operators, and the development of new geographical markets, including China, India, Russia and Brazil – and in line with the corresponding TUI group strategy. At the same time, we will be increasing our product range for older travelers who make relatively little use of social media.

Looking Ahead

Companies and enterprises in the tourism industry that want to use the new social media and platforms will have to adjust their customer communications to play by the rules of Facebook, Twitter, etc. The people using social media – mostly younger – aren't just speaking a different language. Social networks also have their own culture that many companies will have to learn if they want to develop a successful social media strategy for these lifestyle and media worlds. For tourism as well as other industries, success will depend on how companies interact with their customers in the age of Web 2.0 and 3.0. This means:

- Companies will need to be good listeners. Social media offer a wealth of user-generated content about products and companies, which companies can systematically evaluate and use for product development purposes. Through careful monitoring of blogs and other social media platforms, companies can spot trends and even signs of trouble brewing.

- The Internet and social media create transparency. Companies must face up to this. Cover-ups, walls of silence, evasive action, message control: these tactics won't help. Social networks are forcing companies to adopt a culture of honesty and to live up to their brand claims.

- Transparency, openness, honesty and agility – these values from the realm of customer communications via social networks can help within companies to initiate internal transformation processes. To accomplish this, social media need to become firmly anchored and networked in an organization – to provide the seeds of change that will drive the shift to a more customer-oriented way of doing business.

- "Always connected" is now a hallmark of the lifestyle of many younger "digital natives." The line separating private life from work has dissolved. People are no longer working fixed hours in an office and are wedging their online shopping between two teleconferences. If companies and enterprises want to maintain a constant and stimulating dialogue with their target groups on social media sites – and offer their customers something new and unique – then they themselves will have to become fast, fresh and more open minded.

- Facebook, Twitter and YouTube aren't, first and foremost, platforms for marketing communications. Companies that are active in social networks will instead have to address the question: How can I create added value for users? They will have to come up with a very good reason for users to let them into their private lives.

- The value that social networks bring to a company comes in the form of visibility and engagement. Companies that are successful at navigating digital forums will be able to win over a large number of unpaid "brand ambassadors" – people whose stories about their good vacation experiences will be more authentic and legitimate than any company will ever be. And because users are "always connected," the comments and "Likes" of their friends can endlessly spread the word about their good experience with a company.

How will the relationships between tourism industry companies and their customers develop in the future? The web revolution has just begun, and the trends discussed in this article will significantly increase in both power and influence. And practices that are today just innovative experiments will, in time, mature into key marketing and customer loyalty tools. Technology will also continue to develop at breakneck speed and open up possibilities unimaginable today.

One key factor in the implementation of digital strategies – which encompass online, social and mobile applications – will be the question of how to use them to generate new business models and sales revenue, and also how established businesses will have to change to adapt. For obvious economic reasons, the development of social and mobile commerce will be a major focal point for the tourism industry in the future. What to expect? A diverse range of approaches, collaborations and players that are now barely on the radar, and a wealth of cooperative arrangements that we can't begin to imagine.

The decisive factor for our digital strategies and the approaches we take to the transformation will be balanced: on the one hand, implementing new business ideas in a networked structure with our customers and partners and, on the other, making the transition with existing customer contacts into a new type of interaction.

In any case, we are now just getting started with social networks, mobile end devices and the online-supported travel experience.

The Company

TUI AG – previously Preussag AG, is Europe's leading travel group. The company began in the mid-1990s with the transition from a conglomerate into a leisure industry service provider. TUI AG's three areas of business – TUI Travel, TUI Hotels & Resorts, and Cruises – reported total revenues of 17.5 billion euros for the 2010/2011 financial year. In 2011, the company had 73,700 employees.

For further information: http://www.tui-group.com/en/company and http://en.wikipedia.org/wiki/TUI_AG

Summary

The revolution brought about by Web 2.0 has changed the way many people book their vacations. Alongside the intensifying competition among travel companies – which has led to a lesser role for traditional travel agencies – individual customers in particular have gained power and influence. Now they can compare and evaluate travel offers online, for free. A professional website has therefore become an important instrument for attracting new customers and for selling travel products. Mobile access to the Internet and social media have made it possible to offer customers ever-improving levels of service, even after they set out on their trip, and often around the clock.

The role once played by travel tips and recommendations traded among friends has now been assumed by online customer ratings and comments. Take these communications very seriously and learn from what your customers are doing. Social media are the new hotline to the customer.

In an age of total transparency, ignoring or avoiding customer complaints is not an option. What matters today is honest communication that de-escalates the situation – and a prompt reaction. In Web 2.0, the amount of positive customer comments a company receives says a lot about its success.

Above and beyond this, social media has made it possible to develop products individually tailored to customer needs – to tell customers about them directly. Targeted marketing campaigns combined with transparency can provide added value for customers and companies alike, particularly when it comes to choosing a travel operator.

The Author

Mathias Döpfner, born in 1963, is chairman and CEO of Axel Springer AG in Berlin. He has been with Axel Springer AG since 1998, initially as editor-in-chief of Die Welt and since 2000 as member of the management board. During his career Mathias Döpfner held different positions in media companies. Among others, he was editor-in-chief of the newspapers Wochenpost and Hamburger Morgenpost. At Gruner+Jahr he was assistant to the CEO in Hamburg and on the staff of the head of international business in Paris. Mathias Döpfner worked as author and Brussels based correspondent for Frankfurter Allgemeine Zeitung. He studied musicology, german and theatrical arts in Frankfurt and Boston. He is a member of the board of directors of Time Warner Inc., member of the board of directors of RHJ International SA and holds several honorary offices, among others at the American Academy, the American Jewish Committee and the European Publishers Council (EPC). In 2010 he was Visiting Professor in Media at the University of Cambridge and became a member of St. John's College.

Dr. Döpfner co-authored this article with Dr. Clemens Trautmann, who served as chief of staff of the chairman and CEO at Axel Springer AG.

Customer-Oriented Approaches in a Digitized Media World – a Progress Report

Mathias Döpfner, Axel Springer AG

Do we even know anymore who our customers are, what they want and what they do? It's a question that companies have always had to ask themselves; but after almost two decades of digitization and globalization, finding the answer is more urgent than ever before. Even a cursory examination of the question reveals a few surprises for the media industry and a media company like Axel Springer AG.

Formerly, the archetypal reader of the *BILD Zeitung*, Germany's biggest tabloid, was a construction worker who would discuss the day's headlines on his lunch break and then check out the "Page 1 Girl" back in the cab of his truck. Does this reader even still exist? Not really, because nowadays, Germany's construction sites teem with imported labor from Warsaw or Istanbul who don't read the news – or they buy the Turkish newspaper *Hürriyet*. The girl on the front page disappeared for good on International Women's Day 2012 – a change that was made, by the way, based on the recommendations from a reader advisory panel that we formed as part of a customer loyalty and retention initiative. And the proportion of university graduates among visitors to the newspaper's website, bild.de, is now 41 percent.

In sharp contrast, the archetypal subscriber to Germany's daily newspaper, *DIE WELT*, used to be a bank employee and family man who sat down to breakfast with his three children and read aloud to his wife from the editorial page. Is this reader still around? Not really. Nowadays, he is most likely childfree, single or divorced, usually skips breakfast, and if he happens to have time to read the news in the morning, it's a quick check of the headlines or stock prices on his smartphone. Once in a while, he'll read the print version of the newspaper's weekend edition, *WELT am SONNTAG*, on the balcony. Or if he's traveling, he'll check out the electronic version using the iKiosk app on his tablet.

And what about the classical newspaper advertiser? Once it might have been a supermarket chain advertising specials and the latest meat prices with plenty of photos – known as "pork belly ads" in German newspaper jargon. Carmakers were also big advertising customers, booking an enormous amount of space in *AUTO BILD* and the national dailies well in advance of every new model launch. Do these kinds of advertising clients still exist? Not really, because today, fewer and fewer clients have direct control over their own marketing budgets – they've handed it over to media agencies. Customers are booking ads at much shorter notice nowadays. And the customers have – quite rightly – become rather demanding when it comes to evidence that advertising is actually working. In difficult times, when budgets are tight, companies rely more often on performance-based marketing. It used to be all about full-page or corner display ads. Now, customers also expect expert information on things such as "conversion optimization", "predictive behavioral targeting" and "real time bidding".

With the advent of the digital age, traditional assumptions and role models have evaporated into thin air. Customer profiles have become more differentiated, and we now have greater transparency – but also a higher degree of complexity. Customers are becoming ever more discerning – because they're being offered so much more as a result of intensifying global competition. As we've seen in many other industries, the balance has shifted from the supply to the demand side in the media industry – making it a buyer's market. And the customer has become more autonomous and mobile, and has come to expect performance. Customers are also more open to trying new things – or we could say: They've become more fickle. The bonds forged between customers and services or brands have become weaker. When a convincing offer comes along, the customer is willing to give it a try. The perfect is the enemy of the good.

One Product, Two Markets

Even with all of the social and technological changes we've experienced, the basic structure underlying the relationships between media companies and their customers and products have remained remarkably constant. What is the essence of our business model, after all? It lies in the creation of powerful content and media brands that are attractive to readers and users. We then use the resulting mass reach to attract advertisers. Consequently, publishers – and this is an important point, as well as an anomaly in business terms – are present with the same product in two different markets: with our readership and with our advertisers. And for Axel Springer and most of central Europe's publishing houses, each of these markets represents about half of total revenues. The readers are mostly end consumers (B2C), whereas with our advertising customers – apart from the ones who place small classified ads – we have a B2B relationship.

Having a foot in two different markets can, among other things, lead to conflicting objectives in the respective customer relationships, particularly since an advertiser's buying power is typically many times greater than that of an individual reader. So, for example, it may seem to be good business and quite service-oriented in the short term to agree to an advertiser's request for favorable coverage of a product in a news story, to place a link to his e-commerce offerings prominently in an editorial online article or to make the layout of a paid advertorial indistinguishable from that of a regular article. But in the medium term, the results are both inevitable and fatal: a loss of credibility for the media brand among its readership paired with a significant drop in the publication's reach. That, in turn, would not serve the interests of the publication's advertising customers, and they would quickly start looking for a new advertising medium.

This takes us straight to the second anomaly of our industry: It is probably the only one in which management has almost no say in the product contents. Internal organizational measures are in place to ensure that a publisher's management team – which is responsible for selling advertisements – has no influence on what topics get covered and how. Instead, this is decided at the discretion of the independent editorial staff. This strict separation of editorial functions and publishing, of journalism from advertising, is required, first, to bring us into compliance with the legal requirements – and also with the voluntary code of conduct and self-regulation as stipulated by the German Press Council. At Axel Springer, we have gone a step further: Since 2003, we have enforced an internal set of "Guidelines for Ensuring Journalistic Impartiality," which we also made part of a company-wide Code of Conduct in 2011. In addition, at the beginning of 2012, our editorial teams announced a general policy of rejecting press discounts. What may appear at first glance to be merely a set of compliance measures is, in practice, also a form of product management. Credibility and transparency are becoming increasingly important as a distinguishing feature and a reason for choosing our products – for our readership and the advertising market alike.

Exemplary Customer Contact: A Prerequisite and Objective of Digitization

How is digitization affecting the business models and customer relationships of media companies today? Our working hypothesis – not yet disproved – is this: Fewer things are changing than one might think. We need to consider where we excel in our traditional business and transfer these core competencies into the digital world. This is the essence of the digitization strategy that Axel Springer has been pursuing – largely unchanged – since 2002.

- As in the analog world, we are creating powerful brands and attractive content with the goal of achieving a large, high-quality readership. To accomplish this goal, we digitize brand content either organically – for example with BILD.de or WELT Online – or we acquire leading content portals such as auFeminin, Netmums (U.K.) or Onet (Poland).

- Axel Springer markets its mass reach to advertising customers. In the digital world, this means investing primarily in online marketers. Axel Springer recently succeeded in expanding its position as the leading provider of performance-based marketing solutions in Europe, above all through the international expansion of the zanox Group into new markets, the acquisition of the affiliated British networks Buy.at and Digital Window and the Dutch provider M4N. And through the acquisition of kaufDA, we're now also active in the rapidly growing market for online catalogs, coupons and local deals.

- As in the past, Axel Springer continues to utilize the wide reach of its product portfolio to establish lucrative classified ad markets. In the print world, these include job ads, real estate or used-car ads. Consequently, in the online world we are either setting up portals or buying existing ones such as StepStone, Totaljobs, Immonet, SeLoger and AutoReflex. Another reason for this approach is the decision that it is better to cannibalize our own traditional classified ad business than to let others do it.

If you wanted to boil all of these activities down into one simple formula for both the analog and digital worlds, it would have to be something like this: We generate and sell customer contacts. And therefore, our own customer contact, the standard of our own customer orientation and customer loyalty, must be exemplary.

The year 2012 marked an important turning point for Axel Springer: For the first time ever, our company generated revenues of more than one billion euros on digital media activities, more than any other operating segment. Furthermore, this growth is highly profitable. From this strong position, though, Axel Springer needs to pursue the digitization of our business with even more speed and vigor. We intend to accelerate the digital transformation of the entire Group, in order to further bolster our position of digitization pioneers. We intend to accelerate the pace of innovation and shape the fundamental structural transformation of the media industry. Although our print media will continue to make an important contribution to the success of our business for a long time, our goal is clear: We want to become the leading digital media group.

On the Path to Modern Customer Orientation

However, there was a substantial gap between today's claim and reality back in 2006, when we began implementing our digitization strategy at Axel Springer through concrete acquisitions and startups. Our customer orientation was by no means outstanding. Like many other media companies, we had been following the trend of outsourcing sales and service for subscribers and low-volume advertising customers without having any real operational control over the external service providers. The consequences were plain to see. One indicator was the analysis of subscription cancellations: The old newspaper adage – that the average subscription lasts longer than the typical marriage – took a beating, today's higher divorce rates notwithstanding. And the stacks of complaints and subscription cancellations in the CEO's office were getting taller by the day. Things were equally grim for our advertising sales team. To bolster entrepreneurial autonomy at the local level, advertising sales fell under the auspices of our major profit centers. As a result, our advertising customers were being contacted numerous times by different salespersons from different teams. It was bad enough that the sales representatives from our different media brands were completely unaware of each other's activities. Worse yet: In some cases they simply didn't want to know, and wouldn't lift a finger to support cross-brand, cross-medial marketing of our portfolio. Thus, we were unable to fully exploit the potential of the rapidly growing online marketing segment.

In response to that situation, in 2006 we set ourselves a goal: "Making Axel Springer Europe's customer-friendliest media company by 2010." Spoiler alert: We fell a little short of that target, but nevertheless accomplished a lot. For one, among all of Germany's publishing houses, surveys by TNS Infratest have ranked Axel Springer number one for customer retention and loyalty since 2009. However, the goal setting had an even more significant impact internally at Axel Springer: The sophisticated evaluation and ranking systems that we developed in tandem with TNS Infratest – still being used today to measure our successes and setbacks in the area of customer retention and loyalty – have since become firmly established as management and controlling tools. We conduct regular surveys of all of our relevant customer segments: On the advertising side, we survey media agencies, advertisers, and classified-ad customers. And on the sales side, we survey press wholesalers and, of course, several thousand readers and online users. In addition, we include our internal service providers and even departments performing service-related work, such as our legal department, central purchasing and group controlling. It's exactly this latter aspect that underscores our view of customer retention and loyalty as part of a larger, group-wide cultural shift at Axel Springer – one that goes hand in hand with the digitization of our business. The project team heading up our customer retention and loyalty activities is now seen by our other departments as a business partner with real credibility. By working with our respective market-oriented departments and editorial teams after each survey to develop specific measures, it creates genuine added value and benefits.

One concrete example of the value of our customer loyalty tools for our editorial teams was *BILD*'s reporting on the jungle camp reality show from broadcaster, RTL, "Ich bin ein Star, holt mich hier raus," or in English, "I'm a Celebrity, Get Me Out of Here!" The series was broadcast at the same time as one of our surveys was being conducted, and the customer loyalty scores for *BILD* were unusually poor. We followed up on the survey by conducting a qualitative analysis of the results, and discovered this: When the participants in the camp faced a test or when candidates gave up, fought, or had affairs, *BILD* reported in a sober, newsroom tone. But for *BILD* readers, this completely missed the mark. They saw the show as more of a reality-based satire. We were able to use this insight to adjust our reporting of the show's next season – with measurable results in newsstand sales and our ratings. The editorial team also took this insight one step further in the online coverage: For the last season of the show, the BILD.de team provided a satirical running commentary on the jungle camp goings-on, which were read on mobile devices by large numbers of viewers as they watched. Incidentally, this marked the first time that we actually experienced the "second screen" trend, in which TV viewers use another device to interact while watching a show.

Our initiative to become a more customer-oriented organization also resulted in a very important decision about our company's structure. When we founded Axel Springer Media Impact in 2008, we created an integrated, cross-media marketing unit. The goal: an integrated, "one-face-to-the-customer" approach that offers our advertising customers access to our whole portfolio and range of media products – digital and analog – through one dedicated contact partner. The decision to implement highly centralized customer relations for our advertising marketing, which we arrived at through specific error analysis, was to become a trend in our industry. Today, almost all of the big publishing houses have integrated marketing units in one form or another.

From Advertising Placement Platform to Creative Partner

The dynamic changes we've seen in the way people use media have posed a lot of major challenges for marketers like Axel Springer Media Impact. The creation of cross-media, integrated structures has allowed us to manage these changes. And by the same token, advertisers, too, now have a wider range of new and more complex marketing approaches and solutions to choose from. Target groups are more fragmented, and there are now many more channels for reaching them. This creates the opportunity to transform ourselves from an advertising placement platform to a creative partner for effective marketing solutions.

Increasingly, this will center around working collaboratively with our advertisers to both develop and execute concepts tailored to meet each respective marketing need and to the wide range of available marketing channels and media markets. To accomplish this, marketers will no longer be relying solely on the more classical print and online communication channels, but will also use a mix of elements such as mobile ads, video, social media and reader testimonials, point-of-sale activities, events or private-label media. Consequently, Axel Springer was the first German media company to introduce and report a multimedia reach for its brand *DIE WELT* throughout all channels – print, web and mobile. The targeted expansion of our own portfolios – plus the inclusion of third-party marketing materials, where necessary – allows us to realize practically seamless advertising campaigns. Advertising campaigns supporting a company's marketing goals in this way could be called a 360-degree approach.

With one of its most recent campaigns, "The Faces of Israel," Axel Springer Media Impact proved that we can successfully design this kind of 360-degree approach through close cooperation with advertisers. The goal of this particular campaign, which was commissioned by the Israel state tourism ministry, was to promote Israel as a tourism destination with the motto, "Show Israel Your Smile." We created a contest for our readers which two people – a romantic couple, friends or relatives – could enter by explaining why they wanted to visit Israel. We publicized the campaign and contest through ads in several different Axel Springer AG print titles, including *WELT*, *BILD*, *BILD am SONNTAG* and *Bild der FRAU* as well as online at *WELT* Online and BILD.

de – and complemented these efforts through the use of social media. We took the 10 pairs of Israel fans with the most convincing entries and invited them to a casting event. The winners selected by our jury were sent on a 10-day trip to Israel; Following their trip, their travel experiences became part of a Germany-wide ad campaign.

To successfully develop and execute this type of 360-degree campaign, it is vital to establish a direct and timely exchange of information between the marketer and the advertiser. It's not rare for campaign start-up and preparation phases to last from six to even 12 months in this area. When it comes to their own media products, marketers typically have the most competence and expertise. They're the best judges of when and how ads will be most effective across their portfolios. This runs counter to the supposed trend of automatically giving external media agencies the authority to call the shots when it comes to advertising budgets. A cooperative and trusting relationship between the publisher and advertiser is essential for a mutually beneficial and successful campaign. In the future, marketing representatives – who have expertise in the full spectrum of communication possibilities – will need to become more strongly networked with their counterparts on the advertising side who are responsible for products and brands. Successful campaigns will serve to foster a relationship of mutual personal trust between them.

Interestingly enough, we're also seeing that customer contact plays a key role in pure online marketing, too, although at first glance – with its ad-serving, targeting and tracking solutions – it is considered to be more technology driven. The structural shift from classical to digital marketing has finally started to affect as conservative a sector as retailing – which for many years relied on flyers and circular ads as its main marketing tools. We can meet the demand for a digital equivalent of these methods with services such as KaufDA, or, alternately, the Bonial International Group, and by making a retailer's ads available to shoppers online both via mobile apps and at home, using the geodata of the advertiser's stores. The advertiser pays according to the number of customers who actually click on and open a store's virtual flyer. What hasn't changed, however, is the fact that it still takes long-standing relationships with a retailer's marketing team to secure new online advertising business. The very experienced head of our print marketing team, "National Retail," is also chairman of the KaufDA advisory board, and serves as a sort of "door opener" for the Internet entrepreneurs. And for its entry into the French market, Bonial was able to recruit the former CEO of Carrefour as its brand ambassador. Having a personal relationship with your customer is equally important in the online classified-ads business, where maintaining close contacts to real estate agents and car dealers is a decisive factor for success. And this, in turn, also makes real estate, job and used-car portals better able to withstand competition from the eventual entry of technology-based search engines and aggregator sites into the online classified-ads market.

A Paradigm Shift in the Online Journalism of the 21st Century

Since the turn of the millennium, our relationship to readers and users has changed drastically – both quantitatively and qualitatively. The social web and the advent of new end devices have been the key drivers of this change. The number of contacts we have with customers on a daily basis has grown exponentially, and these interactions have turned the relational hierarchy between journalists and readers on its head. But realizing a new level of quality in customer orientation requires the introduction of subscription and payment models for news portals that, when considering that readers have in general become accustomed to getting their digital news for free, represents nothing less than a paradigm shift. In the English-speaking world – for example, at the *New York Times* – the introduction of paid content and paywalls is already well underway. Besides *Neue Zürcher Zeitung*, Axel Springer's *DIE WELT* has been the first national media brand on the continent to make that decisive step in late 2012 by launching a new subscription model for all its digital offerings. *BILD* introduced a premium membership model in mid-2013.

In the past, newspaper publishers would reach their readers once or twice a day – in the morning, when they read the newspaper at the breakfast table, or on the way to or from work on the bus or train. We can see just how much the typical user's behavior has changed by looking at what's happened with the *BILD* brand. Just as before, the print edition of the newspaper is being read predominantly by people either at home in the morning, or before lunch at their workplaces. Following a brief surge in the early morning hours, the number of users accessing our site via online or mobile steadily increases over the course of the mid-morning hours. The number of users accessing BILD.de peaks at noon. And we're seeing another peak among users accessing the site via the *BILD* iPhone app at around 10 p.m. – exactly the time that the downloadable PDF of the next morning's edition becomes available. Many users then do some intensive surfing on BILD.de and BILD Mobil until after midnight and use the apps. Each medium has its own peak viewing time, and all of them combined ensure full availability of our media content.

It's interesting to note that each individual channel for itself – print, online and mobile – is reaching a record number of readers. The print version of BILD is still reaching around 12 million people, as before. The BILD.de website reaches approximately 14 million unique non-mobile Internet users: an all-time record. And, taken separately, the mobile version of BILD.de is among the top-10 news portals ranked by reach. We are also seeing an increase in the utilization of our BILD apps, through which we are selling well over 100,000 digital editions per day. We could see these numbers as confirmation of Riepl's Law, which says that, once established, no medium for the exchange of information and ideas is ever fully replaced or eliminated by other media.

With the further market penetration by smartphones and tablets, we will be seeing yet another surge in our reach. Our challenge here will be to offer our readers a range of products and services optimized to their devices and the usage situation. To ensure this, it will be essential to streamline our internal editorial processes to allow for creation and adaptation of content for each different channel with reasonable effort. The fact that in the period between 2005 and 2008, we became the first German publisher to successfully combine and fully integrate our online and print editorial teams, means that we already have the framework in place for this kind of multi-channel publishing. At the same time, this has enhanced the role of the individual editors as experts for a certain beat or subject – regardless of the content channel. We'll see this trend reflected on both the product side and in our pricing strategies: Instead of paying individually for individual formats, access rights or apps, customers will subscribe to a media brand's bundled services. The New York Times' offering "All Digital Access" is a remarkable success. By offering three basic digital subscription packages, designed to suit common media usage habits, DIE WELT pursues a similar approach. The first results of this premium initiative are rather encouraging, particularly since the reach of WELT ONLINE has remained stable or even grown despite the pay requirement.

In the pre-digital age, there was already a channel available for readers to provide feedback to journalists: It was called the letter to the editor. The emergence of electronic media has created an even faster, more direct and broader range of methods for readers to interact with editorial staff. They have taken customer orientation to a new level – and have also turned the relational hierarchy between journalists and readers on its head. A quick review of the recent history of journalism serves to illustrate this shift in striking fashion:

- In the 19th century, the journalist was, in a sense, an authority figure for readers, proclaiming in editorials how they should view the world. Journalism had a pedagogical force to it: It lectured people. This attitude was reinforced by the way the text was presented, with readers forced to wade through columns of fine print.

- In the 20th century, the relationship between journalists and readers approached that of equals. Editors recognized that they weren't going to stay in business by lecturing the readers and making them do penance. They began to take their lead from readers' tastes. News stories became more emotional and personal; in short, they took on a tabloid feel, even in the so-called intellectual papers. The layout became more important. The visuals, photos, caricatures and comics, illustrations and graphs were added to make newspapers easier to read and understand. Headlines had to draw the reader in – even through sensationalism. The goal was to capture the attention of the reader—who in that day and age could just as well get the news from the radio or television. During the second half of the 20th century, information that focused on providing a service gained in importance because it had a practical use for readers. The editor became the reader's conversational partner.

- In the online journalism of the 21st century, the editor has now become the reader's service provider. The user tells journalists what he or she is interested in reading about. The continuous collection of click rate data is, in effect, market research happening in real time. Through this practice, editors have instant feedback on their readers' priorities and what they want to read more – and less – about. Consequently, the old hierarchy has been completely reversed in the digital age. The reader has, in a sense, become the boss, and the editor has become the employee.

This is the environment in which our industry is currently trying to develop sustainable payment models for digital journalism products and services. And as with print journalism, it's our goal of creating two different revenue streams from marketing and advertising sales. Admittedly, we couldn't be starting from a worse point: Cultural pessimists insist that with the reversal in hierarchy between the media and media consumers, there's no longer a need for journalists who are specially trained in research and news writing. They say this is something users can do by themselves nowadays. User-generated content, blogs and citizen journalism are being hailed as the new face of media. Content created by users has made professional reporters superfluous. Exacerbating this situation is the fact that for more than a decade, our industry has been conditioning readers to expect that high-quality journalism and media content always comes for free.

So what gives us confidence in the face of these realities? The bigger the flood of information becomes, the bigger the need will be for someone to digest and analyze it. This is because, when information is available to everyone at any time of the day or night, it will become all the more necessary to have someone to guide us through this information jungle – someone who can assess and curate the information for us. It cannot and will not be possible for everyone at every time to serve as his own editor-in-chief. Journalism is enriched by contributions from laymen and readers. But they cannot replace professional journalists – nor do they want to. For centuries, there has been a need for quality information provided by expertly researched and written stories. This is a need that we can count on, and that will remain.

Whether we will actually succeed in taking this basic need as a starting point for engendering a widespread, long-term willingness to pay for media-based products and services will be determined mainly by our level of customer orientation. The basic decision to charge readers for access to digital news media will force media companies – thankfully – to review their entire range of content and processes in terms of their "stickiness," i.e. the extent to which they keep users coming back. Together with the results of detailed market research, especially with regard to pricing, Axel Springer can also take advantage of existing tools to measure customer retention and loyalty. We have been collecting index values for our digital products and services every year since 2006. Consequently, we can accurately pinpoint the brands and channels where we need to improve customer loyalty before implementing paywall models. One very promising development for us is the fact that the paid apps for our core brands already show high index values. Readers' willingness to acknowledge the value of digital media by paying for it goes hand in hand with strong customer loyalty.

Alongside a simple method of payment, the most important factor for success will be the quality and uniqueness of the content offered. However, a look at designs of existing online news portals reveals obvious reasons why they enjoy less customer loyalty than their print counterparts. In our attempts to ensure that our websites reach as large a readership as possible and in the race to stay ahead of the competition with a higher rate of page impressions, visits and unique viewer numbers, the reader often falls by the wayside. We need to be honest with ourselves about whether it makes sense to turn our websites into mere "click engines" with things like quizzes and tests and endless online photo galleries – or through the use of boring headlines to avoid being overlooked or assigned low rankings by search engines. The fact that a website – unlike a newspaper or magazine – has no start or end – means that readers can't derive a sense of completion or feel informed. This, too, is not conducive to customer loyalty.

The development of payment models for news portals will probably serve as a catalyst in fostering a more intensive level of customer orientation with respect to both the user and the advertiser. And we'll be able to determine very clearly just how attractive and customer friendly our online content really is based on how many customers decide to pay for a premium subscription following a free trial period, and whether or not we're hitting our sales revenue targets. There is no better indicator of quality than a customer's willingness to pay. If we experience a simultaneous shift in traffic streams, we will need to engage in intensive talks and close cooperation with our advertising customers to communicate the fact that a paying readership is also worth more in the digital world—just as an ad in the *Frankfurter Allgemeine Zeitung*, the *Süddeutsche Zeitung* or *DIE WELT* has an inherently higher impact and price than one in a free advertising flyer.

Taking Stock and Looking Ahead

When we look at the situation of publishing houses and media companies after nearly two decades of digitization and globalization, we see many opportunities and successes. But we cannot claim to have done everything right when it comes to customer retention. The indications to the contrary are impossible to overlook: A sustainable model for the monetization of online journalism in the digital world is still a work in progress. Despite an increased willingness of users to pay for digital services and products, it's still below the level in the world of print media.

Above all, however, we should be concerned about the fact that third-party entities have been able to encroach into value-creation chains and customer relations where publishing houses have traditionally been strong and are now laying claim to a far from insignificant portion of the margins. Increasingly, the advertising market is dominated by big media agencies such as GroupM, Aegis and OMG. Technology brands such as Apple and iTunes have successfully developed platforms for selling media content to readers and users, and now have a 30 percent share of the market from product sales and royalties – and also have a monopoly on the accompanying customer and user data. Globally active aggregators such as Flipboard and Zite (B2C) or Meltwater News (B2B) are taking the content produced by publishers and repackaging it in an attractive, customized and customer-friendly format – which they then monetize through the use of advertising and/or subscription models. On the news portals of established brands we are also seeing a rise in the share of search engine links and social media referrals among total page impressions as compared with direct access, or "brand traffic," as it is known.

When companies neglect customer relations, they become especially prone to this kind of "transfer of power" to third parties. With the transition of media from analog to digital, many publishers have obviously focused on adapting their organizational and cost structures and taken customer loyalty for granted. The task facing us now: bringing about a renaissance for direct customer contact in the digital age. The technological means for accomplishing this – in the form of social media, for example – are substantial. A data-protection environment that restricts the exchange of customer data is a further incentive to foster and nurture direct contacts with customers. We are also seeing promising initiatives in our industry to give precedence to the retention of current subscribers and advertisers over the much more expensive approach of attracting new ones. Open platforms and intelligent, industry-specific solutions help us to win back some of our business from technology providers. One example: the Axel Springer iKiosk, which allows us to offer PDF versions of our own publications and products from other publishers for sale in numerous European markets. In any case, the numerical framework for customer contacts is outstanding. Axel Springer AG alone reaches 53 percent of the total German population with its print products, and our digital products see total traffic of 74 million unique visitors Europe-wide. This places us among Europe's top 20 Internet companies in terms of reach, after such online-only players as Google, Facebook, Amazon, Wikipedia, AOL and Mail.ru.

Media companies must establish themselves as trailblazers and specialists in customer retention and relations in the digital world, too, just as they did for decades in the print business. Placing our readers and customers firmly at the center of our activities and focus may seem like a platitude – but based on what has happened in our industry over the past several years, its importance cannot be stressed enough. And we aren't going to accomplish this by pandering to alleged customer needs, but rather by striking the right balance between intelligent market research and bold leadership. Steve Jobs knew this when he formulated his business maxim: "It's not the consumers' job to know what they want. It's my job."

All of those aspects lead to our strong conviction media companies need to be even more radical and vigorous in transforming their business: For Axel Springer, the tasks extends beyond the digitization of our traditional news outlets and advertising solutions, with the digital ventures being little more than synergetic add-ons. As the strategic goal of 50 percent revenue contribution from the digital business is in close reach, we are going reverse the direction of the business transformation. In this accelerated process, we hope to launch more ventures ourselves and invest more in start-ups and early-stage companies. It is their spirit and culture we need to adopt in the company as a whole. Among others, this is the rationale why we are sending some of our best people to Silicon Valley, the heart of entrepreneurship and innovation: our best journalist, our best marketing professional, our best IT expert and founder. And if any proof of our genuine resolution was needed: The latest fellow in Axel Springer's Silicon Valley initiative serves as head of a printing plant and – not least – also oversees Axel Springer's customer loyalty initiative.

The digital world's ecosystem can perhaps best be described by a quote from Mario Quintana – a Brazilian journalist who is also known as the "poet of simple things." He says that "The secret is not [to] chase butterflies. The secret is to take care of the garden so that they come to you." Only those who adopt this philosophy of customer orientation and product design will be among the winners in the digital age.

The Company

The Axel Springer company was established by the publisher of the same name in 1946. Today it is Germany's largest newspaper and third-largest magazine publisher, and counts among Europe's leading media companies. The company's broad portfolio includes the successful and well-established multimedia brands of the *BILD* and *WELT* groups as well as leading digital companies such as *StepStone/Totaljobs, zanox, auFeminin* or *SeLoger*. Axel Springer is active in 34 countries with more than 230 newspapers and magazines, over 160 websites and 120 apps. In 2012, with more than 13,650 employees, the company earned total revenues of around 3.3 billion euros and an EBITDA of 628 million euros.

For further information: http://www.axelspringer.de/en/artikel/Brief-Portrait_40171.html

Summary

Strong content and media brands attract readers. The resulting mass reach is then marketed to advertising customers. The fact that publishers serve both readers (B2C) and the advertising market (B2B) with the same product may lead to conflicting goals, which must be resolved in favor of journalistic autonomy and the credibility of the media brand.

In online journalism – driven by mobile end devices and the social web – customer contacts have coalesced into anywhere, anytime availability through multi-channel publishing. The possibilities for interaction and continuous identification of content preferences have inverted the hierarchical relationship between the journalist and the reader. However, the reader still has a basic need for filtering, orientation and exclusive information. The necessity to develop sustainable online payment models on the basis of this need will in turn engender an improvement in customer orientation and the quality of journalism, which have sometimes been neglected under ad-financed models.

In the marketing of advertising, publishing houses are undergoing a transformation from ad placement platforms to creative partners, taking a "one face to the customer" approach to work with advertisers to design cross-media marketing solutions (360-degree concepts). Even in the technology-driven areas of online marketing and classified ad business, personal contacts between customers and marketing managers, dealers or brokers is still crucial.

One challenge is the encroachment of outsiders and technology companies (search engines, aggregators, media agencies) into the customer relationships and value chains of publishing houses. Media companies that still have a mass reach and strong subscriber base can also become successfully established as specialists and trailblazers for customer loyalty in digital publishing channels. However, they will only be able to capitalize on these assets, if they drive the digital transformation even more radically and adopt the culture and business logic of digital ventures.

B2B
Business-to-Business

The Author

Marc Benioff was born in 1964. He started his first company, Liberty Software, at the age of 15 in 1979. In 1984, he joined the Macintosh Division of Apple Computers. He earned a Bachelor of Science in business administration from the University of Southern California in 1986 and worked for the Oracle Corporation from 1986 until 1999. In 1999, he founded salesforce.com, and since then has served as that company's chief executive officer and chairman.

The SOCIAL Revolution – How to Transform Your Company into a Social Enterprise and Your Customers into Friends for Life

Marc Benioff, salesforce.com, inc.

In 1999, I quit my job as an executive at Oracle because I couldn't stop thinking about a simple question: "Why isn't all enterprise software like Amazon.com?" Why couldn't business applications be run from a simple website, without software or hardware to install, and costly consultants to hire? Why couldn't we just compute in the Internet, or the cloud, and get away from the data center and all its complexity? It was a pretty straightforward idea, but from the confines in which I sat, there wasn't anything close to a straightforward solution.

That vision led to the founding of salesforce.com. And, over the past decade, this idea gained traction, became known as cloud computing, and exploded into a $150 billion industry that revolutionized the software business. Our startup was launched in a one-bedroom apartment, with our servers in a walk-in closet. Since then, we've grown into the largest tech employer in San Francisco, the only $3 billion enterprise cloud computing company, and the most innovative company in the world according to *Forbes*.

An amazing story. In truth, it all happened faster and it all became bigger than I had ever anticipated. The world changed in ways I never imagined. I should have been content. But I wasn't.

At the start of this decade, something new was happening with the Social Web, and it was making a significant impact on our daily lives. Suddenly, a new door opened to a world of new possibilities. I became obsessed with another simple question: "Why isn't all enterprise software like Facebook?"

As we were focused on bringing enterprise computing into the cloud age, Facebook redefined consumer computing and helped ignite a social phenomenon. This technology – with features like feeds, profiles, and groups, and the ability to use them on any mobile device – changed everything for consumers, and it began to change the world. It ignited a social revolution.

With technology that was social, mobile, and open to everyone, we began to see a profound shift in which power is possessed by individuals. Wired citizens could rally crowds, gain global attention, and nearly topple established political systems with Facebook and Twitter posts. There's been much written about the Arab Spring and the role of social media in the revolutions in Tunisia, Egypt, and Libya, and we see new stories emerge every day. In a similar vein, we've seen how individuals can damage companies by posting a single YouTube video. Think about "United Breaks Guitars," which is probably now Dave Carroll's most famous song and which wreaked havoc on United's brand.

At salesforce.com we observed what was happening – how these technologies were becoming adopted and adored – and we knew that there would be profound implications for all businesses. We saw how managers in companies – once the "elite" – no longer controlled the conversation with employees or with customers. It became clear that if we didn't find a better way to create more authentic and meaningful relationships with customers and employees, a "Corporate Spring" and a "CEO Spring" would be next (And for some organizations, it has happened. In the U.S., Netflix lost 800,000 customers and $13.4 billion in market cap for not listening to customers, and the Susan G. Komen Foundation executive responsible for driving a decision that alienated constituents resigned after much public backlash).

What we've seen time and again is that the adoption of new technologies doesn't stop for anyone. With this in mind, we took on a "social" perspective. We built Salesforce Chatter, a Facebook-like social network for the enterprise and invested in reinventing all of our services – sales, customer service, collaboration and more – to make them social.

We achieved our incredible success by embracing the cloud, but we transformed our company to go faster, become more transparent, and achieve better alignment with employees, customers and the community by embracing social. I like to say, "We were born cloud – but we've been 'reborn' social." As a social enterprise – a company that embraces social technologies to facilitate employee collaboration and engagement with customers in entirely new ways – we're able to listen, share and innovate better than ever before. As a result, we excel at things we've never even tried before – things people told us we would never be able to do. We are constantly learning how to delight customers and employees in new ways, and we are receiving the benefits of their engagement, their loyalty and their friendship. We've achieved more – and it's been easier, less expensive, and more fun than I would have predicted even a few years ago.

Let me sum it up: I've spent 30 years in the technology industry, and I've seen the most profound and most exciting changes in the past two years. And, it's just the beginning.

Welcome to the Social Revolution

What I love most about my job is the continuous evolution of the technology industry. Every 10 years, a radical new paradigm of computing emerges, and every cycle brings 10 times more users. From mainframes (1970s) to minicomputers (1980s) to PCs and LANs (1990s) to cloud computing on the desktop (2000s), the only constant has been change. But now, we are embarking on the most far-reaching shift yet. We are living in the post-PC revolution. The mobile and social Internet, fueled by amazing advances in hardware and in software, will define this decade as the one with the most profound potential.

For the first time, we are seeing a simultaneous hardware and software revolution. Software is evolving with social networking, driven by sites like Twitter, YouTube, and Facebook; a phenomenon which now has nearly one billion active users. It's incredible to consider that in 2009, Facebook surpassed Google in terms of total users; it is now the website where Americans spend the most time. The Internet as we know it is going away; Facebook is the platform where we congregate to do everything from getting news to writing messages, and swapping photos to sharing music. The stats on Facebook are mind-boggling: If Facebook were a country, its population would make it the third-largest nation on the planet. Fifty percent of users log in every single day; people spend 700 billion minutes on the site a month, and it's so sticky in our culture that its creation story became a No. 1 movie in the U.S.

How Facebook has impacted our culture, our society and even our civilization is what fascinates me most. It has altered the way we define who our "friends" are and it has changed how we think about sharing and collaborating. With the "Like" button, Facebook took an oversaturated, meaningless word and made "liking" something bigger, easier to communicate, and more significant than ever before.

We have quickly welcomed and embraced these interesting behavioral and cultural changes in our personal lives. Time spent on sites like Yahoo and Hulu is declining, while time spent on social sites such as Facebook and Groupon is growing exponentially. Nielsen[1] finds that 22 percent of all time spent on the Internet is considered "social."

---

1 http://blog.nielsen.com/nielsenwire/online_mobile/social-media-accounts-for-22-percent-of-time-online

At the same time, hardware is being reinvented by mobile devices like the iPhone and iPad, which are replacing desktop and laptop computers. People love tablets: The iPad scored higher than any product before it on the American Consumer Satisfaction Index, and Oprah Winfrey has declared it to be her "No.1 favorite thing ever." Morgan Stanley called the iPad the "fastest ramping mobile device ever." And it's not just relegated to the world of Apple. Google activates 900,000[2] of its Android devices a day.

What's most interesting is how the hardware and software revolutions are symbiotic: People who access Facebook through an app on their mobile device are twice as active on the site than non-mobile users. The average mobile user now spends 81 minutes a day using mobile apps, 9 percent more time than they spend surfing the Web, according to analytics firm Flurry. More than four billion apps have been downloaded from the Appstore. Furthermore, according to a Morgan Stanley report, the number of people who access the Internet via mobile devices will surpass desktops and laptops in 2012[3].

I just threw a lot of data at you to highlight how quickly the world is changing, but really, what does any of this mean for business? What does reading a Facebook newsfeed on my iPhone mean for my company? In a word: everything.

I believe that how well a company leverages the hardware and software developments under way will determine the winners and losers in business in the future. We are still in the early days, but we are on the cusp of a mass awakening. There are now more than 500 million people who access the Internet via a mobile device and the use of mobile apps will grow at a double-digit rate, according to a recent report by IDC[4]. It's a global phenomenon: China has more mobile phone users than the US has people.

It's staggering to think that the iPad, a device that was not available until 2010, is now the machine I use to run my entire business. I'm not alone. Whereas 71 percent of all chief information officers forbade tablet use in the enterprise in 2010, 51 percent of them purchased tablets for employees in 2011. Now, they are rolling out iPads en masse. Carl Bass, the CIO of Autodesk, runs his whole company on iPads. These changes are being adopted in the enterprise because employees want to work with these new tools. According to IDC, mobile devices are be-

2 www.pcworld.com/article/257289/over_900000_android_devices_activated_every_day_says_goggles_rubin.html, IDG News, June 11, 2012
3 Morgan Stanley, The Internet Mobile Report, December 2009
4 IDC, "A Consumer Revolution in the Enterprise," June 2012

coming the new enterprise desktop for more than 50 percent of the workforce.[5]

What exactly do we mean by the next generation of cloud computing? This chart spells out the advances.

The Evolution to the Social Enterprise

Last Generation	Next Generation
Type/Click	Touch/Voice
Yahoo/Amazon	Facebook
Tabs	Feeds
Chat	Video
Pull	Push
Create	Consume
Location Unknown	Local
Desktop/Notebook	Smartphone/Tablet
Windows/Mac	Cocoa/HTML 5
Fixed	Mobile
Closed architecture	Open Architecture
Transactional	Conversational
Individuals	Networks

Weaving a social context into business is rapidly becoming a prerequisite for success. Ten years ago we used cloud technologies to become faster, smarter, and more innovative. And, as a result, salesforce.com grew into the first $1 billion cloud computing company. At the start of this decade we were able to double our revenue to $2.3 billion in two years. We grew fast in a very challenging economy because we adopted new technologies and a new framework of thinking that I call SOCIAL, an acronym for: Speed, Open, Collaboration, Individuals, Alignment and Leaderless.

5   IDC, Worldwide Software Business Solutions 2010 Top 10 Predictions: The "New Normal" for Enterprise Software, February 2010

S: **Speed** – Everything is happening faster.

O: **Open** – Companies need open environments that embrace transparency and build trust.

C: **Collaboration** – People use new tools and new ways to share information and organize to solve challenges.

I: **Individuals** – Anyone can start something and gain traction faster, deeper and cheaper than ever before.

A: **Alignment** – It's more important than ever to be laser focused as a team, and social media makes it easier than ever to articulate – and reinforce – the vision and values that create and inspire alignment.

L: **Leaderless** – Traditional "command and control" is over; social leaders are neither the elected nor the elite. Power has moved to the periphery; anyone can empower, inspire and enable.

Contrary to what many business people assume, SOCIAL should not be feared or ignored. It is a movement happening in society and one which is being embraced by customers and employees, and therefore must also be reflected in our companies and products. The path to do that is through new technologies. I am using these SOCIAL principles and new social technology to successfully manage my fast-growing business. I believe that any company – large or small – can benefit from these same principles and practices.

Bridging the Social Divide

We are now at a tipping point where enterprises are recognizing the need for change. Our customers are social. Our employees are social. But our businesses are not social. The social revolution has created a social divide. We need tools that work smarter, make better use of new mobile devices, and fully leverage the opportunities of the Internet and a generation of individuals that are savvy about its advances.

Public social networks like Facebook, Twitter and sites like Yelp have the biggest impact on how brands are perceived – more than any other tool that's been developed in the past 100 years. While a brand used to be a collection of memories initialized by companies, it is now a series of conversations instigated by customers. Today customers have more of an ability to influence a brand than its marketing department does. It's no longer possible to continue to sell products and services, or run businesses the old way, when individual customers have more power than ever before. We must leverage new social tools that give pivotal information about who our customers are and what they like – information we use to delight them in new ways and make them our friends.

One of my favorite examples is how the Dutch company KLM, one of the world's largest airlines, not only actively delivers customer service via Twitter, but also uses the power of social networking to understand its customers. KLM created customer social profiles – contact information from customers made richer by including information harvested from Facebook, Twitter, and elsewhere on the social Web – and put this social intelligence into action. As passengers who checked in on Twitter arrived at gates, KLM flight attendants greeted them by name and gave them a personalized gift—something that the passenger could use on his or her trip, or enjoy when they returned home. For example, one woman who was going hiking in Rome was given a watch that tracks distances and walking speed. Another customer, who had tweeted he was going to miss his team's biggest soccer game of the year while on a trip to New York, was surprised with a Lonely Planet guide to New York with the best soccer bars highlighted.[6] This was not a huge effort in terms of numbers. Maybe KLM gave 40 gifts. But the ripple effect was amazing. That month the KLM Twitter feed was viewed more than *one million times*.[7]

It's not just publicity, though. Using the data on the social Web to get to know customers more deeply helps companies make better decisions, and do so with unprecedented speed. For example, the sports drink brand Gatorade uses social media monitoring service Radian6 (salesforce.com bought Radian6 in 2011) to collect analytics on the number of times Gatorade, its competitors, and related athletes and sports-nutrition topics appear in tweets, Facebook pages, and public chats and analyzes the data to know how to respond. Case in point: Gatorade discovered a lot of buzz on social media about a song by rap artist David Banner it was featuring on its commercials, and within 24 hours, it put out a full-length version of the song and distributed it to Gatorade followers and fans on Twitter and Facebook.[8]

In another example, Dell, which uses Radian6 technology to monitor 22,000 online conversations about the company a day, discovered negative dialog around a new laptop launch and it also identified misinformation that was being reported. The social media team took the information it found to the product experts, who were able to address the issues and Dell was able to use social media to immediately respond with clarifications and the correct information. The result? They in-

---

6 http://www.digett.com/2011/01/11/klm-surprise-how-little-research-earned-1000000-impressions-twitter
7 http://aboutfoursquare.com/klm-surprise/
8 http://mashable.com/2010/06/15/gatorade-social-media-mission-control/

stantly saw more even-toned coverage about the new laptop, says John Miles, the CIO at Dell. They also saw an impact on sales.

Social networks are not just about leveraging the public sites we know, like Facebook and Twitter, but companies can create secure private social networks where they can engage with employees, customers, or even products. Yes, products.

Take for example what Toyota, the biggest car company in the world, is doing with its product social network. Toyota came to meet us after they had experienced a difficult two years because of problems with their braking systems. They had gone through Congressional investigations and lost trust with customers. Toyota needed a way for its cars to share information with its drivers – if its tires were too low, or if its battery needed to be recharged. Toyota needed its cars and drivers to be more connected and with a product social network; we could create the world's first social car.

We created Toyota Friend, a private social network for Toyota customers to communicate with the company, their dealership and their cars. Powered by Chatter, Toyota Friend provides product and service information and maintenance tips. For example, if your electric or plug-in car is running low on battery power, Toyota Friend notifies you to recharge in the form of a private "tweet"-like message. It can also send you directions to the nearest service station. It will tell you when it's due for maintenance, or if the tire pressure for your partner's car gets low. It sends alerts about possible problems and drivers can schedule a service appointment via a link to the service center. The service is also accessible through smartphones, tablet PCs, and a range of other mobile devices.

I believe this product social network will transform the car ownership experience—and take the auto industry into the future. It's already inspired similar services, and I believe soon companies in every industry will have ways to connect their customers to their products.

The Social Transformation

As Toyota transformed into a social enterprise, so did salesforce.com. We learned that not only could our products have social attributes, but that all of our internal business processes could be redefined to be social as well.

The social revolution had radically changed sales and marketing, putting the customer in the driver's seat, with everything from pricing to product information available in real time from trusted social connections. But we found that sales reps could also leverage these phenomena. The same social revolution that is empowering buyers is providing salespeople with an abundant supply of sales intelligence as well as with tools to strengthen and extend their connections.

That inspired us to change the way we sell. The old way of selling meant going to a prospect's website, reading the marketing materials, and trying to incorporate the essentials into a PowerPoint. Overachievers might dial up a prospect's customers, competitors, or vendors. But realistically, most salespeople only had time to shout over to the next cubical. But "social sales" could change everything and massively increase productivity. Instead of cold-calling with a generic sales pitch, we could identify the members of a decision-making team and reach out to them with a custom proposal tailored to their particular business goals. Rather than digging through old e-mails in search of everything from product specs to winning presentations, we could log into an internal collaboration tool, like Chatter, and find everything in one place. Reps no longer had to spend hours tracking down data in multiple apps or hunting for the most up-to date documents in e-mail, multiple servers, and intranets. They just had to log into their sales app from their mobile device and hit the collaboration tab. All the relevant documents are clustered around each open opportunity, along with members of the extended sales team, providing unprecedented expertise and visibility into each and every pending deal. With these new tools, questions are answered immediately through company-wide crowdsourcing, and reps uncover best practices – without ever asking for advice.

We've seen amazing things happen. Jim Steele, our chief customer officer, was on his way to a customer's office at Canary Wharf in London when he realized that he was not adequately briefed. Chatter had just been turned on at salesforce.com, but Jim hadn't yet used it to assist him with customers. But on this day, with no other option and nothing to lose, he thought he'd give it a try. He logged onto Chatter and typed into his status bar that he was meeting with this particular CEO in 15 minutes and asked for any insights. He immediately received several responses with helpful guidance.

The best part of the story comes next, though. Jim was so excited about this new way of collaborating with the organization that during the meeting with the CEO he pulled out his BlackBerry and began showing off his Chatter feed and demonstrating how the app worked. As the CEO was looking at his newsfeed, a message popped up. Sam Chung, a sales operations executive, posted that it was serendipitous that Jim was meeting with his "largest delinquent customer in the world."

"Is this a joke?" asked the CEO. Then he immediately called the CFO, who confirmed the company was late with the bill. The CEO says he never would have known. We were wired the payment right away. Not only was Jim more prepared for his meeting with the help of connecting to his network, but this invoice likely would not have been paid until weeks later had the finance people in our organization not been following Jim on Chatter. Private social networks provide new ways for us to collaborate across oceans, across departments and across hierarchies.

We now all use Chatter to collaborate and tap the "knowledge of the tribe" to sell better and smarter. Another time, Jim was pitching our service to a prospective CTO who asked some challenging and specific technical questions. Rather than have someone do the research and get back to the CTO in a few days, Jim entered the questions into Chatter during his lunch meeting. Four minutes later, he received the first of 11 Chatter responses to the post – all of which succinctly answered the customer's technical questions. Two months later, he signed the deal.

This instant access to the knowledge of the entire organization is now part of the sales playbook at salesforce.com. We no longer have to wait for answers or for one person to complete work. We have achieved collaboration that is untethered to time or location. It's helped us win some of our biggest deals with customers like Coca-Cola and GE. Our customers have incorporated it as well. Dan Petlon, vice president of IT at Enterasys, was following his usual habit of logging into Chatter and reviewing open opportunities when one deal caught his eye. Dan knew the company because his friend was the CIO. But the Enterasys sales rep wasn't talking to his friend; he was trying to sell to someone at a lower level. Dan introduced the sales rep to the CIO, and together, they closed the deal.

"We've been able to move deals forward by sharing information that would have been buried if not for Chatter," Dan says. "We ended up closing a record number of renewals, and I think Chatter helped by accelerating the pace of deal closures."

For salespeople who embrace new tools and techniques, social technologies create a new opportunity to offer the right solution at the right time while forming richer, more rewarding relationships. Thanks to new tools that aggregate customer activity on different networks, fantastically rich databases of information are just a few clicks away from any salesperson at any stage of a deal. Contact databases are already being replaced by social profiles that include not only a person's job title and e-mail address, but also their most recent public tweets, blog posts, and forum comments.

Social profiles help companies understand customers better – and that makes them more competitive. Consider this story of social transformation with Jinya Ryokan, a traditional inn in Japan that was built on the grounds of a Shogun encampment dating back to the 13th century. Jinya prides itself on its careful attention to its customers' needs and providing them with an excellent experience. Ever since the inn's founding more than a century ago, information on guests – their reservation status, their likes and dislikes – had been kept on paper. It wasn't a perfect system, and sometimes inconvenienced guests.

Two years ago, Jinya began to transform into a social enterprise when it created social customer profiles, which included information on guests' booking status, recent stays, and preferred dishes and brands, even their allergies. Employees updated customer profiles online, in real-time, from their smartphones and iPads. Using Chatter, employees could share this information and collaborate to provide guests with world-class service. Jinya also keeps track of customer conversations and feedback on public social networks like Facebook. Their conversations are captured and stored in their CRM solution along with customer histories so when they get inquiries from these customers, they have everything they need to know about them all in one place. With more robust data, Jinya has been able to increase its level of service. Takako Ono, the Front Desk Manager, says that it "has helped us attend to every detail and to serve guests on an individual basis."

These ideas and strategies can be used across many lines of business. For example, at salesforce.com we create social profiles of our candidates to help us recruit, one of our most important business functions. We gather public information to gain insights into each candidate's qualifications for the position. We look at presentations the candidate might have on YouTube, data on where they went to school, where they are working, and business affiliations from LinkedIn, and determine what topics they have expertise in via Twitter. For example, we might learn that the candidate is expecting a new child and tired of a long commute; we can use this information to approach her with an offer that will better satisfy her needs.

The universe of candidates is enormous on the Web. By using analytics and algorithms, we can segment and prioritize our candidates, narrowing down a pool of 50,000 to 500 that are best suited for certain opportunities. We rely on research, such as the stock price of their current employer and whether or not they are fully vested to determine the most appropriate time to approach them. By knowing more about prospective employees, we are able to determine which candidates will be the best fit for our organization and we are able to increase the chances of getting them in the door.

Companies that think socially are not only better able to attract – and also retain – top talent. New graduates entering the workforce right out of school are often appalled by the technology employers use to run their companies. They are more productive at home than they are in the office. They don't know how to use old computers, they look like relics removed from time capsules. CEOs around the world are experiencing this phenomenon. "Companies that don't use social collaboration internally will find it harder to recruit talent and lose significant competitive advantage," says my friend Lord Jonathan Rotheremere, the chairman of the European media conglomerate and owner of The Daily Mail (DMGT).

In many ways, the way we work is very dated. Most companies are defined by pyramid-like systems that resemble the papal hierarchy and military structures, with the highest-ranking people at the top. The top ranks control the flow of information throughout the organization. That made sense in ancient times, but it is not very well designed for today.

The old systems of working do not best enable or leverage the potential contributions of individuals, and yet this collective body is what defines any organization's success. Furthermore, knowledge workers demand a new way of work where they are enabled to collaborate with the best across the organization, where they may access real-time information, and where they can be appreciated. Today's workers value recognition for work – not just financial rewards – and we need real-time services that can help motivate them in the workplace. We've instituted this with Rypple, a social performance management company we bought in 2012. With Salesforce Rypple, companies can engage and align every employee – to set goals, manage objectives, and provide feedback and recognition – all from within an internal employee social network. The service is designed for today's employees, incorporating badges and other social gaming concepts that keep them engaged and motivated and give managers and peers visibility into their achievements in real-time. Companies like Facebook and LivingSocial are using these apps to evolve their management process from a once-a-year, top-down performance review to something that is integrated into daily work, where they can finally make a meaningful impact on performance. And they are seeing the results in happier and more productive employees that make significant contributions to the company.

The Social Imperative

We need to embrace what I call "The Facebook Imperative." We need to transform the business conversation the same way Facebook and other social sites like Twitter have changed the consumer conversation and created incredible loyalty. In Egypt a man named his daughter Facebook, in honor and gratitude for how the site helped protesters overthrow Muhammad Hosni Sayyid Mubarak. In Tunisia, graffiti reads, "Merci Facebook." When have we ever seen "Merci Microsoft?" "Merci Oracle?" "Merci SAP?" Never. But social technologies are changing civilizations and they are changing companies.

We now have an enormous opportunity in front of us. A true paradigm shift occurs when the barriers of entry are removed for everyone. The innovation and rapid adoption of social networks and social apps means that managers no longer hold an informational advantage. The thought leaders who have always talked to each other – but who may have been unknown to a larger group – are now enabled by modern apps. New social models provide a way to immediately leverage the knowledge across an organization. People with expertise and relevance are instantly looped in, can participate in the conversation, collaborate, and make contributions more simply than ever before.

I have seen salesforce.com fundamentally change more in the past two years than we have in the past 10. And I have seen our customers transform into social enterprises to connect to employees and stay closer to customers, anticipate their needs, enable transparency, build trust, and deliver amazing service.

The Social Revolution is the next major shift in enterprise computing. Companies that adopt these trends – companies that transform themselves into social enterprises – will connect with everything that is important and lead in the next decade, and beyond. I think it's the most exciting and most rewarding time to be in business.

Thank you, Facebook.

The Company

Salesforce.com was founded in 1999 by Marc Benioff, who has served as the company CEO and Chairman since then. Salesforce.com is a pioneer in cloud computing for business applications. The company has become the market leader in this area. It has a market capitalization of over $10 billion, and counts major international companies such as Burberry and Symantec among its customers. Salesforce.com is a founding member of Eurocloud Deutschland / Eurocloud Germany and is a member of BITKOM.

For more information: www.salesforce.com, http://en.wikipedia.org/wiki/Salesforce

Summary

There's no revolution without change. And the social revolution has caused a paradigm shift that couldn't be more far-reaching in its impact: Social networks have become a fixed element of our everyday lives. People publicly share their knowledge and personal experiences; the way we communicate has changed; and in this public sphere, consumers have more power than ever before.

The effects of the social revolution – heightened by the enormous spread of mobile end devices – represents a new and promising opportunity for companies of all sizes. But to take advantage of this opportunity efficiently and profitably, companies will first need to bridge the gap that separates them from their employees and customers. In our private lives, we're already "social," but not in our businesses. It's only when companies finally enter the social age that they'll be able to realize the full potential of their employees and relationships with customers and, in turn, to compete successfully as innovators.

So how do companies successfully enter the networked age? And how will they be able to generate added value from the social web? As examples from Dell, KLM and Toyota have shown, they will be utilizing cloud technologies that are social, mobile and transparent to revolutionize their sales and marketing, internal communications and product development activities.

Being a part of the social age means being part of a fundamental change that will continue to shape companies in the future. Values such as transparency, trust, the ability to listen – and flat hierarchies, too – will become ever more important.

Welcome to the age of the social enterprise.

The Author

Rolf Buch was born in 1965. He studied mechanical engineering at RWTH Aachen University, where he also completed a degree in business administration. In 1991, he joined the Bertelsmann Group. He served as a department head at Lettershop from 1991 to 1993 and was later appointed as a senior department head. As of 1999, he was the product line manager with Direkt Marketing Fabrik. Starting in 1996 he also held the position of CEO of Bertelsmann Services France.

From 1999 until 2002, he was the managing director of the Bertelsmann Services Group. He was a member of the executive board of arvato AG and the CEO of arvato direct services from 2002 until 2007. From January 2008 on, Rolf Buch served as the CEO of arvato AG and as a member of the Bertelsmann SE Executive Board. In April 2013 he was appointed as Chief Executive Officer of Deutsche Annington Immobilien SE.

The Fragmented Market – Services in the Digital Age

Rolf Buch, arvato AG*

In 1999, the year when the Bertelsmann Print and Industry division was renamed arvato AG, Germany's then chancellor, Gerhard Schröder, on a visit to the CeBIT high-tech trade fair in Hanover, remarked that he would like a computer that he could talk into. At that time, digital cameras with a sensational image resolution of two megapixels were available for 2,000 deutschmarks. Intel broke the 800 MHz barrier with its Pentium III processor. The first MP3 players were presented to the public – with a capacity of 30 minutes of playing time. And just under 17 percent of the German public had Internet access.

Today, nearly 75 percent of all Germans use the Internet. Digital cameras with double-digit megapixel specifications are now relatively cheap. Today's PCs boast Porsche-like processor speeds, leaving the now obsolete Pentium III in their dust. We play our digital music on pods and pads with storage capacities that could almost be called unlimited. So, now that things have reached this point, all we need is a device that gives us access to all the information we want to use, whenever and wherever we want it: It's called a smartphone – which, incidentally, fulfills Schröder's wish from 1999. You can ask it whether you will need an umbrella next week, for example, or when your next appointment is due to start, and how to get there.

The technological changes in information and communication technology, with the evolutionary leaps getting larger as the innovation intervals get shorter, are just one example of the way the tumultuous digitization process is changing everything – for everybody: industry, commerce, trades and manufacturing, governments and public administration, customers and citizens. On top of that, owing to the fact that digitalization also means networking, the various worlds are becoming more closely linked and intertwined all the time. Boundaries are blurred, and reciprocal relationships are forming – resulting in more cooperation and division of labor. This is in turn leading to a steady increase in work for service providers – because the complexity of digital processes coupled with the accelerating pace of technological advances is forcing companies to focus on their own product or – in

* Rolf Buch was chief executive officer of arvato AG from January 2008 to December 2012.

the trade sector – on their own goods. Whether they make physical goods such as cars, mobile phones, televisions and cameras, or develop content such as application systems, games, music, films – more than ever before, companies are well advised to clearly define what tasks are part of their core competencies and what processes can be handled better and more efficiently by external service providers.

Inventory management, sales, repair management, payments, customer acquisition, customer service and customer loyalty – all of these activities lend themselves readily to outsourcing. More and more companies are discovering the impact on their bottom line of knowing as much as possible about their customers. A service provider can help to leverage additional potential in these areas. Most service providers have learned to think consistently from a customer's standpoint. They focus on the customer, especially when they offer business clients – from any sector – services related to their products, or when they tell them how they can transform their business model for the new, digital age. Service providers may know nothing about developing new drugs, but they are highly skilled in the quick and secure IT-based shipment of those drugs to where they are needed, and in the fastest and most secure invoicing methods. Service providers know nothing about building cars, but they know car buyers. From experience, they know that getting people excited about a product and then building customer loyalty is harder in our digital age than at any time in the past. At the same time, the use of online sales channels can boost sales.

The Internet Puts the Customer on an Equal Footing

The World Wide Web has given customers a much bigger say in things, while putting them on an equal footing with the vendor. In many cases, initial timidity in dealings with sellers and goods has given way to a professionalism that plays a role in shaping opinions: Customers are becoming influencers who guide other consumers' purchasing behavior with ratings and reviews.

Only a few years ago, a customer looking for a certain product or service still had to work hard to piece together information to compare quality and prices. Now, with just a few clicks, the same customer can find out everything he or she needs to make a decision by visiting specialized blogs or comparative portals. The market is becoming more transparent for the buyer. This is shaking up the old hierarchies in the relationship between the buyer and seller, so that the customer is indeed being crowned king.

This is because seller-buyer communications have also undergone fundamental changes. Back in the days of classical media – radio, television and the newspaper – the customer was wooed with advertisements, commercials and marketing campaigns and then left to their own devices. Dialog was virtually non-existent. For seller and customer communication, it was a "one way street." One side was transmitting and the other was receiving. A customer who wanted more information had to rely on the competence of the sales person they happened to be dealing with. Any dispute or dissatisfaction was unpleasant for all concerned. In general, there were no consequences in such cases for the company because, after all, they only involved individuals who were on their own with their disappointment.

Today, by contrast, almost any dissatisfied customer becomes an acid test, because communication is increasingly taking the form of an entirely new and direct kind of dialog. And customer feedback has become a currency of its own. It's part of a trend that has only just begun, and is set to undergo dynamic growth. A company that is unwilling to communicate, or is clumsy, unfriendly or incompetent in its communications, may suffer consequences that would once have been inconceivable. The Internet not only intensifies dialog; it can also increase it exponentially by starting with a single incident and then gathering, pooling and channeling the experiences and opinions of millions. In a worst-case scenario, a wave of outrage – sometimes referred to in the hard-hitting world of social networks as a "shitstorm" – can come crashing down on a company or a product, and may even obliterate it if the company reacts too late, ineffectively, or not at all.

The networked world has spawned better-informed consumers who are more demanding, individualized and flexible. It has also given them more power. However, the vast range of choices available has also left consumers bewildered: They want the kind of orientation that a company can offer, for example, in the form of assistance with frequently-asked questions (FAQs) or 24-hour online support service. From the supplier's standpoint, on the other hand, it has become increasingly difficult to reach customers, as they are constantly moving around – sometimes on the go with a mobile device, sometimes online, and sometimes showing up at the old-school point of sale. What's more, it is now quite common for a customer who cannot find a desired product in a brick-and-mortar shop to order it online while still on the premises via terminal or smartphone. In the World Wide Web, the potential customer may be spending time in a niche occupied by like-minded hobbyists, posting messages on Facebook, writing e-mails, checking out offers in online shops, playing games, working, reading books or listening to music. Companies have to adjust to this reality, and their own, external communications must be geared to it.

Digitization makes things like communication and networking more complex, but at the same time simplifies them, for example because it enables companies to find and recruit new multipliers. With the improved availability of information on the customer side, sellers are also gaining new possibilities: More and more people are willing to provide information about themselves, their needs and desires – both in social media and when making online purchases. In the same way the customer uses digitization for increased market transparency, it also helps sellers to get to know their customers better, improve their target group management, fine-tune their message or even to avoid losses from poorly targeted advertising. For customers who reject transparency and prefer to protect their personal data, the classical service channels are still open to them, or they can simply order from a mail order house by catalog.

Basically, it isn't any different from the old-time general store: In business, knowing your customer is the name of the game. That is the only way of targeting communications individually to give customers the feeling that they are highly valued. This in turn makes them more likely to select and purchase goods; but a detailed knowledge of the customer must come first, before a business can even present them with a suitable offer. In the springtime, someone who owns a barbecue is more likely to need related products such as tongs, the right cuts of meat, sauces or even a fire extinguisher. The owners of a mom-and-pop store could readily retrieve the necessary information to identify that kind of business opportunity from a wealth of experience. Today the network generates it using treasure troves of data.

Walk the Walk – Or Hit the Road

Knowing individual end customers – with all of their needs and wishes – and possessing the ability to strike the right tone when communicating with them is the key qualification for any service provider that claims to be qualified to handle customer relationship management for entire companies. At the same time, such a provider must be aware that it is vital both to perform the specific tasks professionally and to assume the role of a brand ambassador for the client. That is because, regardless of what an integrated service provider does, its service must be in keeping with the image and promise of the client company, with regard to technology as well as content. A company working for Audi, for example, must reflect the carmaker's *Vorsprung durch Technik* claim in the technological excellence of all of its services. The same applies to innovative Facebook or YouTube formats and on the telephone, owner's manuals with appropriately appealing designs, print ads and other marketing activities.

And conversely: In the Internet age, nothing is more dangerous to a company's reputation than false promises. For example, when a TV is rated as inferior and overpriced in product tests, and the discussion boards on various consumer electronics forums are filled with the complaints of unhappy buyers, it doesn't take long before inflated advertising claims are seen for what they are. One consequence of the new transparency is that advertising that is completely at odds with the truth is nothing but laughable. Companies that try to position themselves as champions of sustainability, only to be publicly unmasked for "greenwashing," become painfully aware of this fact.

Crumbling Loyalties

But even those who make an honest effort to produce excellent quality and deliver what they promise cannot afford to sit back and relax. The networked world feeds the prevailing societal trend away from long-term ties. Whether it comes to personal relationships, loyalty to a party or tying oneself down with a newspaper subscription: Loyalties are fraying and people are willing to change direction abruptly and make a fresh start at any given time. In markets, this often means a high customer churn rate and volatile sales, driven above all by the online product review portals already mentioned, whose strong impact is comparable to that of product ratings in online communities.

Nowadays, it is a common practice for travelers planning a weekend getaway to Munich, for example, to book the cheapest online hotel offer instead of staying at the hotel in the same class that they liked so much on their last trip. And many of us are familiar with the customer in the electronics store or elsewhere who looks at the price tag on a laptop or smartphone and then pulls out a mobile device to do some comparison shopping on the fly. With special apps, shoppers can point their smartphone at a bar code to get technical specifications of a product or access blogs discussing the pros and cons of the item in question. As a result, the retailer's store is increasingly becoming a showroom of the boundless market in the network.

Amazon – the King of Customer Loyalty

Amid the increasing availability of – seemingly – better and better bargains, in times of weakening loyalties, it may be instructive to take a look at the company that has been hugely successful at acquiring customers and hanging on to them: the online book seller, Amazon.

Since it was established in the 1990s, Amazon has shown the world how to connect with today's new breed of customers, who are equally flexible and demanding, how to listen to them and how to use technology to meet their needs. Factors behind the company's success in beating numerous competitors to emerge as the world's biggest online retailer include three aspects of vital importance today: relentless customer orientation, user-friendliness in all processes and – the key point – trust. Trust makes everything happen that now defines state-of-the-art e-commerce: simple, transparent sales processes on all platforms, a broad product range with easy-to-use search functions, fast delivery, start-to-end shipment tracking and – above all – secure payments through a variety of channels. For many of these things, Amazon was the first to offer them, thus building a lead over the competition. And it keeps adding to that lead through constant adjustments to its business model. The company is already doing what any entrepreneur would be advised to do today: It is always on the move. And the adjustments it makes are not mere tweaks: It constantly adapts to changing technologies. One example is the Kindle e-reader. It exemplifies yet again how Amazon never stops reinventing itself, but still remains what it was from the very start: a virtual department store.

What can we learn from this example? It shows that, in the digital age, a strong brand now means even more than before. It also proves: Those who stay on top of customers' expectations, pick up on them and take them a step further, develop the technologies to implement the insights thus gained, and get the product or service out into the marketplace in a timely manner and in perfect quality – those are the businesses that will succeed.

Most important, however, is the following lesson: Only those who succeed in taming the clutter of the network through integration on a single platform and structuring it so that users can quickly, easily and securely find the products and services they are looking for – only those companies have a chance of making it to the very top in the digital market.

Integrated Services: a Decathlon

B2B service providers face a mirror image of that situation. All companies in the service sector will claim to be doing their utmost to listen to their customers and act in their interests. That is the basis for a successful, mutually beneficial business relationship.

The prospects of success are better for suppliers that are able to bundle all of the relevant processes and act as the sole point of contact for every conceivable issue and provide expert guidance through all ramifications of supply chain and customer relationship management. The service provider of the future will be the integrated service provider: the decathlete among service providers. The specialists who only excel at the high jump or javelin will not get very far.

Integrated service providers build a world of services where customers get everything they need – and, if possible, a little more, with a view to making strategic adjustments.

Against the backdrop of digitization, that means, first and foremost, acknowledging that organized industrial structures, with their fixation on mass production and standardization, need to be broadened to embrace the new dimensions of individualization and fragmentation. This is reflected in the new, multifaceted communication channels mentioned above, through which businesses must maintain customer contacts in very diverse ways. For printed materials, for example, it means producing catalogs that address every user by name, and customized owner's manuals for carmakers that cover the exact combination of features selected by the car buyer. This, in turn, impacts the handling of orders and deliveries, for example for the retail sector, which must set up its e-commerce logistics not only for volume, but also for individual service.

People Still Have the Upper Hand

There's one thing that we have to acknowledge: The digital world will probably never completely displace the analog one, because people will presumably never entirely immerse themselves in the virtual world. Lots of people want to own an e-reader. After all, it's handy and can store a large number of books. However, they don't want to say goodbye to their Sunday newspaper or the sensation of leafing through a beautiful book. We will be listening to downloaded music with increasing regularity, but sometimes we will still go back to a CD or – now making something of a comeback – put a vinyl LP on a turntable.

Many people love web art, but still hang old-style prints above their sofa. People want the old and the new. They want everything – everywhere and at all times.

That means that, although brick-and-mortar retail stores are dwindling in number, they will not die out completely. And they are being replaced by new businesses with new technologies – in the case of CDs, for example, with sophisticated digital storage technology and download platforms. The music industry was the first to undergo the painful experience of watching its old business model – which basically amounted to bundling every hit song with 11 other tracks onto a CD – fall victim to the fragmentation possibilities of digital media.

Without doubt, the powerful impact felt with the arrival of the digital age triggered a paradigm shift. But it did not completely wipe out what was there before. It is apparent that what Josef Schumpeter called the "creative destruction of innovation" can sometimes stop short of a complete revolution. In many cases, it's a matter of processes and developments that need to be watched and supported. It's all about floating – the ability of our service providers to adapt to the disappearance of some needs as others emerge, and the question as to which technological solutions are most suitable for meeting those needs. Sometimes a brick-and-mortar retailer can expand into the networked world, and sometimes an e-commerce platform finds its way into the mall. The transformation goes both ways. No search engine is used more often to generate information than Google. But the soft skills such as knowing how to get a smartphone to a customer or how to organize customer service cannot be found on any website. That's a set of knowledge that has to be acquired first.

The dynamic of the processes driving the advance of digitization will continue. As long as markets and customers demand it, service providers will have to perform the stunt of being "retro," up-to-date and future-ready at the same time. They have to be equally excellent on the web and in print. While still turning out classical advertising calendars, they must master digital marketing concepts for social media platforms. They must find a way to take content prepared for tabloids with a readership in the millions and put it online in a way that, under the special set of rules governing the networked world, does not harm the profile and image associated with the print product. And they will have to understand the difference if they do the same thing for a scientific publishing house. When expanding into the various channels – print, radio, TV or online – every product must be designed to remain true to its brand roots. SternTV, for example, the TV program produced by the Stern publishing house in Hamburg, must be different from that firm's flagship *Stern* magazine, but still recognizably carry the DNA of the "old" Stern. The same applies to the Stern brand's presence in Facebook, Twitter and other social networks. The service providers tasked to carry out these transformation processes must therefore have an almost psychological sense of how the client's brand works. Thus, if the integrated service provider is a decathlete, then customer orientation is the discipline where medals are won or lost.

The same applies when service providers work on behalf of retailers or industrial customers. They must be equally familiar with the e-commerce platforms of major fashion houses and the shelves and racks of brick-and-mortar retailers. They need the same familiarity with analog customer loyalty and payment systems as with their digital counterparts. They need to know the right way to digitize a printed Microsoft textbook so that learners all over the world can work with it. When providing services for an airline, they have to know how to respond to a letter of complaint written by a premium customer and frequent flyer. But when the client is a mobile phone company, they must be equally skilled at striking the right tone when a stressed-out customer calls the support line for help with a new phone.

Service for the end customer is and will remain the ability to act in the client's interests by finding the appropriate approach – technically, factually and in human terms – to every situation.

Digitization as a Growth Driver

The consequences of digitization for the service sector are limited to two effects: It means that the pool of potential customers will expand to include the companies that have directly emerged from digitization: companies such as Google, Apple, Amazon and eBay. And it will result in technological changes to all of the processes that were previously strictly analog. Consequently, digitization harbors growth potential for service providers, assuming that they have the necessary high-tech expertise and understand the changes it will require from them and their business customers. And that requires a panoramic view of the various technological developments and the upheavals taking place in the customer industries. For example, if there is a proliferation of new paid services via smartphones and cloud streaming, it will be necessary to address copyright issues, set up encryption technologies and organize micropayment settlements.

The digital dimension will also play an increasing role in shopping at supermarkets and malls: A catalyst of this trend is the functionality available now or in the near future to users of smartphones. The user receives a message when milk, cheese or cold cuts are running low in the refrigerator, and with a scan of the bar codes, can arrange for home delivery the very same evening. And if the user decides to head for the supermarket instead, the smartphone – using the previously entered digital shopping list – navigates quickly to the desired products and can even display special offers that may be of interest. At the cash register, payment is also handled via smartphone. Nor will a customer need to go to a furniture store to shop for a new bedroom suite. When shopping at home, he or she gets help from a smartphone, tablet PC and augmented reality: the computer-based extension of normal sensory perception. By inserting the desired piece of furniture into a camera image of the living room, the shopper can see exactly how well it matches the existing decor. In the same way, shoppers can virtually try on glasses or clothing, compare different items and then place an order.

Smartphones and other mobile devices can offer their users all of these things and much more, thus unleashing a permanent shopping revolution, with obvious consequences for all sellers: They will have to leave behind their old ways of doing things and face the new, virtual world to utilize it for their businesses.

In the future, this new world will inevitably include what is referred to as "the Internet of things," i.e. the increasingly interlinked world of real products with the virtual, networked world. Today, for example, printer cartridges are already tracked via chip technology to monitor the ink level. Before the ink runs out, a request to order a replacement cartridge is sent to the manufacturer's site. This intermeshing of real products and the virtual information world is not limited – as described above – to the retail sector, but shows an overall trend to expand into increasing numbers of areas. For example, specialized providers are already selling systems to allow home heating to be controlled via smartphone apps. And once smart grid technologies become more widespread, homeowners will also be able to use their smartphones to retrieve information on times of day when electric power is cheaper, so that they can switch on the heating or air conditioning system a little earlier if necessary. On their return home, the temperature is back to normal, and they have saved money. Similarly, the driver of a networked car can receive constant updates en route on the location of the cheapest nearby gas station, the best authorized dealer or the nicest hotel. The car of the future will do more than just get people from A to B; it will also be a platform for all kinds of information: a digital device. And, in the future, the augmented reality glasses now being developed by Google will project information into the user's field of vision relevant to whatever he or she happens to be looking at.

Whatever we might think about the possibilities created by digitization, and regardless of the debates they may trigger in society – the task of a service provider, above all, is to spot technological trends early, make them part of new business models and explore the opportunities for developing additional business around the high-tech inventions. One thing is clear: The more customer contacts are created through digitization, the more intensively dealers and manufacturers will be doing business in entirely new ways with new customers – and the more they will need a service provider who understands how to handle customer-relationship management on the basis of completely new technologies. What's more: The best-qualified company for this task is the one that is active in as many industries as possible, enabling it to gain insights that it can use in a mutually beneficial way for itself and its customers. Put simply: The best qualified candidate is the one with the best network.

The Art of Staying Flexible While Growing

The higher a service provider's level of integration and the more wide-ranging its customer base becomes, the more profitably it can work for its client. But size alone is no advantage. The benefits of size come into play only if growth does not put an end to flexibility – because it is only by retaining the ability to pay attention to detail, regardless of size, that a business can fully exploit the growth potential harbored by digitization. This is a prerequisite for optimally managing the challenges posed by the fragmentation of markets and the individualization of customers.

At this point, allow me to remark that arvato AG, as part of the Bertelsmann Group, has lived Reinhard Mohn's philosophy of delegating responsibility right from the start. In the "entrepreneur within the enterprise" tradition, "Ms. Microsoft" is now responsible for handling all services that we perform for the software giant. We have a "Mr. Lufthansa," who is in charge of our activities on behalf of that airline. There are many other examples of how that concept, developed by Mohn, of the company within the company, making its own decisions and largely autonomous from headquarters, is a perfect fit for the qualification profile generated by today's digitized world. Working in small, manageable units, employees have a good grasp of all the details as well as their own sensibilities and gut feelings for special developments and needs that may vary considerably, even for companies in the same industry.

This applies in particular to the more than half of the 60,000-strong arvato workforce employed at the many foreign locations on all five continents, who also function as our antennas out there in the wide world. The ability to spot individual trends in digitization is almost always a matter of sensitivity. Sometimes these trends are not immediately apparent, and take shape only gradually. They emerge almost unnoticed from a garage or a dorm room and suddenly take an industry by storm.

The paradox of the networked world is that it is getting bigger, but is still made up of tiny elements, because the world is nothing but the sum of its parts – countries, people, mentalities and possibilities. Only those who take this fact into account and are capable of being both – the global player and the local hero – and, in their global activities, learn to take into account the different languages, sensitivities, laws and customs, will be able to fully exploit the new growth markets and achieve success in globalization. Another essential aspect is the will to keep learning from new customers in new countries to benefit from their views, demands and products. That applies both to service providers as well as their client companies. We see, therefore, that it's only logical that more and more companies, faced with the increasingly complex market structures, are concluding that the best way of coping with this complexity is to focus on their core business. After all, a modern company generally has enough to do just to manage the product-related knowledge that is accumulating ever faster through more and more channels. Today's carmakers, for example, have to dedicate research and development capacity to much more than engines and chassis design. Now, as I have described, more emphasis is being placed all the time on user-friendly, in-car IT solutions. Audio, navigation, on-board computers and all kinds of information systems are becoming increasingly integrated, and their digital and analog design is gaining in importance – at least in the premium segment – as a key factor for convincing prospective buyers.

The Service Provider Becomes Part of the Client Company

Consequently, the more companies are able to offload activities that get in the way of their core business, the more their outsourcing activities will, in fact, become the "insourcing" of the knowledge and skills of a service provider. This effect becomes all the more pronounced when, over the course of time, there is no other option for companies seeking to profit from the advantages of digitization than the harmonization of data systems and the networking of people and information. As a result, service providers are now much more tightly intermeshed with the client company than in the pre-digital age. The more intelligent and sophisticated the processes become, the more intensively the parties cooperate in the sharing of tasks. From that perspective, the service provider can sometimes become part of the client company: The result is a sort of joint venture, and service providers increasingly find themselves playing the role of business consultants who can actually put into practice what they present in their PowerPoint slides.

In any case, integrated service providers always work close to the heart of the client company. When you are aware that it can take just one ill-considered comment by one clumsy employee on the Facebook page of the client company to unleash mass outrage or – equally disastrous in the online world – to make the client a laughing stock, then you have an inkling of how important communication services have become in the digital age. And when you are in a position to process billions of clicks a day for Internet companies, and then filter out the ones to which charges apply, and handle the billing – then you may potentially be capable of making one mistake on that day, which naturally may prove infinitely more costly than in the days when invoices were sent out by regular mail. Digitization has put things on a much larger scale, and in particular has inflated the dimensions of responsibility on the part of the service provider and the dimensions of trust on the part of the customer.

The Business of the Future

Sports stadiums and markets have always lived by the Olympic motto: faster, higher, stronger. Today, however, the records are falling faster than ever before, and those who want to mount the podium must see beyond the hectic tumult of everyday business, driven by constant IT innovations, to analyze the foreseeable megatrends closely, place them in the context of technological progress, and arrive early at the right conclusions for their own business and that of their customers.

For example, what will today's demographic trends mean for the service sector? What does it mean that average lifespans will keep getting longer, but that people's health may deteriorate as they age? Can service providers be part of the solution to help avoid a further explosion in healthcare costs? Could smartphone apps help to analyze moles on a person's skin and warn of cancer risks? Or can they send reminders to patients with chronic conditions requiring exact drug dosages and also ensure that a refill is delivered before the old one is used up? Health insurers and pharmaceutical companies are exploring these possibilities because patients who fail to take prescribed drugs as directed not only runs the risk of having their condition worsen; they also contribute to rising costs.

And another thought: Could the dire state of public-sector finances – probably with no prospect of improvement in the foreseeable future – represent an opportunity for service providers? Could they – as in the health care sector – provide intelligent solutions to keep costs from spiraling completely out of control? Without doubt, public-private partnerships will play a larger role. Even today, more and more public authorities, both here in Germany and abroad, are plagued by staffing shortages and empty coffers, and are exploring options for handing over services such as payment management, digital archiving or digital commerce to private companies.

Another of the megatrends is definitely education. As industrialized countries become increasingly dependent on research and development, and with employees facing rising expectations at all levels of the workforce, education is indispensable for personal success and for the success of entire countries. What's more, the faster-paced turnover of knowledge can be handled only by those who make use of digitization themselves. That is the only way of genuinely staying on top of things. The innovation cycles in some fields have become so short that books, with their relatively long production and sales lead times, are of limited use for communicating brand-new knowledge – unless it is presented in e-books or digital textbooks that allow seamless inclusion of social networks or user-generated content.

But there are some constants that will remain unshakeable in the future, including the insight that service businesses always depend on people as individuals. That's because a company relies above all on the successful management and cooperation of its employees, regardless of the number of new communication channels.

Consequently, whatever a service provider does – in the digital or analog worlds alike – the human factor remains crucial. That's because our clients entrust us with their greatest treasure: their customers. This, in turn, automatically means that, when hiring staff, we can't just look at their professional knowledge and qualifications, i.e. the good references. Instead, as the decisive factor, we have to consider above all the social skills of a potential new hire: empathy for people, a willingness to work in a team, share knowledge and network with others, and a clear understanding that people who put themselves ahead of the customer have no business in the service sector. Our industry is – and will remain – the wrong place for a big ego.

The Company

Arvato AG is a 100 percent subsidiary of Bertelsmann SE and has a 175-year history. As one of Europe's leading BPO service providers for end-customer processes, arvato designs and implements tailor-made solutions along integrated service chains for business customers all over the world. These solutions cover the entire range of activities related to customer care and CRM services, supply chain management, financial services and IT services. With more than 68,000 employees, the company generated 5.4 billion euros in sales in the 2011 financial year.

For more information: http://www.arvato.com/en.html

Summary

Concentrating on core competencies: Against the backdrop of a steady rise in the complexity of digital processes flanked by accelerating technological developments, it is becoming more important all the time for companies to focus on their own core competencies, and to outsource all processes that can be handled better and more efficiently by external service providers.

Customer focus: As a factor for business success, knowing as much as possible about one's customers becoming more important all the time. Professional service providers can help companies to utilize untapped potential in this area because they have learned how to keep their thinking consistently attuned to the customer's viewpoint. The Internet and social media make it possible to maintain much more intensive customer contact. It allows vital information to be gathered about customers' behavior and desires and used in a targeted manner for product development and marketing.

Putting the customer on an equal footing: The networked world has given customers a bigger say, and has made them more demanding, individualized and flexible. A company's online presence results in a high degree of transparency, which also means responsibility. Customers are quick to see through misinformation and false promises. The confident and assertive customer becomes an influencer whose ratings and reviews in turn affect other consumers' purchasing behavior.

Loyalties are crumbling: The sheer diversity of products and services and the limitless opportunities to compare them make it harder to forge lasting ties with regular customers. At the same time, the Internet, social media and related technologies present a wide range of opportunities to communicate with consumers and retain them as customers through innovation and the element of surprise.

People come first: A company's success depends primarily on its employees. In addition to technical know-how, the necessary soft skills for dealing with customers are indispensable.

The Author

Michael Heinz was born in 1964. After studying business administration at the College of Applied Sciences in Ludwigshafen, he completed an MBA at Duke University in North Carolina, USA. He joined BASF in 1984 and served in various management positions for the company, including delegations to the USA, Ecuador and Mexico. Since 2011, Michael Heinz has been a member of the board of executive directors of BASF SE, responsible for the divisions Dispersions & Pigments, Care Chemicals, Nutrition & Health, Paper Chemicals, Performance Chemicals and Advanced Materials & Systems Research as well as *perspectives*, an internal program to bring the BASF business models in line with the needs of customers in all relevant markets.

"We Create Chemistry" – The Strategic Development of Customer Interaction at BASF

Michael Heinz, BASF SE

BASF Customers and Products

BASF is the world's leading chemical company. Our product portfolio is highly diversified. It extends from oil and gas exploration and production and classical chemical products such as acrylic acid and butanediol to specialty products such as raw materials for coatings, engineering plastics and crop protection products. The BASF customer base is almost entirely made up of companies that use BASF products to make their own products or perform further processing with them. Consequently, our business is clearly focused on B2B customer relationships.

Our very extensive product portfolio is structured partly on the basis of chemical value chains, and partly by the wide range of industries of our customers, each with its own special requirements. BASF thus covers a broad spectrum of business segments with a variety of market drivers. As a result, we have a highly complex portfolio of customer relationships. Every strategic decision has numerous effects, and therefore has to be backed by differentiated approaches. The success of BASF is rooted not only in the effectiveness of our innovative products, but also in close cooperation and long-term partnerships with customers. Social networks in the broadest sense have therefore always been very important to BASF. But even now, direct, personal customer relationships still play a far greater role than the digital media versions of such relationships. Nevertheless, the basic principle of social media – global networking – also presents opportunities to B2B companies: It facilitates even closer cooperation with customers and the involvement of other partners, up to and including end consumers.

Customer Relationships as a Pillar of Our Strategy

Historically, BASF has owed its success above all to its leading position in production and technology. This was – and is still – based on a continuous flow of innovations combined with the utilization of synergy effects from various chemical value chains. We call this approach – with its unique cost advantages – the "Verbund" principle. It is one of our strengths, enabling us to use resources efficiently. At large production sites, the manufacturing facilities are closely linked. This results in efficient value chains that extend from basic chemicals right through to high-value-added products such as coatings and crop protection agents.

But the competitive advantages, which remain in effect even today, are no longer enough to guarantee long-term success. Today's chemical markets are characterized by fierce price competition, in which Asian rivals as well as companies with cheaper access to raw materials flex their muscles. With the exception of new process technologies, the innovation potential for classical chemicals has been dwindling for years. Trailblazing molecular innovations are becoming more and more scarce.

If we want to set ourselves apart from the competition in the long term, we must therefore create a specific added value for the customer that other market participants cannot truly match. For this reason, in 2003 BASF adopted the slogan "We help our customers to be more successful" as one of our four key strategic principles. In our current overall strategy, this principle has become "We innovate to make our customers more successful." But: How can this goal be implemented in a company which – as described above – is active in so many different industries, markets, countries and steps along the value chain?

BASF's answer: Each and every business unit must be consistently aligned with the needs of its own customers. In practice, this means making the entire company more customer-focused – and winning over the whole workforce, from sales and marketing, to research and development right through to production and logistics.

But what are the concrete customer needs that BASF wants to focus on? Depending on the business segment, this may mean reducing the customer's process costs, being flexible while offering a broad product portfolio, or supporting customers with their innovation processes. To take into account the very diverse customer needs and success criteria in the various business segments, BASF created six differentiated customer interaction models (CIMs). This sets the parameters for BASF's role in this submarket: The CIMs not only determine the product package for and the interaction with the customer, but also how we can define internal processes, organizational models and competencies.

BASF uses six customer interaction models (CIMs) to align itself with customer needs

Trader/transactional supplier (TTS) • numerous, largely anonymous buyer-supplier relationships • spot market behavior (transparent market pricing, with prices agreed on a short-term basis depending on supply and demand)	**Lean/reliable basics supplier (LRS)** • certain product/service differentiation is evident to customers despite generally high level of standardization in the market • service reliability and constant product quality are important buying factors	**Standard package provider (SPP)** • customers with a need for certain breadth of product/service offering but not prepared to pay for complete customization • customers able to configure own packages
Product/process innovator (PPI) • customers seeking for superior performance products/services and expecting frequent innovations • high R&D spending needed to meet market needs • pricing based on value creation for customer	**Customized solution provider (CSP)** • customers willing to partner with supplier to jointly develop solutions and innovations • customers seeking for customization of product/service to fulfill their specific needs	**Value chain integrator (VCI)** • customers open to outsourcing of parts of their own value chain • highly integrated processes and work forces between supplier and customer through utilization of synergies in the delivery of products/services

Trader/Transactional Supplier (TTS)

This model is suitable for transparent spot markets in which customers shop for products that meet standard specifications at the lowest possible price. The customer/supplier relationship is limited to the individual transaction. There is little or no loyalty to individual suppliers. The implementation of this model requires minimal cost structures, flexible pricing and professional risk management.

Lean/Reliable Basics Supplier (LRS)

This model is used for serving customers who want to pay low prices for standardized products, but place a premium on highly reliable quality and delivery. Experience shows that customers in LRS business segments are willing to reward BASF's reliability with a small price premium. However, a lean organization and highly efficient processes are needed to be profitable here.

Standard Package Provider (SPP)

This model is used for customers who want various product/service packages to choose from, but are unwilling to pay for a tailor-made solution. It can be implemented only with a clear understanding of the needs of individual customer segments and clear rules for doing business and managing the use of commercial, technical and logistics services in line with these needs.

Product/Process Innovator (PPI)

This model is used in business segments in which customers value outstanding performance criteria of products and complementary services. For these customers, the price tends to play a secondary role in the purchasing decision. Implicitly, they are willing to bear the costs of constant product improvements. The implementation of this model calls for a thorough understanding of our customers' technical problems and trends, high R&D expenditures and outstanding expertise in the launch of new products.

Customized Solutions Provider (CSP)

This model is appropriate for customers looking for very specific solutions not available as "off-the-rack" products. In these cases, BASF enters into an exclusive, cooperative partnership with the customer to develop innovative solutions that provide a competitive edge in the customer's industry. Within the framework of professional key account management, BASF provides the customer with dedicated resources from sales, engineering services and product development.

Value Chain Integrator (VCI)

Some customers are looking for ways of outsourcing entire levels of their internal value chain to an outside supplier. Sometimes the motivation is the desire to focus on core competencies; for other customers, cost reduction is the main factor. In such cases, BASF takes on the operation of selected production stages and assumes responsibility for the cost and quality of the intermediate product in question. Payment is then made on a per-unit basis for the intermediate product, and not according to chemical prices.

Over the past few years all BASF business units have defined their CIMs in a systematic process and made them a key element of their business strategy. But only consistent implementation and constant review will ensure that business activities are in fact aligned with the actual customer needs and market situation.

The Implementation Process – From Theory to Practice

Offering customers exactly what they really need and what they are willing to pay for – that is the goal of CIM implementation. Depending on the customer requirements, the focus may be placed on expanding the range of products and services or on boosting efficiency in order to offer competitive prices. In any case, the goal is to take a differentiated view of our customers' needs and their contributions to earnings, and to align our overall marketing mix (products and services, prices, sales channels and market communication) accordingly. The CIM implementation follows a clearly structured process:

1. **Market analysis:** In the first phase, current customer needs are identified by sales and validated through surveys.

2. **Customer segmentation:** The basis for a differentiated structuring of our marketing mix is a needs-based segmentation of our customers. Typical BASF customer segments are price-driven buyers, value optimizers, service buyers and innovators.

3. **Product portfolio optimization:** The next step is to optimize the product portfolio in line with customer needs. This includes the clear positioning of the products according to the customer segments.

4. **Marketing channel optimization:** The goal here is to optimize the mix (e.g. direct sales, pull marketing, dealers, e-commerce, among other channels) to achieve the required levels of customer proximity and efficiency.

5. **Service optimization:** The commercial, technical and logistics services are tailored to the needs of the various customer segments.

6. **Pricing methodology and structure:** Through optimized pricing, we ensure competitiveness and profitability. This includes incentives for stable customer relationships as well as agreements for a fair allocation of economic benefits between the customer and BASF.

7. **Market communication:** Through consistent communications tailored to the target groups, particularly through sales, we ensure that the value of our products and services is transparent to our business partners and that the trust that forms the foundation of our customer relationships is being upheld.

8. **Customer concepts:** As the basis for a dialog with the customer in a spirit of partnership, and also for internal coordination purposes, the sales unit systematically plans customer-specific activities.

For better support in making the CIM concepts part of everyday business activities, BASF is currently setting up a customer interaction portal. This IT platform will serve to anchor our strategic decisions in operational processes through differentiated transaction rules, pricing and customer relationship management.

The Future Strategy, "We Create Chemistry" – Focusing Even More on Customer Relationships

To further enhance the differentiation potential and align ourselves even more closely to customer needs, BASF has shifted the focus in its portfolio in the direction of end customer-driven businesses – a move underscored by several acquisitions in recent years. With the take-over of Engelhard, for example, we have added the key business segment of catalysts for the automotive industry to our product range. And the purchase of Cognis makes BASF a leading supplier of chemical solutions for the consumer goods sectors of home care, personal care and food & beverage.

BASF is now continuing on this successful path: The key of the current corporate strategy is "We create chemistry" – another expression of the fact we do not just produce and supply chemicals, but also work with our business partners to develop and implement new solutions. In line with this slogan, our strategic principle for customer orientation is: "We innovate to make our customers more successful." Which means that BASF is pushing ahead with its efforts to expand partnerships with customers and other market participants. Moreover, we will be working even harder in the future to utilize synergies between business units to offer our partners innovative, sustainable solutions. That is how we have re-envisioned the classical "Verbund" principle for today's world. At the same time, the focus of our innovations will shift: away from the invention of new molecules, and towards customer-specific solutions and functional materials and systems.

For example, BASF develops complete formulations for its end customers in the Personal Care and Home Care segments to meet the needs of consumers. In our segment Functional Solutions, chemicals are produced for use as multi-material systems in new applications – for instance the combination of epoxy systems, foams, adhesives and coatings needed for the design of the rotor blade on a wind turbine. At the same time, a cross-divisional development team works on all of the other materials needed to build wind generating equipment, from construction materials to the lubricants needed for the turbines themselves.

To start with, the implementation of the new strategy requires an in-depth understanding and intelligent marketing approaches for entire industry value chains, in some cases extending all the way to the end user ("think B2C, act B2B"). Now, with customers at several points along the value chain in many industries, and with its intensifying efforts to build a network with downstream market stages, BASF is developing into a solutions provider for entire industries.

The close alignment of innovation processes with business partners and other participants in the value chain will also become more important in the future. What we envision is problem solution partnerships involving all relevant parties in an industry or application field, in which all partners contribute their own expertise to solve a given industry problem in existing markets or prospective growth areas. BASF is already pursuing approaches like this today in some key innovation areas. In the Battery Solutions business segment, for example, we have acquired a stake in the U.S. technology company, Sion Power. We are now working together with that company on an innovative battery technology to decisively boost the development of electric mobility through lower costs and improved battery range performance. In the Water Solutions segment, with the acquisition of inge watertechnologies (inge GmbH), BASF is seeking improvements in the production of ultrafiltration membranes through synergies between chemistry and other sciences. As a result, we are evolving from a supplier of flocculating and coagulating agents for waste water treatment to a system supplier for water treatment.

Through internal industry and customer teams, we will continue in the future to intensify our focus, across business units, on industries and innovative key customers. With this – to some extent virtual – organizational structure, we are creating a counterweight to the business units which, in many cases, are still geared towards product lines, while ensuring that we are aligned with the requirements of our target industries. Just one example: For the automotive industry, one of our most important customer sectors, with 7 billion euros in annual sales, BASF is the biggest chemical partner. Six different BASF divisions supply this industry with products ranging from coatings to catalysts, and from plastics to brake fluids and engine coolants. BASF-wide global account teams and a global Automotive Steering Committee ensure that we are positioned as a strategic partner of the industry. In addition, the Steering Committee promotes the creation of unique solutions for our customers, embracing elements of diverse technologies in such strategic areas as lightweight construction, energy efficiency and interior temperature control. One outcome of this strategy is the development by Daimler and BASF of the smart forvision concept car that achieves outstanding energy efficiency through weight-saving plastics, a polymer wheel rim suitable for high-volume production, innovative, high-performance insulation materials, organic solar cells and infra-red-reflecting dyes.

The Possibilities and Limits of Digital Media in the B2B World

At BASF, the direct, long-term interaction with individual customers has already become routine – in contrast to many B2C companies. This personal customer relationship is much more intensive, for example, than interactions via social media. Consequently, digital media will not replace personal interactions with customers in the B2B world. Depending on which CIM is involved, however, they could provide valuable support. Under the various CIMs, this is taking shape as follows:

The Trader/Transactional Supplier and Lean/Reliable Basics Supplier CIMs

Since 2001, BASF has enabled key accounts to use the Elemica e-commerce platform for ERP-integrated order settlement and supply chain networking. Many customers that place great value in a reliable supply have taken up this offer. For smaller customers and dealers, digital channels are increasingly replacing personal interactions. The majority of BASF's strategic sales partners use the company's proprietary "WorldAccount" e-commerce platform to retrieve information on products and applications and settle transactions. In emerging economies, social media – especially Facebook – are playing an increasing role in making contact with new customers. In regions where BASF does not have its own sales offices, this can serve as an efficient tool to complement direct interactions with customers.

The Standard Package Provider and Product/Process Innovator CIMs

Some BASF business units (for example crop protection and automotive refinish coatings) operate in highly fragmented markets where they simply cannot maintain a personal relationship with every customer (such as individual farmers or car repair shops). Digital marketing helps to gain a better understanding of the market, to communicate efficiently with customers and even to offer certain services online. In South America, BASF has established an Agro Interaction Portal where farmers can view maps showing the extent and severity of pest infestations. They can also upload photos of infested plants. After analyzing the pictures, BASF experts send suggestions for appropriate crop protection measures via e-mail. In this way, the customer receives quick and cost-effective support, and the company gains a better insight into customer problems, which in turn benefits the innovation process for products and services. Another example is the Body Shop Mall, set up by the North American Automotive Refinish Coatings unit. Car repair shops can log on to this portal to place orders that are then handled by BASF sales partners. This enables BASF to learn about the needs and behavior of the product users at a level of detail that would have been inconceivable under the classical dealer-based business model.

With this tighter focus on customer industries, the understanding of the entire value chain of our customers is becoming increasingly important in innovation-driven businesses. Digital media can facilitate the issue-driven and solution-driven dialog with downstream stages in the value chain, right through to the consumer ("think B2C, act B2B"). BASF employees are already active as bloggers, for example on industry-specific platforms. The emergence of internal corporate collaboration platforms may open up additional opportunities. For example, the possibility of systematic web tracking of the proprietary platforms may help to gain a deeper understanding of markets that may prove useful, for example, in developing target group-specific communication for new product launches. In addition, to aid in the development of new products, crowdsourcing campaigns could be launched, involving customers, suppliers, and above all consumers. This would enable us to gather specific ideas, test prototypes and plan the rollout of the new product.

Customized Solutions Provider and Value Chain Integrator CIMs

In the future, Web 2.0-based collaborative functions will enable us to create protected platforms for joint innovation projects with some business partners. BASF already has the internal, web-based social network connect.BASF in operation. This has developed into a central forum for the exchange of knowledge and ideas within the company. With modern portal solutions, connect.BASF could be selectively opened up to customers and external partners in the future.

In the dialog with the public and as part of a proactive approach to issue management, social media now represent an important channel. To implement our strategy of developing sustainable solutions for our business partners, the exchange of ideas with various elements of society via Facebook, Twitter, etc. delivers valuable input: First, we learn what issues are seen as priorities for solving sustainability problems. And second, we gain opportunities to recruit multipliers for our sustainable solutions.

These various examples show how digital channels are helping BASF to interact directly with previously anonymous market participants and interest groups. However, these channels can "only" be a complement to our established communications: For the most part, personal contact between sales units and customers remains irreplaceable. Moreover, under the BASF strategy "We create chemistry," it will actually become more important.

Conclusion

BASF is active in many different markets and business segments. To be in a position to offer solutions in every area tailored as closely as possible to customer needs, BASF manages its business segments on the basis of six customer interaction models (CIMs) based on idealized customer types. They are distinguished above all by the type and intensity of customer relationships. The specific CIM of a business unit is implemented by systematically aligning the marketing mix with customer needs. This customer-oriented approach is also reflected in the company's overall strategy: In response to the changes in the chemical markets, BASF is increasingly focusing its innovation efforts on growth segments (new industries such as wind energy) and customer-specific problem-solving skills, while leveraging synergies between the various business units. This strategy requires an even more active approach to shaping customer relationships. Although the use of digital media presents interesting opportunities – which are indeed being used more intensively – it cannot replace personal interactions with our business partners on a large scale. Consequently, the BASF sales units will have an even more important role to play in the future. With the initiatives I have mentioned, our company is developing the necessary skills to reach an even higher standard of professionalism in supplier-customer relationships in the future at both the strategic and operational levels. This represents the continuation of BASF's transformation to a customer-oriented system solution provider, and demonstrates every day that we do not just produce chemicals, but rather live by the slogan:

"We create chemistry."

The Company

BASF SE, established in 1865 as Badische Anilin- & Soda-Fabrik, is now the world's biggest chemical group with approximately 111,000 employees in more than 80 countries. The company has its headquarters in Ludwigshafen am Rhein, Germany, and operates more than 370 production sites around the world. From its beginnings as a paint factory, BASF has developed into a chemical company with a portfolio ranging from chemicals, polymers, refining products and crop protection agents to oil and gas. An outstanding milestone in the company's history came in 1913, with the world's first facility for producing synthetic ammonia. Decisive developments for BASF in the 1950s and 1960s included such innovations as Styropor expandable polystyrene. One of the company's strengths from the very beginning up to the present day has been the "Verbund": the intelligent networking of production facilities, energy flows and infrastructure as well as know-how and customers. In 2011, the total sales of the BASF Group amounted to 73.5 billion euros.

For more information: www.basf.com and www.deutschland.basf.com/ecp3/Germany/de/ content/aboutus/index

Summary

Customer focus: "We innovate to make our customers more successful." That is a core principle of the BASF corporate strategy. To make this principle a reality, the entire company – in particular across all business units – must be consistently customer-oriented. This includes getting all employees involved, from sales and marketing to research and development right through to production and logistics.

Interaction: To take into account the very diverse customer needs and success criteria in the various business segments of BASF, customer interaction models were defined. These models not only define the company's product package for the various customers and how it interacts with them, but also how to define internal processes, organizational models and competencies.

The human factor: In the future, direct personal contact will remain unchallenged as the key approach to the customer. Depending on the customer interaction model, however, digital media can be valuable for supporting and complementing customer contact. Most order handling is already carried out through e-commerce platforms. Proprietary, protected online portals and collaboration platforms support the networking of BASF employees and make it possible to open up internal know-how networks and innovation processes to customers. This enables BASF to find even better solutions for its customers.

The Author

Prof. Dr. Siegfried Russwurm was born in 1963. He studied production engineering and earned a master's degree. Between 1988 and 1989, he was employed with the Chair of Applied Mechanics at the University of Erlangen-Nuremburg. Dr. Russwurm initially joined Siemens in 1992 as a production planner and project manager for the company's Medical Engineering Group. He subsequently held a number of different central management positions, including head of Siemens Motion Control Systems Division. In 2006, Dr. Russwurm became a Member of the Group Executive Management for the Siemens Medical Solutions Group. In 2008, he was appointed to the Managing Board of Siemens AG as the head of Corporate Human Resources and Labor Director. In 2010, Russwurm was appointed CEO of the Industry Sector; in addition, he was given responsibility for Africa and the Middle East as well as for the Corporate Information Technology, Corporate Quality Management and for the Corporate Security Office at Siemens. Since 2009, he has served as an extraordinary professor in mechatronics at the University of Erlangen-Nuremburg. Dr. Russwurm is also a member of the Supervisory Board of Deutsche Messe AG.

Networking for Greater Industrial Productivity

Dr. Siegfried Russwurm, Siemens AG

Steady growth in the variety and complexity of today's products is posing new challenges for industrial enterprises – and will continue to do so into the future. Consumers are demanding more and more products that are tailored to their needs, and they do not want to wait for them. Online tools for configuring a new automobile are now available to let shoppers build their virtual dream cars, select the options and features they want from the myriad possible combinations, and even change their preferences shortly before the car is delivered. This trend will become more widespread in other markets as well. For the manufacturing industry, it means production on demand and production planning in real time. Modern production systems must be increasingly flexible and offer greater performance, but they also have to enable ever shorter innovation cycles and time-to-market for manufacturers – combined with faster response times. Ultimately, the goal is to control, manage and process enormous volumes of data while handling a wide range of variants and dealing with the resulting complexity. Customer and product relationships are in a state of fast and continuous change. This is just as true of business-to-business (B2B) transactions as it is for business-to-consumer (B2C) relationships.

The key to mastering all of these challenges is networking. Networking means a fast and consistent exchange of information and direct communication with customers and other stakeholders, for example about products and processes, as well as the incorporation of specific customer needs in one's own development processes.

It can take place at **three levels**:

1. networking in product development and production process

2. networking between manufacturers and customers

3. moderated networking of customers with customers

The possibilities for networking at these three levels are provided by today's broadband communications technology and the increased performance of computer processors, but especially by the use of new media. Providers and customers are now able to communicate directly, quickly and flexibly via a wide range of channels. Thanks to this close interconnection, it is possible to anticipate trends and developments in the end-customer arena and to offer business customers the necessary tools, production equipment and services in upstream stages of production. At the same time, this intensive and interactive communication strengthens customer loyalty and promotes close collaboration.

Networking in Product Development and Production Process

The networking of product planning and engineering processes is the decisive factor in reducing development times and speeding up time to market – and thus in increasing productivity and flexibility.

To get products ready for market more quickly in the future, product and production planning will have to run in parallel instead of sequentially. With conventional, sequential engineering methods it would be impossible to master product complexity and the volumes of data that have to be processed in product development and production planning and, at the same time, to make products available in a way that meets time and market expectations. But with parallel product and production planning, it is possible, for example, to plan a new car model, its various features, components and modules, all tools and processes needed for its production, cycle times, logistics relationships and the like in a single, end-to-end process – quite a complex task. This challenge can only be met using industry software that provides a holistic development environment along the whole value chain – with a shared database that is consistent over the entire lifecycle of products and production facilities. Something that sounds quite straightforward in theory has been found in practice to be extraordinarily difficult. For decades, the industry has been talking about the necessity and ways of optimizing the interfaces between development and production.

Collaborative Product Data Management (cPDM)

That is the task of modern product lifecycle management (PLM) software such as Siemens' Teamcenter, which is among the world's leading collaborative product data management systems (cPDM). Teamcenter bridges the gaps between the various parties involved in the product development and production process, and networks them closely with each other. To that end, the program handles uniform product and production data along the entire value chain and manages that data – keeping it available around the world, location independent and consistent at all times. Uniform CAD (computer-aided design) and CAE (computer-aided engineering) models, simulation results and specifications, parts lists, manuals and assembly instructions are always exactly where they are needed – when they are needed.

Researchers and product designers, suppliers and engineering companies thus no longer work as isolated stations in the product development and production process. Instead, they are able to collaborate with one another as if they were working in the same office. Teams with members spread throughout the world can exchange information more easily and make necessary modifications.

Applications for Mobile Devices (apps)

In the meantime, these software solutions can even integrate mobile devices by way of application programs, or apps. With Teamcenter Mobility, for example, a custom-made iPad app supports the exchange of data when on the road or anywhere on the factory premises, assuming broadband mobile access or a WLAN connection is available. With the app, users can add their own files, create relations and trigger active processes. This enables them, for example, to respond quickly and directly to situations as they arise on-site.

Networking Between Manufacturers and Customers

In addition to networking in product development and production process, there is a second step in which the focus is on promoting networking with customers through integrated, interactive communications tools. There are several ways to establish relationships with customers and other stakeholders and make these relationships as direct and intensive as possible. Three are described below:

- e-business offerings
- communications via social media and
- open-innovation processes.

E-business Offerings

Online shopping is nothing new. Some time ago, the B2C enterprises exploiting the many and varied possibilities of Web 2.0 were joined by growing numbers of manufacturers who use this direct business relationship as a form of B2B customer care. For example, Siemens customers can find a wealth of information and transaction services on various online platforms, such as the "Industry Mall" and the "Service and Support Portal" (cf., 8), which are interconnected via suitable interfaces. The online catalog and ordering system for the full range of the company's automation technology is also directly linked in some cases to the procurement systems of large customers.

Customers around the world can configure products for their own specific needs, check availability and place orders via several different electronic channels – and thus minimize delivery times. These networked platforms offer support services, downloads and operating instructions designed to make it easier for customers to decide which product is the right one for their needs. It is also possible to download a customized manual for certain products. Online access is available around the clock and is easy to understand, so it is appropriate for a wide range of customers. Every month, tens of thousands of users from around the globe visit the Industry Mall.

Communications via Social Media

Even more customers and prospects make up the audience for new media and social networks. Particularly popular channels for social customer relationship management are Facebook, YouTube and Twitter. At Siemens, we encourage our own experts to contribute their know-how to online forums.

It is impossible for a large company with international operations to speak to its customers with a single voice via social media. It is more practical to have several voices communicating in different languages and dialects, but to ensure that they all communicate the same content. Three principles make certain that the employees use social media in an efficient and profitable way:

- All employees with a PC at their workplace have unrestricted access to social media.

- These employees are regularly provided with content that they can post in social media. That is particularly true for experts with extensive technical knowledge; some of them are given very specific information for Twitter feeds or other platforms.

- Employees receive professional support in the proper use of social media. That includes tips on the benefits and risks of using the new media.

All of these measures make it possible for sales representatives or product managers to address their customers in an individualized way via social media. And that's not all: Active communication by many company employees through social media also makes the company more aware of criticism or bad reviews and enables company experts to weigh in with useful factual information without delay. It takes quick responses and active participation in social networks to gain credibility in online communities.

In addition to this networking with customers on the part of individual employees, there is also a centralized use of social media channels. In this way, not just experts, journalists and users are provided with information, but also "digital authorities" such as bloggers – via a central Twitter channel, for example (@siemensindustry). On YouTube, one can find more than just image films; there are also video tutorials for many products and much more. Several of our Facebook accounts have met with a very strong response: The one for Siemens Water Technologies, for example, has more than 1,400 followers. And a wide variety of apps, such as "Siemens Industry References," "Siemens Industry Online Support," "Siemens Explorer" and "Siemens SIRIUS eAssistance" make the most of these increasingly popular digital and mobile communications channels. In many different ways, then, we engage in the discussion on specific topics, which ideally can move from social media to the trade press and from there to general-interest and business publications.

Open Innovation as a Form of Communication

Since communication via social media is interactive, it is also excellent for exchanging industry-specific knowledge and gathering information that can be used in product development. Open innovation is a good way to do that. This concept describes an approach in which a wide range of external skills, abilities, developments or suggestions – including those from experts, customers or suppliers – are integrated. Under this method, companies gain the ability to respond quickly to technological changes and changing markets. For example, Siemens was ranked first for its knowledge management and open innovation activities in the study "The European Most Admired Knowledge Enterprises" (MAKE), conducted in 2011 by the international market research firm Teleos. The company received top marks in the category "Creating Value from Customer/Stakeholder Knowledge," among others.

TIA Portal as an Example of a Successful Open Innovation Process

One example of a successful open-innovation process is the development of the Totally Integrated Automation Portal (TIA Portal), an engineering framework with which manufacturers can control all planning and production processes from a single user interface, from development to assembly and commissioning and on to maintenance and the extension of automation systems. Soon after its launch, the portal was seen in the automation industry as a pioneering innovation. This leap in technology was only possible because the TIA Portal was not developed, tested and checked behind closed doors; Instead, the work was done over the course of several years together with pilot customers in a range of industries around the world and with various perspectives and needs.

The open innovation project was first presented to selected customers, and their special needs and possible conceptual changes were discussed in detail with them. More than 80 user interviews resulted in about 5,000 pieces of qualified feedback. After analysis, the results were integrated into a working software prototype. In a second and more complex step, some 50 customers worldwide were invited to work with the prototype in a field trial. It was closely monitored to see how well the customers were able to solve test tasks and where they might run into trouble. In addition, the customers provided detailed feedback regarding their work with the prototype.

The customers involved included such diverse companies as the Chinese tool company, Shanghai Dahua Network & Electric Technology; the Chinese power plant technology manufacturer, Yantai Longyuan Power Technology; the German stainless-steel processing company, Butting, and the U.S. software company and system integrator, Solvere. They all made use of the opportunity to have their experience incorporated in the new software. As a result, the TIA Portal has a high degree of usability and has satisfied real-world requirements perfectly from the very start. And it was not just another new product for which users first had to be found – they were already there right from the launch date.

Moderated Networking of Customers with Customers

The third level of networking builds on direct communication among the customers themselves. Siemens enables and organizes this communication through its Service and Support Portal, for example. The portal is the central point of access for technical information and services related to products and solutions. It's here that customers can find 300,000 documents in six languages; they include everything from manuals and certificates to updates and patches for both current and older programs and equipment. The portal also offers sample solutions, frequently-asked questions (FAQs) and access to technical support. Around 750 global experts, product managers and translators ensure the quality of the content. Each month, industrial customers visit the service portal – which is free of charge – more than a million times; on some days there are more than 50,000 visitors.

Strong Customer Loyalty Thanks to the User Forum

Particularly strong customer ties are forged by the portal's user forum, where customers can network with other customers. Siemens moderates these discussions and evaluates them. The forum was set up in 2004, at a time when the interactive Web 2.0 was not yet on the radar at many other companies, and it quickly became a huge success. In the period from 2009 to 2011 alone, the number of daily visits grew by 137 percent. Today, 15,000 visitors view the forum discussions and post a total of 400 to 500 new messages daily. A total of 124,000 active users are registered.

They can exchange their ideas and opinions in the professionally moderated forum and support each other with tips and practical suggestions on topics ranging from general automation technology issues to detailed issues concerning the assembly or operation of products, plants or solutions. In these discussions, employees contribute their own thoughts to encourage the users' exchanges or to answer specific questions, but so far, more than three-fourths of all postings that have helped solve a problem have come from external users of the forum. In total, the users discuss an average of 1,000 English-language and 200 German-language technical queries each month. More than 80 percent of these queries are solved in the forum discussions.

Certificates for External Experts

Forum users who are deemed to be particularly active, and whose contributions stand out because of their high quality, can be officially designated as "experts." That honor brings with it certain privileges. For example, these users can highlight topics they regard as especially interesting or chat in a closed user zone. These experts are given a certificate each year. This represents a valuable distinction for many of them that they can use in other contexts to demonstrate their technical credentials in certain areas. At present, 52 external experts from 13 countries are working in the user forum of the Service and Support Portal. Most of them are employees of external companies who invest their time and effort in the forum for reasons of personal interest, but also in the interest of their own companies.

Both customers and the company profit from the open-user forum of the Service and Support Portal – a classic win-win situation. The forum gives customers direct access to reliable information about products, systems and applications. That information can come from the moderators or from other users who may have dealt with similar issues in the past and can thus give a practical answer. In this way, all users can increase their technical knowledge and get help with problems at any time – quickly and at no charge.

Crowdsourcing

For businesses, these open-user forums bring three main benefits. The first is the ability to involve users in what is called "crowdsourcing." A practice-driven knowledge base grows from the users' questions and the expert answers given by the community. The evaluation of forum discussions provides feedback concerning customer behavior and ultimately leads to greater success with future product developments and sales activities. This approach is currently being expanded. In the future, for example, forum discussions will be systematically evaluated to identify customer requirements – from training needs and desired product features or improvements to new forms of cross-selling.

Greater Customer Loyalty

The second benefit is enhanced customer loyalty. An active community is built up, with regular contests held to find and honor the most active users over a certain period, for example. Winners can be rewarded with certificates or high placements in online rankings or the like. As a result, customers do not just feel that they are taken seriously – ideally, they also feel a strong sense of identification with the company.

Case Avoidance

Last but not least, an open user forum also has cost advantages. For the same level of user traffic and the same problem-solution quota, the operation of the forum costs just a tenth as much as a continually updated, high-quality FAQ resource. And it would cost a hundred times as much to operate a qualified call center. Since every customer can use the forum, and the postings are indexed in an integrated search engine, many users find quick answers to their problem – and do not need to contact central technical support or the experts in the regions. This case avoidance greatly reduces costs in the entire service and support area.

Conclusion: Networking Pays Off at All Levels

All forms of networking described above have their own immediate purposes, of course, but they also have one overriding goal in common: boosting customer loyalty. As has been seen, it works – and it is a good investment, too.

Networking is the rapid, seamless exchange of information. Consequently, it results in a higher degree of adaptability to today's markets, which are changing faster and more radically than ever before. Thanks to networking at three levels – in product development and production process, between manufacturers and customers, and in the moderated peer-to-peer networking of customers – we can address the needs of our customers in a more individual manner, offer them tailored solutions, respond more quickly to market and customer needs and shorten innovation cycles and time to market. That helps to make customers realize that they have a partner at their side who understands them and who provides them with the support they need to increase their productivity, their efficiency and thus their competitiveness.

The Company

Siemens AG was originally founded in Berlin in 1847 as the "Telegraphen-Bauanstalt von Siemens & Halske" by Werner von Siemens and Johann Georg Halske. In just a few years, it expanded from a family operation to an international company. In 1866, Werner von Siemens discovered the dynamoelectric principle and recognized the economic significance of his discovery. At the end of the 1870s, high voltage engineering began its relentless advance, allowing the company to grow steadily over the following years. The year 1949 saw the successful relocation of Siemens & Halske headquarters to Munich; the headquarters of the Siemens-Schuckertwerke moved to Erlangen, with the company retaining a secondary location in Berlin. Today, Siemens is present in over 190 regions of the globe and is a market and technological leader in the sectors of Energy, Healthcare and Industry as well as the Infrastructures and Cities segment. A total of around 370,000 people are employed with Siemens worldwide, and in 2012, the company had sales of 78.5 billion euros.

For more information: http://www.siemens.com/history/en/

Summary

Increasingly, customers are demanding products and services that are tailored to their individual needs – without having to contend with long waiting times. Modern production systems therefore need to become more flexible and offer greater performance because customer and product relations are in a continuous state of change. This is true for both B2C and B2B relations.

Networking is the key to tackling these challenges. It means a quick and consistent exchange of information, direct communication with customers and other stakeholders – for example, about products and processes – and the incorporation of specific customer needs into a company's own developmental processes.

This can take place at three levels:

1. networking in product development and production process

2. networking between manufacturers and customers

3. moderated networking of customers with other customers

The possibilities for networking at these three levels are provided not only by today's broadband-communications technology and the increased performance of computer processors, but above all by the use of new media and social networks.

Product and service providers and customers now possess the ability to communicate and exchange ideas via a wide range of diverse channels – quickly and flexibly. These tightly intermeshed links make it possible to anticipate trends and developments in the end-user arena, and to offer business customers the necessary tools, production equipment and services in upstream stages of production. At the same time, this intensive and interactive communication strengthens customer loyalty and promotes close collaboration.

The Author

Dr. Heinrich Hiesinger was born in 1960 and studied electrical engineering at Technische Universität München (TUM) in Munich. From 1986 until 1992, he worked as a research associate at TUM. He joined the Power Transmission and Distribution Division with the Siemens Group in 1992, and held a number of positions in various countries until 2000. In 2000, he was appointed president of the Power Transmission and Distribution Group and in 2003, president and chief executive officer of Siemens Building Technologies AG, Zug/Switzerland. He became a member of the managing board of Siemens AG in 2007, and in 2008 was additionally appointed CEO of the Industry Sector of Siemens and head of the corporate information technology department. From October 2010 to January 2011 Dr. Hiesinger served as vice chairman of the executive board of ThyssenKrupp AG, and since January 21, 2011, has held the position of chairman of the executive board of ThyssenKrupp AG.

Gaining Access to the Markets of the Future – How the B2B World is Being Transformed by Modern Information and Communication Technologies (ICT)

Heinrich Hiesinger, ThyssenKrupp AG

Introduction

Modern information and communication technologies (ICT) have already permanently changed our communication habits and will keep doing so as technological progress continues. The same applies to the B2B sector. In some respects this area, too, has already undergone structural changes in response to the emerging technological possibilities.

The challenge for B2B companies is to make intensive use of the technological trends and developments to bolster existing customer relationships and build new ones to leverage the opportunities and potential presented by modern information and communication technology. Featuring prominently among the ways of offering added value to business customers is the transfer of intelligent solutions from the B2C segment, such as social media concepts. This can be backed by specific examples.

The World Needs "More" – And Demands Sustainable Solutions

The global economy is passing through an exciting and challenging phase. In western countries, which have dominated global economic growth for decades, the markets are largely saturated and we are now seeing only moderate gains in output. At the same time, enormous demand is taking shape in the emerging economies. More and more people around the world are catching up with western standards of living. They want to be more mobile, they use more electric power, and they live and work in bigger buildings. They also need more food and other products. With the combined effects of population growth, globalization and urbanization, the demand for consumer and industrial goods, infrastructure, energy and raw materials will continue increasing. In short: The world needs "more."

But, as we have learned, we cannot push growth at the expense of the environment and natural resources. We have to become more efficient in use of energy and raw materials, manufacture consumer goods and industrial products in a more environmentally friendly manner, and make sustainability a priority in the planning of our infrastructure. Long-term success will come only to those companies with the ability to be not just good, but "better," in meeting the demand for "more."

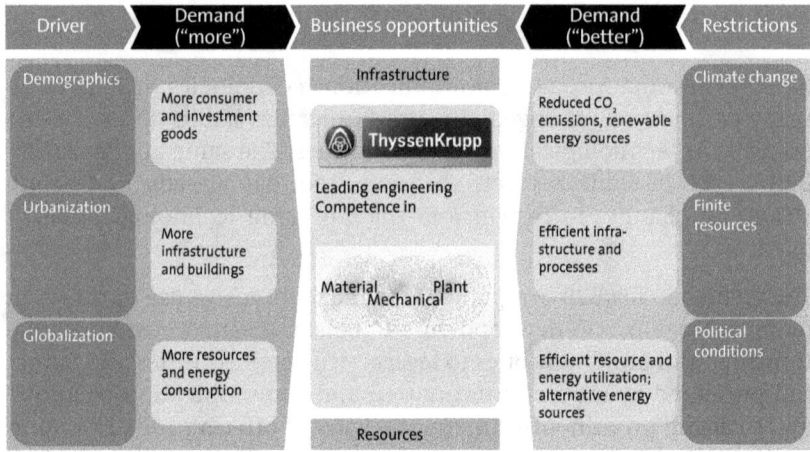

Figure 1: "More and better"

ThyssenKrupp is on the right track to live up to these expectations. We have transformed our company from a steelmaker to a global, integrated materials and technology group. In the three areas – Material, Mechanical and Plant – ThyssenKrupp develops technological solutions and products to meet the increasing global need for goods, resources and energy amid the conflicting demands of growth and ecology. As a result, the group can help its customers to set themselves apart in global competition and produce innovative products while balancing profitability and resource conservation.

Customer Proximity as a Long-Term Success Factor

Key factors behind the success of companies that have effectively competed in the market for decades are a precise understanding of their customers' needs and a set of innovation skills geared to those needs. Ensuring that these factors are in place is a constant challenge for every company, especially when its business activities and the industries and segments of its customer base are as widely diversified as those of ThyssenKrupp.

ThyssenKrupp's range of products and services extends from steel production and related material and logistics services to plant construction, elevators and escalators. It also makes components for the automotive industry, the mechanical engineering sector and shipbuilding, among other sectors. As a result, the group's customers represent the most diverse fields imaginable, for instance the manufacturing of vehicles and construction equipment, aircraft and plastic goods. In these business relationships, ThyssenKrupp, with its divisions, serves the entire customer value chain, starting with raw-material extraction and extending from trading and processing materials right through to spare parts and service activities in the elevator business. The customer groups and segments are also highly diverse, including material buyers, strategic buyers, key accounts, municipalities and countries, retailers and property managers, for instance, as well as private households and internal customers.

But the business segment, industry and customer type are not the only criteria for determining the optimal structure of a given customer relationship. Increasingly, it depends on which information and communication technologies are available and how they can be used.

Information and Communication Technologies are Fundamentally Changing Customer Relationships

The influence of modern information and communication technologies on customer and product relationships is multi-layered and far-reaching. However, we can identify four highly characteristic effects indicative of how companies can offer their customers added value through the use of intelligent solutions:

- objectivization of customer relationships
- individualization of products and services
- customer integration through intelligent processes and
- breaking down communication barriers

The following sections will describe these four effects, supported by examples from the ThyssenKrupp Group.

Objectivization of Customer Relationships

First and foremost, the use of modern information and communication technologies has made customer communication much more efficient and cost-effective. In the past, the focus was on personal contact. Today, by contrast, business processes between customers and suppliers are becoming increasingly digitized and anonymous. The purchasing processes in the car industry are a good example. The dominance of personal contacts between buyers and key account managers is long over. Even today, technical consultation and technical sales still require intensive personal communications. But purchasing processes have become disconnected from those forms of contact to some extent. Requests for quotation are handled through IT systems to which bidders must upload their offer specifications. This results in greater transparency and makes it easier for the buyer to compare bids.

This approach, now in widespread use for procurement in the automotive sector and other industries, is also being applied by B2B companies to their own purchasing processes. For example, more than 12,500 suppliers take part in the more than 12,000 calls to tenders handled through ThyssenKrupp's web-based procurement platforms eBidding and eAuctions. This approach to purchasing is appropriate especially for standardized consumable materials with clearly identifiable quality and performance specifications based on well-defined criteria. This makes the market highly transparent for buyers, who can more easily compare suppliers and switch to different ones if necessary.

From the suppliers' standpoint, on the other hand, this increasing objectivization of customer relationships for standardized consumables is a challenge. Apart from the price, there is hardly any other way for them to set themselves apart from their competitors. As a result, modern information and communication technologies have generally diminished the intensity and importance of customer relationships in the B2B segments where standardized products are bought and sold.

The opposite is true for the increasing number of B2B products that are

- individually tailored to a given application,
- highly complex and require user support or
- complemented by services.

With these types of products and services, the intelligent use of information and communication technology can generate substantial added value for customers.

Individualizing Products and Services

We are seeing a steady rise in the sheer variety of products and services. They are also becoming more complex and are increasingly individualized. At the same time, customers are now more demanding, and want B2B companies to deliver the experiences and services, such as social media, that they have come to appreciate in the B2C sector. The challenge is to provide customers who differ widely in their needs and expectations with the greatest possible variety and range of choices for the product and the related services – and to provide this without overwhelming them. At the same time, the customer relationship must still live up to the same transparency standards. This is made possible through the use of modern information and communication technologies. Especially with smartphone and tablet apps, companies can make it fun for customers to communicate with them.

The service initiative by ThyssenKrupp Elevator provides examples of this approach. This business area pools the Group's global activities in the area of passenger transportation systems. Its product range includes passenger and freight elevators, escalators, moving walks, passenger boarding bridges as well as stair and platform lifts, and also extends to service, maintenance and modernization packages. But elevators and escalators do more than just carry people. They are also the first impression a visitor has when entering a building. In addition to technical performance, the design, tactile characteristics and the reliability of elevators now count for much more. Customers want fast, safe and pleasant transportation within buildings. Architects, contractors and developers also expect more than ever before: Elevators must fit seamlessly into a building's architecture. This applies to such structural characteristics as the shaft dimensions, the desired capacity of the elevator, noise levels and energy consumption as well as the color concept, the choice of materials, the displays and controls, and the lighting concept.

The ThyssenKrupp Elevator service initiative has responded by developing several innovative solutions using modern information and communication technologies to support planners, users and service personnel in the selection, operation and maintenance of ThyssenKrupp equipment. The EVOLUTION® BLUE product line offers a modular concept with more than 7,000 color and material combinations that can be adapted to customer needs. It would be almost impossible to communicate this vast range of design possibilities through conventional communication channels. ThyssenKrupp has responded by creating an app that lets customers get started by playing with the design choices. More experienced customers can use an elevator cabin configurator on the website that also lets them check technical specifications. These computer-based and app-based configurators enable ThyssenKrupp to advise customers on design configurations in the early planning stages. This can then serve as the basis for in-person discussions in which ThyssenKrupp specialists can focus on technical details to round off the advisory services. By pooling the data generated by these tools, the company can spot trends in individual customer segments as input for the product development teams.

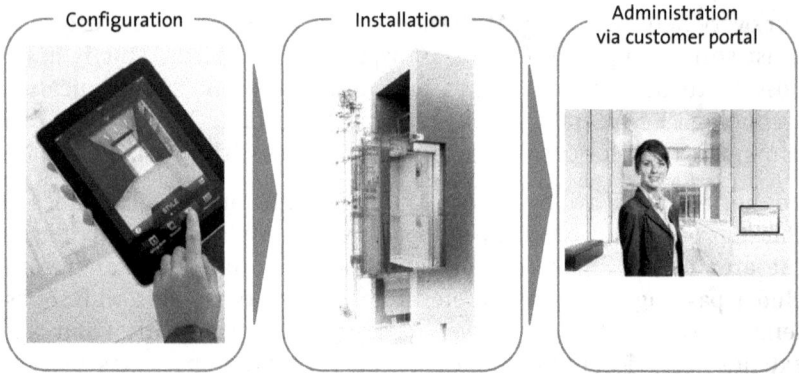

Figure 2: ThyssenKrupp Elevator Service Initiative

These solutions not only facilitate the selection and design of elevators, but also yield additional customer benefits during operations. Through intelligent controls, the elevator can achieve energy efficiency Class A by optimizing traffic flows with the self-learning function. Elevators can also be programmed remotely through the web portal. This can be used to activate priorities for individual floors, for example. To meet customer expectations for quick and reliable availability of data, ThyssenKrupp sets up customer portals to give customers quick access to all business documents and records related to all of their installed equipment: from contracts, invoices, orders, maintenance work carried out by ThyssenKrupp Elevator and pending maintenance queries, through to information on the availability of each individual elevator.

These examples show how electronic communication is complementing personal contact without replacing it. Customer benefits increase and the customer relationship is strengthened. At the same time, customers gain a greater understanding of the company's products. This enables ThyssenKrupp Elevator to remain focused on and responsive to customer needs while continually developing its products and services.

Customer Integration through Intelligent Processes

Another trend resulting from the development of information and communication technologies is the increasing integration within the value chain and closer ties between customers and suppliers through electronic information systems.

Cooperation within value chains allows customers to coordinate their processes more efficiently across stages in the value creation process and expand their range of products and services. Depending on their position along the value chain, B2B companies are seeing their role being steadily redefined as a single point of contact, i.e. that of a coordinator of the upstream activities in the value chain. It is no longer enough for them to offer their own products. Now they must be able to provide services in adjacent fields as well. For this purpose, B2B companies must be capable of completing flexible "docking maneuvers" with the communication platforms of their customers.

This kind of direct link between suppliers and assembly plants is a standard procedure in the car industry. Under just-in-sequence (JIS) manufacturing, the supplier not only ensures that the required parts and components are delivered in time, but also that they are manufactured and delivered in the precise sequence in which they are used. This makes it possible to carry out individualized production and preassembly for a vehicle prior to the components actually being installed. Consequently, manufacturers do not need to keep numerous versions on hand, which enables them to reduce inventories significantly. On the technical side, communications are system-based and are handled via electronic data interchange (EDI), through which current requirements can be retrieved instantly when needed. However, the EDI formats vary by region and manufacturer, which is yet another challenge for automotive suppliers.

ThyssenKrupp Automotive Systems, which operates axle assembly plants around the world as a partner of carmakers, mostly in the immediate vicinity of assembly plants, must be capable of getting a functional communication platform up and running within a very short time. This platform must ensure the networking of all processes between the carmaker and ThyssenKrupp and also between ThyssenKrupp and its suppliers, which are also linked via IT networks. There is enormous time pressure when setting up a new assembly plant. There is generally only six months between the time when a new plant is proposed and the launch of production.

For this purpose, ThyssenKrupp Automotive Systems has created the standardized "JIS-Template" that maps the various EDI standards and ensures the standardized exchange of invoicing data while taking into account the differences across the field of axle component suppliers. To avoid cancelled deliveries whenever possible and ensure quick correction of delivery malfunctions, the data generated in the component delivery process are analyzed immediately. The system sees whether a supplier has replaced so much as a single screw that does not match the specifications without forwarding the product code to ThyssenKrupp. The communication platform ensures links to the carmaker, serves as a liaison between the partners in the value chain, guarantees the quality of ThyssenKrupp's own products, and thus ultimately makes a vital contribution to ensuring product quality for car buyers. Today the template is used worldwide at all locations of ThyssenKrupp Automotive Systems working with plants using JIS processes.

Another example of how ThyssenKrupp is deploying modern information and communication technologies to make its internal business processes and its customer and product relationships more intelligent and efficient is the use of RFID (radio- frequency identification) technology. The slabs loaded on ships at the steel plant in Brazil are automatically identified using RFID tags. These logistics data are exchanged in real time in a standardized format. Due to interference and reflections, the use of RFID in applications involving metal products or in metal environments was long considered an impossibility. There was no way to guarantee reliable detection of transponders or sufficient signal ranges.

The use of this new technology enables all internal and external participants in the value chain to engage in a standardized, real-time exchange of relevant logistics events. This makes it possible to increase crane utilization levels and speeds, shorten laytimes, speed up the loading process, and reduce logistics costs. For the customer, it means shorter average delivery times, greater certainty for delivery dates, and constant availability of the necessary information on the shipment status. As a result, the customers, in particular rolling mills in the USA and Europe, can optimally coordinate their own processes with the arrival of shipments.

With its generic structure, this ThyssenKrupp RFID-Logistics Platform, which has already proven its worth in the steel segment, can be adapted quickly and cost-effectively for new, viable RFID-based solutions specifically geared to the business process in question. Other applications within ThyssenKrupp, for example in plant construction, are currently under consideration. They could conceivably be used to track plant components from the manufacturing facility to the construction site.

Breaking Down Communication Barriers

Modern information and communication technologies are opening up new networking possibilities with customers and suppliers in the B2B world and in direct communications between B2B suppliers and end customers. In the classical B2B business, the B2B customer has typically "translated" customer demands, and in many cases has acted as the only interface to the end customer. This has made it difficult for B2B companies to spot emerging trends and effectively convert them into innovative products. But that ability is a decisive factor in the future success of products, and thus for a company's success. To foresee the needs of end customers and recognize trends at the earliest possible stage, companies must create communication channels to reach them.

This challenge is faced, for example, by automotive suppliers such as the ThyssenKrupp Chassis Group under the Bilstein brand. The company develops and sells products covering the complete range of damping and suspension solutions, and is a preferred partner in motor sports and vehicle tuning. Customer segments include car manufacturers, motor sports and aftermarket parts.

For years now the car, as a product, has seen an unparalleled rise in the emphasis on emotional appeal and individualism. With their products, automotive suppliers make a major contribution to making the desired product features a reality. For the end customer, however, this often goes completely unnoticed. From a marketing standpoint, but also in the interest of heightening the direct awareness of products and customers, direct communication with the end customer makes a lot of sense.

To complement the conventional channels such as print media, motorsport events and brand ambassadors, Bilstein has developed a number of social media initiatives as an additional means of reaching out to end customers, alongside contacts with B2B customers. This includes Facebook, Twitter and RSS feeds as well as blogs and microsites with brand ambassadors. Examples include the Performance2 marketing campaign and the "Dream Curves" customer campaign, which invited car enthusiasts to mark their favorite curved stretch of road on a virtual map.

The various social media measures have opened up bi-directional communications with end customers. They are also proving highly effective for reaching the 18–25-year-old age group. ThyssenKrupp Bilstein gets unfiltered feedback from end customers and can find out directly from them about their needs and experiences with its products. This is a major contribution to building the brand. At the same time, the insights gained are used as direct input for product development. Ultimately, this is also beneficial to the carmakers' mass market business.

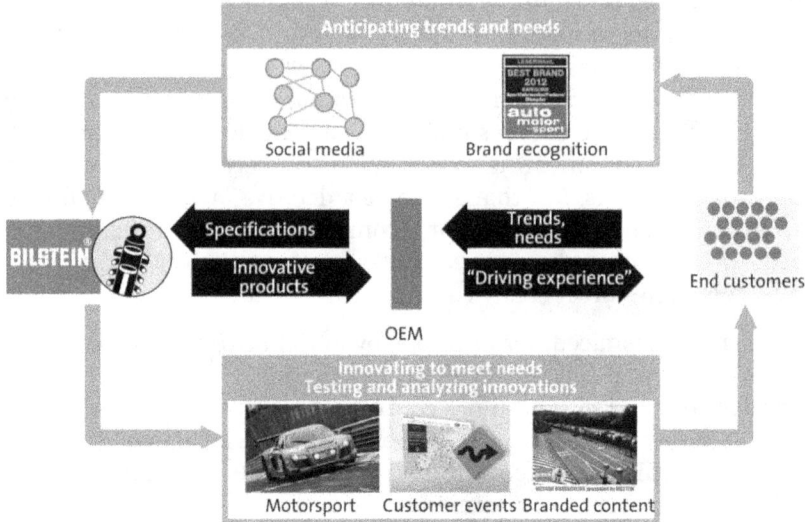

Figure 3: "Breaking down communication barriers"

Outlook

The rapid development of technologies will present opportunities for more applications. Major forces driving this trend include improvements in the performance of semiconductor chips, software, the speed and intelligence of networks, as well as advances in sensor electronics and transponder technology.

Except in the case of standardized consumables, for which the sales processes are becoming increasingly rationalized and objectified, customer relationships are looming larger in almost all B2B segments as the trend towards more complexity and individuality in products and services gains momentum. As a result, buyers need more support and explanations.

B2B companies must respond to changes in their customers' communication and consumption habits resulting from the spread of digitization. Many B2B customers are transferring experiences and services from their personal lives to the B2B world and expect to be offered similarly user-friendly solutions.

Consequently, the motto "more and better" not only relates to the rising global demand for consumer goods and industrial products, infrastructure, energy and raw materials. It also applies to the customer relationships of the future. "More" is also what the B2B customer wants – in terms of service and customer orientation. Modern information and communication technologies will enable companies to be "better" at satisfying these needs than before – and in particular to be more efficient, faster and more user-friendly. Consequently, the companies who spot these trends early and implement them with intelligent solutions will have a clear edge over their competitors.

The Company

ThyssenKrupp AG was formed in 1999 through the merger of Thyssen AG with Fried. Krupp AG Hoesch-Krupp. The merger of these two companies, each with deep roots in the Ruhr District, yielded one of the world's largest technology groups. Today, ThyssenKrupp has a global workforce of 170,000 employees in some 80 countries, working on product solutions for sustainable progress. In the areas Material, Mechanical and Plant, the group helps its customers to gain an edge in global competition and to produce innovative products profitably while conserving resources. In the 2010/2011 financial year, the company had total sales of 49 billion euros.

For more information: http://www.thyssenkrupp.com/en/konzern/index.html

Summary

As products and services become increasingly complex and require more explanation and support, the development of more advanced information and communication technologies also creates opportunities for B2B companies to solidify existing customer relationships while attracting new customers.

Intelligent solutions from the B2C world such as communications on public or closed platforms can be used by B2B companies as well to bring about an open dialog with their various target groups. With online planning tools and apps, customers can be involved in the development process from an early stage, long before orders are finalized. The networking of production and logistics processes along the order settlement process forges closer ties between customers and suppliers by enabling them to exchange information in real time.

For B2B companies, the added value of modern information and communication technologies relates mainly to the following possibilities:

1. **Objectivization** of customer relationships through technology-based communication standards and platforms

2. **Individualization** of products and services, supported by the understandable representation of complex solutions with IT-based tools

3. **Customer integration** through intelligent processes and bidirectional integration into customers' communication platforms

4. **Breaking down communication barriers** to foster brand growth and product development

B2A
Business-to-Administration

The Authors

Prof. Dr. Thomas Bieger was born in 1961. He is the president of the University of St.Gallen (HSG), where he is also a professor of business administration, with a special focus in the tourism industry. In addition, he is the director of the Institute for Systemic Management and Public Governance of the University of St. Gallen (IMP-HSG). He has published extensively while conducting research, consultation and teaching activities, specializing in service management, network management, destination management and regional economy management, at various universities (including the University of Innsbruck, the Vienna University of Economics and Business, Università della Svizzera Italiana in Lugano and the University of Otago in New Zealand). Since 1996, he has held supervisory board appointments with various companies in the service sector and has served as the general secretary of the International Association of Scientific Experts in Tourism (AIEST) and the chairman of CEMS (Global Alliance in Management Education).

Dr. Michael Lorz was born in 1979. He studied international business administration at the University of Macau and Hanze University, Groningen, Netherlands. He completed a Master of business studies degree and CEMS studies at the UCD Michael Smurfit Graduate School of Business in Dublin and RSM Erasmus University in Rotterdam, and completed a doctorate in management at the University of St.Gallen (HSG). From 2005 until 2008, he held sales and marketing positions with the Scottish & Newcastle Group in Edinburgh, Chicago and Antwerp. At the University of St.Gallen (HSG) he was instrumental in founding the Office of University Development (consultation, relationship management, and fundraising), and has headed the Office since 2010. Since 2013, he is also managing director of the HSG Foundation.

Customer Relationships Between Private and Public Value

Thomas Bieger and Michael Lorz,
University of St.Gallen

Owing to globalization and the associated opening of markets and technological progress, more and more companies and organizations, including former public-sector entities, now operate amid the conflicting forces of a purely market-driven approach and state control. They face the challenge of simultaneously generating private value for their direct customers and owners and public value for the public at large. This has a considerable impact on customer relations, as the definition of the traditional customer is split into three functions: The direct user, or the classical end user, frequently pays only a small fraction of the total cost of the product or service received. The process of commissioning and specifying the product or service rests mainly with the generally public-sector entity that purchases it. The general public often finances it through fees and taxes.

The organization and the monitoring of the efficiency of these multi-layered customer relationships requires the management to develop new forms of thinking and approaches. In this regard, a specific challenge constitutes the partially conflicting goal-oriented and task-oriented modes of thinking within a company.

The University of St.Gallen (HSG), on the one hand being a public university, and on the other an organization with approximately 50 percent private funding, is a good example of an institution which, – like many transportation companies or hospitals, – operates in the space between private and public value. Consequently, this chapter not only examines the phenomenon of the increasing importance of management between the state and the market, specifically concerning the multi-layered nature of the customer relationship. It also presents a picture of how HSG is responding to these new challenges in order to be able to offer concrete courses of action for management.

Management Between Private and Public Value: a Megatrend

Many sectors and fields of activity originally characterized by a public mandate to provide services have been deregulated or even outsourced of the public sphere in order to remain competitive in an environment transformed by globalization and market liberalization. As a result, the state is increasingly becoming a "guarantor state" (Schedler 2000). Instead of performing the necessary public services itself for the population, it ensures that the necessary service level is "guaranteed" by commissioning services or public procurement (Schedler and Proeller 2006). For Switzerland, areas formerly covered by state services were structured in a five-ring model based on proximity to the state or the market (Figure 1).

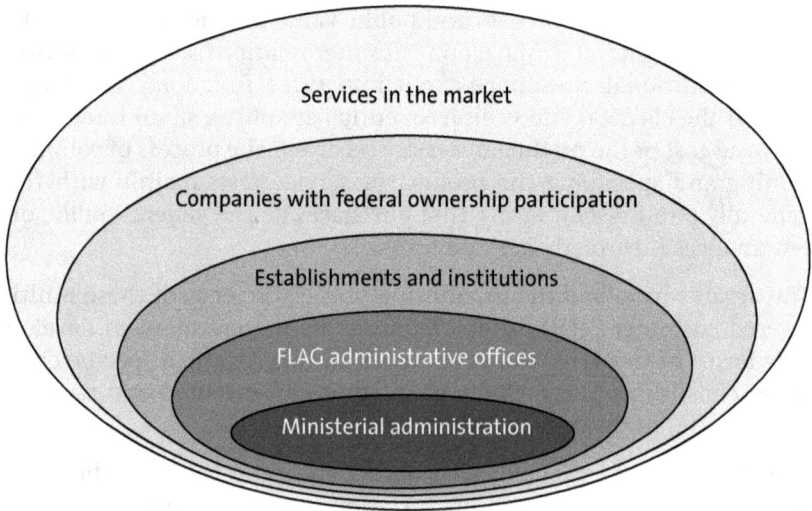

Figure 1: Model of sovereign activities in Switzerland
(Source: Lienhard & Kettiger 2011; FLAG = Management with service commission and global budget)

A core administrative authority should carry out activities only when they concern sovereign activities in the narrow sense, such as law enforcement with decisions in the form of contestable rulings. Organizations in the healthcare sector, such as hospitals, or in public transportation, such as the Swiss Railways, are now managed as independent companies, but with sole or partial state ownership. Many services such as emergency and security services are now procured on the market. In this sense, an ever-increasing part of the services formerly provided under hierarchical, state-controlled management are now shifting towards the market.

Contrary to that trend, the financial crises and subsequent sovereign crises, due in large part to the globalization of financial markets, resulted in many industries previously operating entirely in the private sector being forced to accept government aid. Through multiple effects of globalization – such as feedback effects on labor markets or the natural environment, but also the general trend towards a greater need for protection and public order on the part of the population resulting from increased prosperity – the overall regulatory influence of the state is becoming more prominent in more and more sectors. This applies not only, as described above, to banks and financial institutions, but is also spreading to a widening range of formerly private-sector products. To that effect, an increasing number of sectors are moving away from purely market-driven behavior towards a logic and management more typical of the public sector. To maintain sales and profits, it is becoming increasingly important not only to reach end customers through marketing, but also to seek to influence regulatory authorities and public-sector customers through policymakers.

To predict the future situation of an industry exposed to the conflicting forces of the market and the state, it is helpful to understand the drivers of regulation. Some of these influences may be summarized as follows:

Societal reasons, above all increasing prosperity, which the public wishes to have protected. The fragmentation of society through differences in income and wealth is also resulting in a transformation of traditional values. What was once anchored in traditional notions of values or as morality is now being called into question through different lifestyle concepts and a wider range of choices. If the role of the middle class as a stronghold of values and moderation is changing (see Münkler 2010), then more external guidelines are needed, defined through regulations, for example in the area of leisure services or the consumption of alcohol, tobacco, etc. In addition, ageing societies subject to rapid, externally imposed changes, frequently attempt to control the dynamic of change by regulating aspects still under their control to maintain their prosperity. Expressed in terms of system theory, what is involved is the balance between stabilizing and dynamic elements (see Ashby's Law).

An explanation in political science terms for increasing regulation is the effect of crises and shocks. Each crisis results in new regulations:

For example, global illnesses result in tighter hygiene regulations. In the wake of each new regulation and each new law institutions are set up to operate them. Such institutions and regulations are extremely difficult to eliminate after a crisis is over (see Brecht's Law).

Globalization is among the important economic reasons for increasing regulations. Deregulation practically always implies a further regulation of market conditions – for which regulatory authorities are established. For example, the deregulation of the electric power market in Switzerland led to a flood of laws and ordinances, and of course also resulted in the establishment of the regulatory authority, ElCom (the Swiss Electricity Commission). Each regulation or new law requires refinements, amendments, and then, in turn, further regulations to block efforts to evade their provisions. A typical example is accounting standards: New regulations aimed at transparency and objective information primarily inspire those concerned to look for creative ways of getting around them.

Economists also attribute the increasing regulatory density to industry interests. According to theories of political economy (see Downs et. al. 1957), the interests of well-organized producers prevail over heterogeneous consumer interests because the prospect of profits makes it profitable to invest in lobbying, whereas the costs of information and participation in the political process are rarely worthwhile for the individual citizen. In an unregulated, open market, it is usually possible to earn only modest profits. Life is much more profitable in a market fenced off with regulatory barriers to entry and red tape. It is no accident that industry lobbyists are becoming more numerous in every center of government. Supranational regulators such as the EU are actually even more attractive objects of lobbyist attention due to the greater range of their rulings and regulations (Olson et. al. 1982).

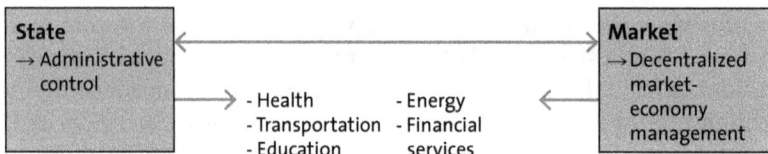

Figure 2: Management between the state and the market
(Source: Authors' own representation, with reference to Bieger, Gross, Laesser 2011:339)

Against this backdrop, we can postulate an actual convergence: It is becoming increasingly common for purely state-owned companies and organizations to be exposed to market conditions, at least to some extent; at the same time, increasing numbers of companies that previously operated in a strictly market-economy environment are subject to the logic of the state, i.e. the public sector, at least in some parts of their operations (see Figure 2). In the future, the degree to which a company or industry is affected by the logic of the state will be determined by the extent to which the drivers described above come into play. This will result in differing levels of regulatory density along the market-state continuum, depending on the sector.

The main differences between management in a pure public-sector operation as compared with a company oriented towards the private sector / market are reflected chiefly in the different customer and stakeholder groups and the importance of these groups. This also results in different goals for an organization or company, and in that context, also in different rationalities (Rüegg-Stürm 2011).

Importance of Stakeholders and Customer Groups

Purely public-sector companies are financed entirely with public resources. In extreme cases, customer satisfaction may be very poor, and the amount of service provided to customers may be low or negligible. As long as the service is deemed necessary and meaningful by the general public and in particular by politicians, it will continue to be financed and, if need be, customers are forced to consume it. The focus of management in this type of "public organization" is thus almost exclusively on ensuring its reputation and legitimacy in the eyes of the general public and policymakers.

By contrast, a company operating entirely in the private sector must generate sufficient value to ensure cohesion among all stakeholders (Rüegg-Stürm 2004) and, thus, naturally earn adequate returns as a basis for satisfying current and deferred customer needs. To achieve this objective, services are offered in accordance with customer wishes to the extent that this is possible and profitable in the regulatory environment.

Management in areas between the state and the market needs both of those forms of logic. The concept of the traditional customer splits, generally into three functions (see Figure 3). On the one hand, users must be satisfied through good performance, which in this case means meeting the needs of end consumers. In many cases, the users must cover at least a portion of the necessary revenues or the related costs, for instance through the fares paid to public transportation companies or tuition fees at universities.

Orderer in the form of state authorities or commissions define the type and volume of services to be provided. In the area of public transportation, compensation agreements are signed with public transportation authorities to define timetables, the fleet of rolling stock, and thus the capacity. In education, the education ministries define the courses of study and the associated capacities to be offered. For these authorities, a public value must be created as the sum of the personal value to the customer and the contributions to state policy objectives.

The services are financed by the general public through mandatory fees and taxes. If the public no longer acknowledges the legitimacy of a service, it will lose its political support, which will have an impact on the entity that orders it and on the orders placed. In organizations operating between the state and the market, the management must therefore spend a more or less substantial portion of their time for public communications and efforts to maintain the reputation and justification of the services produced.

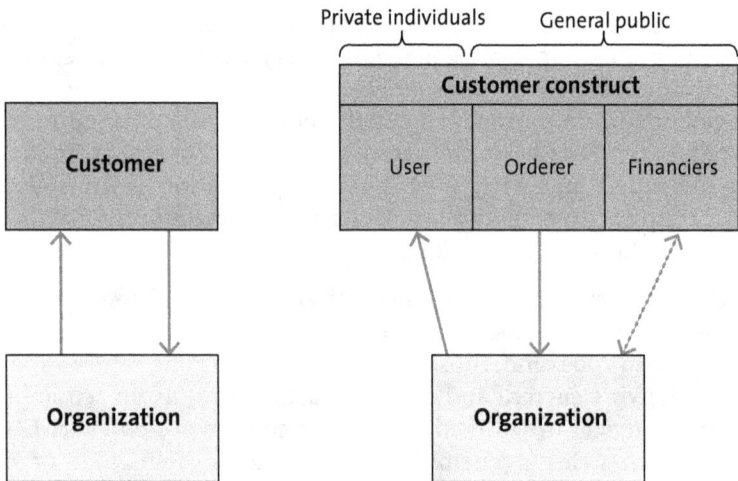

Figure 3: Customer relationships between private and public value

Accordingly, for some time now marketing experts have been discussing the multi-dimensional challenge of engaging in marketing for end users, on the one hand, and, on the other, attempting to influence, via metamarketing – which is, in principle, stakeholder-specific marketing (see Hult, Mena, Ferrell and Ferrell 2011) – the public and, through the public, policymakers, and thus the conditions for delivering the services as well as the buyers.

Public versus Private Value

Because of these differences in the significance of stakeholders and target groups, the expectations for a company with regard to value creation and public reputation vary. A company operating purely within the market must primarily generate private value in the form of customer value for the target group and company value for the owners. The more a company is not only subject to purely market economy management, but also state management as well, the greater the need will be to generate public value. In the same context, value contributed to the general public plays a role. The following diagram uses the example of an airline to illustrate conflicting forces between public value and private value.

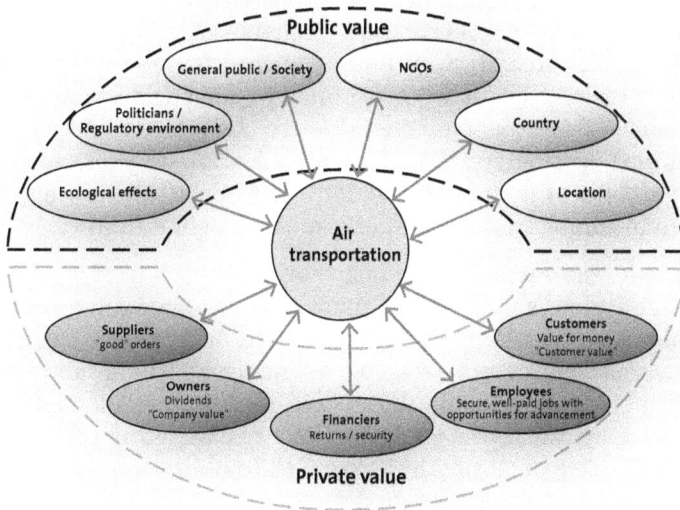

Figure 4: Public versus private value

Differing Rationalities

The differing values to be generated and the differing objectives are the result of different rationalities within an organization. Rationality can be defined as "a specific way of thought, speech and action that follows a consistent and logical pattern. It is a filter that influences the perception of the environment and provides the construction logic of an individual's or group's very own reality." (Schedler and Gross 2011). When a group is primarily geared towards securing its legitimacy in public space, it is shaped by other values and also through a different culture. Identical facts are seen differently. In the area of human resources policy, for instance, the different rationality may increasingly result in personnel decisions no longer being made only from a business management standpoint, and instead being governed above all by the logic of society as a whole, i.e. a communicative logic (public impact). The effects of this change extend as far as the cultural artifacts of the companies – language, symbols, and processes.

As described above, in a company operating between the state and the market, we can assume that customers are multidimensional because the functions of customers are split into the subfunctions of users, orderers and financiers. This is also reflected in a "more complex" manner of thinking and acting on the part of the institutions. There is an increase in the number of target parameters, and business targets such as customer value and company value are complemented by societal and political parameters. Within an organization, this also results in different modes of thought and action – and hence rationalities – that are often in competition or even in conflict with one another.

For example, the part of the company or institution in direct contact with end customers may wish to maximize customer value, so that a classical marketing rationality will dominate. By contrast, the part of a company concerned with securing financing and maintaining contacts with policymakers and buyers will be dominated by a political logic. This may result in a value void due to conflicting rationalities, and thus to a lack of clarity in company policy.

Concretely, the orientation according to different objectives and rationalities has effects on the management of employees and the incentives offered to them. Areas more concerned with end customers and customer-value incentive systems can be operated on the individual level on the basis of quantitative targets. This is less feasible, however, in areas oriented towards public value and the public space, largely due to the diverse goals pursued. For similar reasons, the share of variable compensation is also lower in companies and organizational units positioned closer to state management. Through the specific compensation and promotion systems, there are interesting feedback mechanisms related to culture and thought structures. For example, companies operating in the public space are likely to attract employees with different motivation structures than purely market-driven companies, which in turn will affect the culture.

Accordingly, the particular challenges facing the management in organizations between the state and the market consist of:

- dealing with a large number of stakeholders and customer groups: direct customers in the form of end customers and indirect customers in the form of parties ordering the services as well as the general public, which pays for them.

- coping with complex systems of objectives between private and public value, and

- dealing with the sometimes competing rationalities that require different and occasionally mutually contradictory management instruments.

The University of St.Gallen Between the State and the Market

Using the example of the University of St.Gallen (HSG), the following section now discusses these challenges with a view to present tools and possible courses of action. The University of Economics, Social Sciences, Law and International Affairs was jointly established in 1898 by representatives of the business and political community. It enjoys a long tradition of actively fostering entrepreneurship, manifested in particular in the approximately 35 research facilities and institutes as well as the Executive School. In line with this, it has the highest quota of self-financing of any public university in the German-speaking countries, with the state contributing just over 50 percent of the total budget. The university has about 8,000 students (including the activities related to further education) and 2,000 staff members, and is thus comparable in scale to a mid-sized corporation. With the autonomy granted to it decades ago, the HSG successfully operates between the state and the market.

Customers and Stakeholders – between Financing of Positive Outcomes and Repayment

The HSG performs research work, carries out teaching under the Bologna system, offers continuing education programs and services, and also conducts applied research. Services and continuing education are offered on the market on a break-even basis. Research is financed through third-party state funding, and also through funding from the private sector. The Bologna part of the teaching has an interesting form of hybrid financing. As a public university, the HSG is prohibited by Swiss law (particularly by the Inter-cantonal University Agreement) from charging tuition fees covering all costs. The Canton of St.Gallen, which supports and owns the university, is committed through its management of the university to provide basic funding to subsidize educational services. The federal government and the cantons in which the students reside, finance the studies of "their" students through designated payments. The annual tuition fees paid directly by students, as beneficiaries, currently amount to 2,400 francs for Swiss students (2013). For foreign students there is a non-financed remainder due to the absence of the contributions from a home canton. Consequently, they must pay 4,252 francs per year. Students personally and directly finance approximately 15 to 26 percent of the cost of their studies.

The objective from an economic standpoint is to use the publicly funded contributions to finance a good with positive externalities to ensure that a sufficient quantity of this good is produced (Hanushek and Kimko 2000). The universities are thus in a situation that is for instance comparable, structurally if not materially, with that of public transportation or public health providers. In their case, too, the production and/or consumption of services is subsidized by the public sector in the pursuit of higher policy objectives (environmental targets, the aim of creating social balance and enabling participation in society in the area of public transportation, health-policy objectives in the area of health institutions) and to pay for positive externalities.

The HSG thus relies to a large extent on securing legitimacy and political support in the public sphere, primarily in the Canton of St.Gallen, but also in Switzerland as a whole. Tuition fees for students at the HSG, which is among Europe's leading business universities, are – compared with similar universities abroad – inexpensive, as it is a subsidized service. Consequently, there is a very strong demand, particularly from Europe. As a result, the number of places for foreign students has been limited to 25 percent since the 1960s.

Against this backdrop, interesting challenges arise: For example, due to the large and rapid increase in the size of the student body, marketing does not primarily serve the purpose of attracting students. Instead, it plays a central role in maintaining the university's reputation and building the brand, which is becoming increasingly important in international competition. Another objective is to employ target group-specific marketing to ensure the desired diversity among students and, for example, to increase the share of students from non-German speaking countries.

Conversely, information and communication activities are very important in the public sphere. For example, the university leadership conducts regular dialogue with the parties represented in the cantonal parliament. The university also recently began scheduling annual press conferences open to the public. This direct contact with the general public and the visibility of the university, for example by maintaining and expanding public events on campus, is also highly significant. One of the further aims of the media activity is to report about the university openly and transparently. An increasingly important aspect is issue management, with which the university attempts to be proactive in identifying and addressing critical issues.

The public sphere in which the university seeks legitimacy consists mainly of the region. Consequently, the emphasis on its regional roots is an important aspect deliberately embedded in a regionalization concept. The concept rests on three pillars: creating encounters, offering platforms and fostering knowledge and technology transfers with regional companies. Opportunities for encounters are brought about through the organization of regional events, a new event series, HSG Life, and an innovative format designed to create a discussion forum within the region. Another important aspect is raising the awareness of employees and graduates who function as ambassadors for the university in the region. Platforms are offered through public lectures and visitor programs (for example, an open-house day). Maintaining the campus as a publicly accessible space for culture and dialogue is of great importance to the university leadership. Through public programs offering events and lectures outside the university's core area – for example in theology and the humanities – the university also tries to reach broad target groups. In the area of knowledge and technology transfer, the university carries out pro bono projects, opens up access to international networks for the region, and hosts specialized international congresses there.

In connection with these activities, new media are steadily gaining in importance. The conventional website must meet the needs of direct users through information and tools for bookings and registration. However, as a public institution the university must offer more. Consequently, extensive information is offered on the university and its strategy as well as the discourse taking place there. To create public customer value, a sophisticated, widely accessible research database has been set up. Well in advance of the campus expansion project, the university is developing an internet platform to inform and communicate with the public, years before the necessary referendum takes place.

Communication as a public institution in social networks is especially important, in particular for the early identification of public concerns and for dialogue, for end users and the general public. In this area, the HSG plays a leading role. In a comparative report on Swiss universities in June 2012 (Gielas 2012), it was highlighted as a notable exception with a well-structured concept. The HSG has established a presence on the three social media portals with the biggest reach: Facebook, YouTube, and Twitter. In each of them, the university has set up color-coded thematic sections to address specific target groups. This makes it easy for prospective or current students and researchers, for example, to look for the information they need and to contact the university.

Public versus Private Value

For the measurement of private value, there are established methods and instruments. Definitions, including operational implementation and computation models, have been developed both for the measurement of customer value – in the sense of the value to the customer (see Bieger and Belz 2006) – and for the company value, which is important to the owner (see Spremann and Dietmar 2010). There are also cause-and-effect models showing the interrelationships between the various forms of private value (see Figure 5).

Number of customers

Perceived costs

Willingness to pay

Revenues

Risks

Customer benefit

Perceived benefits

Customer value

Customer loyalty

Operational data

Free cash flow

Company value

Investments

Growth

←--→

Utilization of customer value
(through sale of products and services and/or sale of customer contact)

Utilization of company value

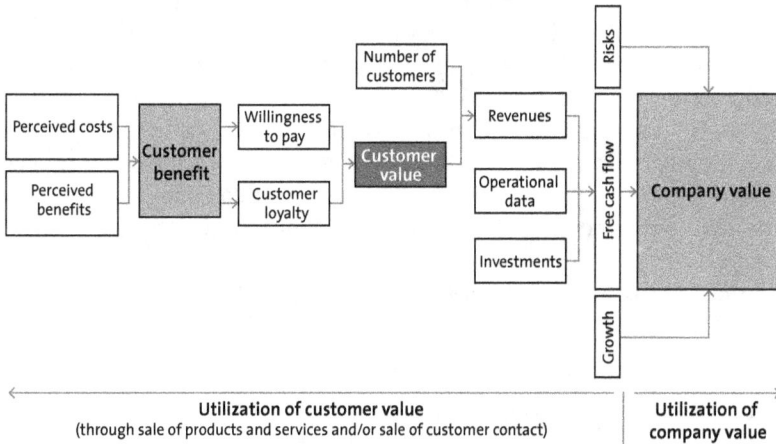

Figure 5: Relationship between customer value and company value
(Source: Bieger and Reinhold (2011:49), with reference to Matzler (2000))

For public value there are various approaches. For example, environmental, ecological and social accounting methods have been developed (for definitions see Capaul and Steingruber 2010; Dierkes, Marz and Antal 2002, among other sources) with corresponding classifications and benchmarking systems. On the basis of the concept of "sustainability" (see the Brundtland Report, 1987, among other sources) or a "triple bottom line", effects in the natural, social, and economic environment are measured.

The HSG has been managing its impact on the natural environment for a long time: For example, individual motor vehicle traffic is controlled using a trip-based model, and a parking management system is in place. Since 2011, the university has applied this system to motorcycles as well, which is unique in Switzerland. In a preliminary study for a carbon footprint audit, one of the biggest sources of emissions was shown to be business and congress travel. This is where environmental goals (minimizing such travel) collide with the objectives of fostering the growth of young talent and the strategic development of the university's profile.

The societal and economic effects of the HSG are presented in the Regionalization Report, which has been published twice. In addition to the direct economic effects (contributions to regional GDP and purchasing power), the report also examines the effects in the areas of knowledge and skills transfer as well as contributions to society and to the region's cultural life. For example, the 2012 Regionalization Report showed that the value generated by the HSG for the St.Gallen agglomeration amounts to five times the transfer payments of the Canton. It is important for all those concerned that the results of these studies on public value are not used solely for communication with the outside world. Otherwise the search for legitimacy might soon be unmasked as a teleological approach (Ulrich and Breuer 2004). To secure long-term legitimacy, the objective is always – as part of a deontological approach – to take into account the reasonable concerns of the stakeholder groups. Consequently, the data from reports of this kind must always be used within the framework of a constant dialogue and continuous process of improvement.

Managing Cultures and Rationalities

As mentioned above, some areas of the university delivering certain services cover all their costs while competing on the market with other international universities and even with private-sector providers of knowledge and services. This is the case in particular for the further education activities of the large institutes and the Executive School. Other parts of the university, for instance educational activities under the Bologna Programs, are financed to a large extent through public subsidies or also perform a regional public service function, as in the case of the public information mission.

This inevitably results in a closer alignment with markets and a competition-oriented culture in the privately financed parts of the university. Conversely, the publicly financed (core) area of the university must rely to some extent on an egalitarian culture to secure cooperative relationships, in particular in research. Many key individuals with the university operate in both cultures. That is the case, for instance, when a professor is employed by the core university, but at the same time is responsible for a department at the Executive School or for an institute.

A prerequisite for the cohesion of the university and for the smooth functioning of the synergetic exchange between research, teaching and continuing education – in a sense, the university's "integrated business model" – is that all those involved must identify with the various areas. Extreme solutions, for example in the form of incentive systems or also with regard to artifacts, or wording clearly indicative of individual cultures and rationalities, must be avoided. The objective of the overall organization and the contributions of the individual areas must be understandable and transparent to everyone.

Conclusion and Outlook

More and more companies are operating between market-economy and state management. As a result, the customer relationship, the marketing and the overall company management are becoming more multilayered. With the definition of the customer divided into three subfunctions – user, orderer, and financier – it is not only the customer relationship that becomes more complex and multidimensional. The company or the institution, exposed to the conflicting forces of private and public value, is shaped by sometimes differing and mutually contradictory organizational cultures and/or rationalities.

In the concrete cooperation and communication with the various customers and stakeholders (see Figure 6), whose functions frequently overlap and influence one another, the decisive factors are consistency and credibility. Messages intended for end users must not contradict those sent to the general public, who pay for the services, simply because these groups overlap. This is particularly valid against the backdrop of modern communication technologies such as social media, which make information and the communication channels through which it spreads both instantaneous and multilayered.

Organization between the state and the market

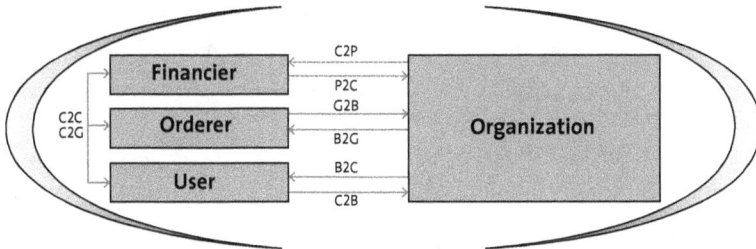

Purely market-oriented organization

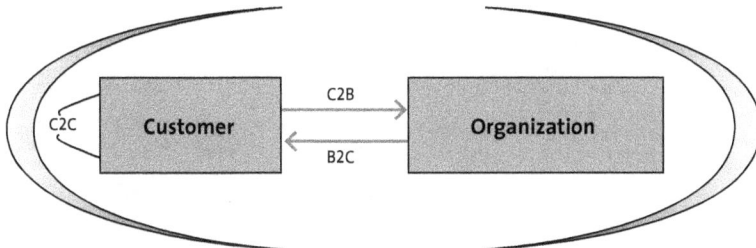

Figure 6: Communication relationships

Bibliography

Bieger, T. Rüegg-Sturm, J., and Von Rohr, T. "Strukturen und Ansätze einer Gestaltung von Beziehungskonfigurationen – das Konzept Geschäftsmodell." In: Bieger, T. (editor); Bickoff, N. (editor); Caspar, R. (editor); zu Knyphausen-Aufseß, D. (editor); Reding, J. (editor). Zukünftige Geschäftsmodelle: Konzept und Anwendung in der Netzökonomie. Berlin: Springer, 2012: 35-61.

Bieger, T., and Belz, C. Customer-Value. Kundenvorteile schaffen Unternehmensvorteile. Second printing. Landsberg am Lech: mi-Fachverlag, Redline GmbH, 2006.

Bieger, T., and Reinhold, P. "Das wertbasierte Geschäftsmodell – Ein aktualisierter Strukturi-erungsansatz." In: Bieger, T. (editor); zu Knyphausen-Aufsess, D. (editor); Krys,C. (editor). Innovative Geschäftsmodelle. Konzeptionelle Grundlagen, Gestaltungsfelder und unterne-hmerische Praxis. Berlin: Springer, 2011: 13-70.

Bieger, T., Gross, M., and Laesser, C. "Geschäftsmodelle zwischen Public und Private Value – Das Fallbeispiel der Schweizerischen Bundesbahnen (SBB)." In: Bieger, T. (editor); zu Knyphausen-Aufsess, D. (editor); Krys,C. (editor): Innovative Geschäftsmodelle. Konzeptio-nelle Grundlagen, Gestaltungsfelder und unternehmerische Praxis. Berlin: Springer, 2011: 331-351.

Capaul, R., and Steingruber, D. Betriebswirtschaft verstehen. Das St. Galler Management Modell. Oberentfelden: Sauerlander, 2010.

Dierkes, M., Marz, L., and Antal, A. B.: Sozialbilanzen. Konzeptioneller Kern und diskursive Karriere einer zivilgesellschaftlichen Innovation. Berlin: WZB, 2002.

Downs, A. "An Economic Theory of Political Action in a Democracy." Journal of Political Theory (1957), Vol. 65. No.

Gielas, A. "Neue Facebook Freunde." Neue Zürcher Zeitung. June 11, 2012: 41.

Granovetter, M. "Economic Action and Social Structure: The Problem of Embeddedness." American Journal of Sociology (1985), Vol. 91. No. 3:481.

Hanushek, E.A., and Kimko, D.D. "Schooling, labor force quality, and the growth of nations." American Economic Review(2000),Vol. 90. No. 5: 1184-1208.

Hult, G.T.M., Mena, J.A., Ferrell, O.C., and Ferrell, L.. "Stakeholder marketing: a definition and conceptual framework." Academy of Marketing Science 1, 2011: 44-65.

Munkler, H. Mitte und Mass. Der Kampf um die richtige Ordnung. Berlin: Rowohlt, 2010.

Olson, M. "The Rise and Decline of Nations. Economic Growth, Stagflation, and Social Rigid-ities." New Haven: Yale University Press, 1982.

Rüegg-Sturm, J. "Zur Rationalität multirationalen Managements." IMPacts 1, 2011: 10-13.

Rüegg-Sturm, J. "Das neue St. Galler Management-Modell." In: Dubs, Rolf (editor); Euler, Dieter (editor); Rüegg-Sturm, Johannes (editor); Wyss, Christina (editor): Einführung in die Managementlehre. Band 1. Bern: Haupt, 2004: 65-134.

Schedler, K., and Gross, M. "Rationalitäten in Verwaltung und Politik." In: IMPacts 1, 2011: 7-9.

Schedler, K., and Proeller, I. New Public Management. third printing. Bern: Haupt, 2006.

Schedler, K. "Gewährleistungsstaat – eine Konzeption für den Staat im New Public Management." Berliner Debatte INITIAL 1 (2000). No. 3: 5-18.

Spremann, K., and Ernst, D. Unternehmensbewertung: Grundlagen und Praxis. International Management and Finance (IMF). Second printing. Munich: Oldenbourg, 2010.

Ulrich, P., and Breuer, M. Wirtschaftsethik im philosophischen Diskurs: Begründung und "Anwendung" praktischen Orientierungswissens. Würzburg: Königshausen, 2004.

The University

The University of St.Gallen was established in 1898 as a business academy. Today it has six schools: the School of Management, the School of Economics and Political Science, the Law School, the School for Humanities and Social Science, the School of Finance and the Executive School. The university's 32 institutes and research facilities are active in research, consulting and continuing education, and are largely self-financed. Today the university, including its continuing education activities, has approximately 8,000 students.

For more information: http://www.unisg.ch/en/Universitaet

Summary

As a result of globalization and the associated opening of markets to broader competition, many companies are operating amid the conflicting forces of the market and the state.

More and more companies that find themselves in this situation face the challenge of generating private value for their direct customers and owners (customer and company value) while generating public value (contributions to public objectives).

A distinction must be made in this regard for marketing to end customers and metamarketing. The latter operates on the conditions governing the production of the service – the public and policymakers – and on the buyers of the service. A company operating entirely under market conditions must primarily generate private value for its owners and customers; state-managed company must generate public value. Nevertheless, the various areas overlap and influence one another.

Customers are becoming multidimensional; Customer relations, marketing and management are becoming more multi-layered.

Communication with the various target groups – especially via social media – must be coordinated. A message intended for end users cannot run counter to the message directed to the general public; that ensures consistency and credibility on the part of the company.

Epilogue

Over the past four decades, information and communication technology has changed our economy and society. The ways we conduct both our business and private lives – for example, the gathering, storage and use of information, or how we shop and communicate with one another – have been transformed. And the discussion about copyright law on the Internet, for example, clearly illustrates issues related to information and communication technologies are penetrating more deeply all the time into our political and social processes. Our world has been changed by IT before: Fifty years ago, with the arrival of the first computers in companies; 30 years ago, when the personal computer started to become commonplace; 20 years ago, with the start of the relentless advance of the Internet; and 10 years ago, when electronic commerce emerged. But when these transformations were occurring, nobody could have anticipated the far-reaching changes we face today. And all experts agree: We are nowhere close to reaching the end of the series of transformation processes triggered by information and communication technologies.

This book is proof that the issues related to the digital revolution are well established on the agenda of the people in charge of major multinational corporations. In their contributions to this book, the 17 CEOs, top managers and leading researchers show that they are paying close attention to questions of digitization and networking. The top managers are certainly aware that very few companies could stay in business today without IT. But developments in just the past few years, with Web 2.0 (the Internet with a user-feedback channel) and Web 3.0 (the Internet of Things and Services) and the arrival of mobile computing in our everyday lives, show that structures, processes and business models are being transformed yet again. It will be important for companies to take advantage of these opportunities and play a role in shaping them.

The ongoing process of "consumerization" of hardware and software is leading to changes in the expectations of customers and employees regarding information procurement, communication and interactions. More and more users are integrating information and communication technologies into their everyday lives. This may be part of the reason why new media are now more firmly established in the business-to-consumer (B2C) segment than in business-to-business (B2B). But even companies with a B2B focus are becoming more digitized and networked with one another. In this regard, the main goal appears to be keeping up with the pace of digitization and networking in the private sphere.

The data generated by customers, products and services as a result of digitization are particularly important. To gain and protect competitive advantages, it will become more important for companies to utilize internal processes in structuring, networking, analyzing, protecting and using this data. Another outcome of the networking of our society is an increase in the amount of data generated through relationships between customers, products, services and companies. This is resulting in relationships and cooperation between people that would otherwise never come about, and the emergence of products and services that could not otherwise exist. At the same time, the new feedback channels are creating opportunities to make improvements in accordance with customers' needs and wants. New technologies and processes now make it possible to collect data generated at different locations in real time and make it accessible at a central location. Key issues pertaining to the ownership and right of use of these remain unresolved. This area still harbors unrealized potential.

The use of social media by companies is now not only taken for granted – it's practically indispensable. And that is true not only for communication with the "digital natives" – the generation that never knew a world without the Internet. It seems practically inconceivable not to take part in this new form of communication. Another consideration: For company decision makers, the digitized, networked world means a loss of control, because it is a world ruled by its own set of rules and laws. Companies that antagonize both existing and potential customers can expect to take a beating on the Internet, with often unrelenting criticism – and should be ready to face the consequences for the company's reputation. By contrast, companies that utilize social media in a targeted manner and are willing to profit from the social revolution of the 21st century will have the opportunity to engage in a direct dialog with their current and prospective customers – or even involve users in the corporate innovations process via methods such as crowdsourcing.

The digitization and networking of our society has yet to reach its apex. The boundaries separating the material world from the virtual one have long since become blurred. The chapters of this book span a wide range of insights, ideas and specific courses of action for managers in the digitized and networked world. They address various aspects of the relationships between customers, products and companies – from yesterday, today and tomorrow. Against the backdrop of the rising dominance of information technology in our everyday lives, it remains to be seen whether we will reach the point of "overrationalization" – where data will allow us to calculate and thus to predict our emotions – a point in which there will no longer be any room for serendipity and coincidence in our professional and personal lives.

Acknowledgements

We would like to thank the following co-authors and contributors to this book:

Carlye Adler

Andreas Büdel, Siemens AG

Dustin Figge, arvato AG

Erica L. Gingerich

Virginia Gomes dos Santos, AXA Konzern AG

Alexander Gulden, ThyssenKrupp AG

Wolf D. Hartmann, ifi Institute for Innovation Management

Hartmut Hasse, BASF SE

Achim Kinter, tabula rasa

Karsten Kroos, ThyssenKrupp AG

Uwe Kattwinkel, TUI AG

Thomas Lueb, BASF SE

Klaus Markus, arvato AG

Christine Maukel, AUDI AG

Jim O'Meara

Toni Melfi, AUDI AG

Caroline Neuenfeld, Deutsche Telekom AG

Jennifer Prinz, Deutsche Telekom AG

Dominik Reinartz, AXA Konzern AG

Barbara Rohner, University of St.Gallen

Jan Runau, adidas AG

Dietmar Scherer, AUDI AG

Andreas Schmidt, Deutsche Telekom AG

Richard Tigges, AUDI AG

Warren Turner

Clemens Trautmann, Axel Springer AG

Christophe Vetterli, University of St.Gallen

Klaus Westermeier

Gernot Wolf, arvato AG

Chrstian Zabel, Deutsche Telekom AG

Saskia Zelt, University of St.Gallen

Glossary

ACTA

Anti-Counterfeiting Trade Agreement: A multinational treaty to establish a set of international standards to fight product piracy and for the enforcement of intellectual property rights. At the beginning of July 2012, ratification of the treaty was rejected by a large majority in the European Parliament.

Accounting standards

A set of internationally recognized regulations created by the International Accounting Standards Board (IASB) determining rules and principles for accounting and financial reporting by companies and enterprises.

Add-ons

The expansion or enhancement of an existing computer program via the addition of smaller ancillary programs. This practice allows for more personalization of the computing experience and convenience for the user.

Advertorial

An advertisement that mimics the design and layout of a journalistic article or editorial format. According to German law regulating the media (Presserecht), an advertorial must be conspicuously identified as such to readers.

Aggregator

A program, vendor or service provider that gathers and reformats media content for distribution to a specific target audience.

Alpha blogger

The blogging version of the alpha male or female. The term is controversial even among bloggers.

API

Application Programming Interface: A program component that allows software programs to communicate with each other and the system.

App

The common abbreviation for "application" now popularized for smartphone or tablet applications that can be purchased online and directly downloaded to a device.

App Store

The portal created by computer maker Apple for the sale of computer programs and applications intended for use exclusively on Apple devices.

Assisted living / Ambient assisted living

A term for intelligent concepts – especially electronic systems, products and services – that help to simplify activities in day-to-day life. These are concepts and products that can be utilized to provide support for people with physical disabilities and also to enhance the functionality of everyday products, for example by integrating a digital "to-do list" into a regular mirror.

Augmented reality

Augmented reality is the computer-aided expansion of our ability to perceive reality. This information can address all modes of human sensory perception. However, augmented reality is often understood as the mere visual representation of information, for example, the use of computer-generated information or superimposed text or graphic effects to supplement images or videos. Augmented reality is employed in the broadcast of soccer games, for example, with the use of graphics (circles and lines) to indicate the distance between a player to the goal during a free kick.

Beta version

The unfinished version of a computer program or website which is made accessible to the public ahead of the product or site launch to allow as many users as possible to participate in the testing process to identify and address potential problems or bugs.

Big data

Extremely large amounts of data that can be processed either not at all or only inadequately using standard programs or tools because the quantity of data is too large to gather, save and analyze. Companies use big-data analysis to gain a competitive edge.

BITKOM

The Bundesverband Informationswirtschaft, Telekommunikation und neue Medien e.V., Germany's Federal Association for Information Technology, Telecommunications and New Media. The association was founded in October 1999 in Berlin, and represents more than 1,700 companies across Germany, among them 1,100 direct members of BITKOM.

Blue tech

A popular term, especially in the automotive industry, referring to energy-efficient alternatives to regular diesel or gasoline engines that produce either no or very low emissions, and which therefore contribute to an overall reduction in air pollution and noise pollution. "Blue tech" is an allusion to the Earth as a "blue planet," and the term is often used synonymously with clean tech and green tech, but is less interchangeable with the term "bio tech."

Blog / Web log

A blog (abbreviation for "web log") is a website that provides coverage of and commentary on specific topics, is often presented in a diary or daily log format and is run by at least one person – the blogger or web logger.

Blogosphere

The entire online blogging world. The community of bloggers and their blogs as a new kind of cultural/informational area of life providing a forum for the exchange of ideas and opinions.

The Bologna Process

The ratification of the Bologna Declaration in 1999 by 29 European education ministers put in motion a series of reforms to make European higher education more compatible and comparable. The main goal of the Bologna Process: To increase mobility, employability and the ability to compete at the international level for Europe's students, a goal that will also be supported by new forms of electronic education and e-learning practices.

Business-to-Administration (B2A)

A term describing business relationships between companies and enterprises and government or regulatory entities.

Business-to-Business (B2B)

A term describing business relationships between companies and enterprises or retailers and distributors.

Business-to-Consumer (B2C)

A term describing business relationships between companies and enterprises with consumers, customers and end users.

Cause marketing

A type of marketing in which "for-profit" companies cooperate with charities or other non-profit organizations, in which a company pledges either a specific donation or percentage of sales for a charity or a cause.

Carbon footprint

The amount of CO_2 (carbon dioxide) emissions produced by a specific activity or through the various stages of a product's lifecycle (from the mining of raw materials through to production, marketing, the use phase and waste disposal), including the environmental impact of these emissions.

Clean tech

Clean tech ("clean technology") refers to a new way of doing business turned into a major trend by investment bankers following the collapse of the dot-com bubble at the start of the century. An umbrella term with an ever-expanding definition to describe technologies such as solar energy, wind power, biofuels and biomass, energy-efficient construction, clean mobility and logistics, intelligent power networks and mobile power supplies through to water treatment technology.

Cloud computing

The network-based supply, utilization and billing of IT services with clearly defined technical interfaces and protocols. Possible services cover all areas of IT, and may range from infrastructure-related services such as computing power and storage through to comprehensive software solutions.

Community

Also called a net community or Internet community. A term for a group of Internet users.

Computer-Aided Design (CAD)

The use of computer software to create technical drawings and designs. Today, special CAD programs can be used to manufacture complex 3-D models.

Computer-Aided Engineering (CAE)

General term for all types of computer-based engineering processes.

Conversion optimization

General term for all methods for increasing the conversion rate (i.e. the percentage of visitors who become customers) of websites and in particular online shops.

Copyright

A copyright grants a creator of intellectual property both legal protection and the exclusive right to use, distribute and sell this intellectual property.

Corporate blog

A blog operated by a company or enterprise and used for both external and internal communication purposes.

Corporate transparency

Management term for efforts to bring openness and transparency to corporate hierarchies and the frequently closed doors of corporations. The term was popularized in German-speaking markets through the book by Volker Klenk and Daniel J. Hanke, Corporate Transparency: Wie Unternehmen im Glashaus-Zeitalter Wettbewerbsvorteile erzielen, published in 2009.

Corporate Wording

Corporate policy on language or wording which, alongside other corporate identity guidelines (such as the logo and corporate colors), requires consistency in company communications whenever possible for such elements as the spelling of the company name, brands and products, standard company terminology, the use of foreign-language or English terminology, units and abbreviations, as well as compliance with a list of desired and prohibited words.

Creative Commons

Founded in 2001, Creative Commons is a non-profit organization that offers standardized, template-style copyright licenses for free to the public for the publication and dissemination of digital media content.

Customer Relationship Management System (CRM)

A corporate strategy that targets customers and customer satisfaction, supported by specialized CRM software.

Cross selling

Any marketing practice that promotes the sale of products or services that complement one another.

Cross-channel communication

The use of different communication channels for advertising. It is often used by television broadcasters as part of their programming.

Crowdfunding

A new way of financing projects in the works. Funding is collected from a large number of Internet users even in very small amounts. It is frequently used to finance art projects and, more recently, film projects. When a project is successful, investors share the profits.

Crowdsourcing

The practice of outsourcing corporate tasks or processes to the labor and creativity of the masses of Internet users. It stands apart from existing models for the division of labor through the addition of the factor of motivation.

CSR

Abbreviation for Corporate Social Responsibility. This describes voluntary efforts by a company, above and beyond legal requirements, in the interests of sustainable development, but above all the implementation of and compliance with social standards in a company's own operations and those of suppliers, and especially those in developing and emerging economies.

Customer interaction process

The relationships between customers. In the best-case scenario, it means customers talking about their satisfaction with a company; in the worst case it can turn into a "shitstorm."

Customer-To-Customer (C2C)

Term to describe business relationships between end customers (private individuals), for example in private auctions.

Data mining

The use of predominantly statistical and mathematical methods for identifying new patterns in a set of data.

Digital inclusion

An initiative that aims to overcome digital marginalization by fostering worldwide access to digital information and services.

Digital publishing / cross-media publishing

Terms used to describe IT tools that enable the automatic publication of digital content on different media channels.

Digital Rights Management (DRM)

Processes used to control the use and dissemination of digital media, above all music and films but also software and e-books.

Direct bank / Direct banking

A direct bank is a bank without a network of physical branches offering banking services mainly via the postal services in the past, and mainly over the Internet today. Direct banks are subject to the same banking supervision regulations as banks with branches.

Double bottom line

A business performance benchmarking that combines two profitability indicators – financial and social. This approach seeks to achieve the greatest possible social impact combined with (usually subordinate) financial benchmarks (e.g. capital preservation).

DSL

An abbreviation for Digital Subscriber Line. DSL is a way of transmitting data via simple copper cables (i.e. telephone lines). It facilitates fast Internet connections with transfer rates of up to 1,000 Mbit/s.

e-auction

Electronic auction in which items are offered via online auction platforms in B2B, B2C or C2C transactions.

e-bidding

Electronic bidding. Refers to the act of placing bids on B2B auction sites.

e-book

A digitized book. E-books can be downloaded from the Internet and read using a computer or a specialized e-reader device.

Electronic software distribution

The direct sale of digital content (for example, software) via the Internet. No data media (CDs, etc.) are shipped.

Embedding

The practice of adding, or embedding, the digital content of one website into another.

Facebook

A commercial, online social media platform that allows users to create, operate and manage social networks. Half of Facebook's users visit the site and their respective online communities on a daily basis. The site was founded by Mark Zuckerberg in 2004; with 900 million members, it is one of the most visited websites in the world. In May 2012, the company held its initial public offering (IPO).

Face-to-face communication

Human communication between individual as it has been done for ages: Face to face, in the form of verbal and non-verbal communication forms such as talking and gesture – as opposed to virtual communication, which is conducted via media channels such as the Internet, television or telephone.

Feed / news feed

Streams of news on the Internet that enable users to track information on websites without having to visit those sites individually.

Flickr

A website that allows users to upload digital pictures and short videos, accompanied by short descriptions and notes, to share with other users.

Flashmob

A large group of people coordinated via social media sites on the Internet, by e-mail or mobile phones, that appears to materialize out of nowhere (in a flash) to participate in activities or events that look nonsensical to bystanders. Originally a non-political phenomenon; now, however, politically or economically motivated flashmobs – so-called smart-mobs – have emerged.

Folksonomy

A distributed, collaborative practice for categorizing digital information and content using tags, or key words. The tags make it possible to retrieve information at a later time. They are subjectively influenced by the various users. The process operates with no system of rules or defined structure.

Geotagging

The assignment of geographical coordinates to photographs. The coordinates are either added to the photo when it is taken via GPS technology or are later retrieved from a map using specialized software solutions.

Greentech

A general term describing environmental technologies, for example the environmentally friendly and climate-neutral production of energy, improvements in the efficient use of raw materials and other products or the employment of closed and waste-free material cycles.

Greentelligence

A new term describing clean tech and green technologies derived from the combination of "green" and "intelligence." Greentelligence was the slogan for the Hannover Messe 2012.

Greenwashing

Any corporate PR method employed to convey the (undeserved) image of an environmentally friendly or socially responsible company.

Group blog

A blog created and run by more than one author or blogger.

Government 2.0 / e-government

The use of digital information and communications methods within government agencies (federal, state or local) or other state-run institutions – or between such agencies or institutions and private citizens or businesses – with the goal of simplifying and expediting information sharing and communications.

GPS

Global Positioning System. A navigation system that uses satellite communications, originally developed by the U.S. Department of Defense for military purposes. Also used increasingly for non-military and private purposes since the mid-1990s, and especially since the end of signal jamming in 2000.

Hosting

The service offered by Internet or web hosting service providers, including online data storage (web hosting), website databases and e-mail hosting.

ICT

An abbreviation for Information and Communication Technology.

iKiosk

An app offered by publisher Axel Springer that functions as a digital newspaper and magazine shop.

Internet of Things

This term refers to the networking of things and objects via the Internet. Once networked, these objects can independently communicate with one another and execute tasks. In the future, alongside computers and other networking devices, everyday items such as cars, consumer products, power meters, healthcare devices or even articles of clothing will be connected to and controlled via Internet, and will also be able to communicate independently with one another. This will be made possible by tiny microprocessors – often invisible to the human eye and built into objects – that will communicate via radio frequencies.

Internet newsroom

An online tool that allows a company's corporate communications team to utilize social media to provide customers, journalists and other interested parties with company information.

Just-In-Sequence production (JIS)

A concept from procurement logistics. It is an advancement in just-in-time-production, under which the supplier is now responsible not only for delivering goods in the right quantities at the right time, but also in the correct order.

Livestream

The real-time (live) online broadcast (stream) of video or audio data, which can be received and played by users on their own computers.

Long tail principle

Term based on the shape of a graph of sales of a range of products shown in decreasing order of unit sales, with infrequently purchased items on the right. For online sellers with low inventory costs, it may be more profitable to offer these less popular products.

LTE (Long-Term Evolution)

A new wireless data communication standard. It is the successor to UMTS and enables a significantly faster mobile Internet connection. For rural regions without access to DSL, LTE will be an option for providing users with faster Internet connections.

Mapvertising

A specialized form of online marketing that uses online map services such as Google Maps to place digital ads, for example on rooftops in the 2-D or streetview modes.

Mashup

The melding and blending of elements taken from two different websites (for example, interactive maps). The mix or mashup can lead to entirely new and interesting online projects.

Metadata

Data containing information about other data.

Microblogging

A form of blogging in which bloggers publish online messages and posts, generally in 200 characters or less.

Moblog

A term that fuses the words "mobile" and "blog," a moblog is a blog created or managed using a mobile device such as a smartphone.

MP3

An encoding format that allows the compression of audio data to reduce the overall size of stored data. In principle, this compression removes the tones on the higher or lower ends of the range of human hearing. Depending on the degree of data compression, there can be a significant decline in sound quality. MP3 technology is currently the most widely used format for the archiving and dissemination of music on the Internet.

Multi-channel management

The sale of goods and services through different sales channels to make the shopping experience most convenient for the customer.

MySpace

A social networking website similar to Facebook that allows members to create online profiles free of charge with photos, videos, blogs, online groups and other content.

Network neutrality

A principle promoting the value-neutral transmission of data on the Internet, calling on Internet service providers to give their customers access to all data, unaltered and at the same level of quality, regardless of the data source, target audience, content or data service package the customer is using.

Net Promoter Score / NPS method

A method for measuring customer satisfaction based on a company's recommendation quota. An NPS score for a company is calculated by asking a representative group of customers how likely they would be to recommend the company to others.

NGO

Non-Governmental Organization: An NGO is a group of people pursuing certain goals, often in humanitarian or environmental fields, without the involvement of governments.

Online shop

A website on which a company offers products or services for sale.

Open innovation

The opening of an organization's or company's innovation process. This enables it to make strategic use of the outside world to expand its internal innovation potential.

Open-source principle

Open-source software (OSS) is a term for software programs offered free of charge to the general public. The source code is also made available, and users are permitted to modify it, copy it and distribute it to others free of charge.

Paid-search marketing

Search engine advertising. This refers to the placement of special search results shown when Internet users search for certain terms. It is a business model used by many search engine companies.

Pay per click

A billing model in online marketing that allows a user to make online payments automatically with a single click.

Peer2Peer network / Peer-to-peer network

A computer network in which all computers on the network communicate as equals (peers). In pure Peer2Peer networks, all computers have the same authorizations and can both utilize and provide services.

Permalink

A permalink is one that links to a specific article on the Internet so that users can provide links to older materials.

Pirate Party

A new political party that demands more transparency and participation, especially with regard to civil rights, direct democracy and citizen involvement in the political process. It wants reforms of copyright and patent law, open access (i.e. the free exchange of knowledge) and freedom of information, and improved privacy protection laws and data privacy for the Internet. In its very first attempt, in recent state elections in Germany, the new party was able to win seats in four state parliaments. Opinion polls suggest that the Pirate Party has a good chance of repeating that success at the federal level. The wave of change triggered by the "Pirates" and the utilization of the new possibilities of the digital age has also affected the economy. Companies are under heavy pressure to become more transparent and change their corporate strategies accordingly. The party wants to make its slogan "Ready for change" a reality everywhere, above all through the erosion of hierarchies, equal rights and full information access, and implement new policies for a society where life is shaped by the Internet.

Plug-in hybrid

A motor vehicle powered by a hybrid engine with a charger that allows it to plug in and charge its battery using the electrical power grid. This allows the vehicle to be driven in an "all-electric" mode to a limited extent.

Podcasting

The production and presentation of audio or video data files via the Internet. Podcasts are available at all times, independently of any broadcasting schedule, and can be accessed as often as the user wants.

Point of sale

Also known as the "point of purchase," a point of sale is the location where a sales transaction takes place. From the customer perspective, this is the point of purchase; from the seller perspective, it is the point of sale.

Post / Posting

A comment or contribution to an online forum or blog. Posting is the act of making this contribution or comment.

Predictive Behavioral Target

Process of combining online usage data and site registration or survey data from a small of users and projecting it onto the entirety of users with the aid of mathematical algorithms. This makes it possible to produce targeted online advertising for various target groups.

Pro-bono project

A project mainly intended to serve the public good, and not the interests of the company.

Prosumer

A combination of the words "producer" and "consumer." A prosumer is any user or customer who simultaneously takes part in the production process, for example by providing suggestions for product or service improvements. Often used in the context of social media.

Public-private partnership

A public-private partnership is a government service funded and operated with private-sector capital and expert know-how. In many cases, the partnership is either partially or completely privatized.

Requests for Quotation

A standard business practice for inviting suppliers to bid on a specific contract or project. A generally non-binding request for prices for specified services or work is sent to suppliers believed by the principal to be capable of completing the work.

RFID technology

Radio Frequency Identification technology. RFID is used for the tagging of objects or living creatures with radio transponders that emit data detected and read by RFID receivers. Referred to in common usage as "radio tags," RFID transponders are particularly important in logistics.

Semantic web

A new concept for the further development of the World Wide Web and the Internet. According to this concept, all of the information available on the Internet will be assigned a description (semantics), so that it can be understood and processed by machines.

Service provider

Companies that provide services enabling computers to connect to the Internet.

Shitstorm

A slang term for a flood of negative commentary and criticism on social networks directed at individuals, companies, institutions or products. It involves countless users publicly voicing criticism that is frequently off-topic, unprofessional and insulting.

Smartphone

A mobile phone that, in addition to telephone functionality, can also function as a computer with an Internet connection and as a camera. Many smartphones can use additional programs (apps).

SMS

Short Message Service. SMS is a text messaging service that enables users to send short messages via mobile phone. It is also sometimes available for use on landline phones.

Social commerce

A form of Internet-based commerce with a strong focus on customer involvement and customer-to-customer communication, for example in the form of recommendations, comments and ratings.

SOCIAL management

According to Marc Benioff, the secret to success for modern enterprises can be summed up in one word: SOCIAL, which stands for Speed, Open, Collaboration, Individuals (everyone can make a difference), Alignment (everyone pulling together) and Leaderless (the absence of rigid top-down management structures).

Social media

A term for digital media and technologies that enable users to communicate with one another, or exchange media content with other individuals or entire communities. Some forms of social media are primarily intended to facilitate interpersonal communication. Others are used partly for interpersonal communication, but their main focus is on user-generated content.

Social networking

The act of communicating or operating in online social networks.

Social software

Any software that serves to promote communication and cooperation among users, for example in connection with social media activities. Social software can be utilized to create and manage online communities on the Internet.

Splogs

A combination of the words "spam" and "blog," splogs are blogs lacking any significant content, deliberately packed with keywords. This causes them to be found by search engines, which maximizes clicks and therefore revenues.

Stakeholder

Any person who has an interest in the progress or results of a process or project. A financial stake is not required. The definition also includes parties that at first glance appear to have no stake, such as customers or employees.

Sustainability

According to the Brundtland Commission definition, sustainability is the "Long-term development that meets the needs of the present without compromising the ability of future generations to meet their own needs." Around 300 years ago, Hans Carl von Carlowitz, the head of mining operations for the court of Kursachsen in Freiburg (Saxony), formulated a principle of sustainability in his 1713 book, Sylvicultura oeconomica. He called for sustainable forestry practices – that the amount of timber harvested should be limited to the amount that could be replaced by reforestation efforts including the seeding and planting. Carlowitz is therefore credited with inventing the concept of sustainable yield forestry. Nowadays, sustainability efforts are focused on harmonizing economic, ecologic and social priorities, preserving of cultures and limiting effects on human health.

Tablet PC

A portable computer designed to be as compact and lightweight as possible, with a touch-screen keyboard in place of a regular physical keyboard.

Tag / Tagging

Tags are key words assigned to online posts, articles or webpages to enable targeted online searches. Tagging is the act of assigning tags to specific data.

Terms of service

A set of business conditions defined by Internet service providers for the use of their services.

Tracking

The practice of keeping track of users on the Internet. Many websites constantly track their users and visitors. Tracking services make it possible to analyze users' online behavior.

Tweet

A short text message of 140 characters or less that is sent using the Twitter social networking site.

Twitter

An online communications platform founded in 2006. It can be used for the posting and dissemination of short messages (tweets).

Unique user / Unique visit

Terms describing the frequency and number of visits to a website. IP addresses are used to count the computers from which a website is accessed.

User-Generated Content (UGC)

Content created by the users, and not the operator, of a website.

Viral communication / Viral marketing

A form of marketing used in social media and networks, often with unusual, attention-grabbing content, to increase brand awareness.

Virtual world

A world artificially generated using computers and the Internet, which numerous users can "visit" and "occupy" simultaneously.

Web 2.0

A term defining the Internet not only as a means for the procurement and dissemination of information, but also, increasingly, for active involvement of users in the content.

Web 3.0

Web 3.0 builds on the foundation of "the Internet with a feedback channel," or Web 2.0. It can be described as the "Internet of Things and Services." For example, products and devices are assigned their own IP address and can send status updates on the Internet. At the same time, with the help of artificial intelligence, online searches in Web 3.0 will be semantically analyzed, so that users can conduct more individualized or less precise searches than before.

Web browser / Browser

A web browser or browser is the software that facilitates the navigation and presentation of Internet content. The most widespread web browsers include Microsoft's Internet Explorer, Apple's Safari, Mozilla Firefox and Google Chrome.

Webinar

An interactive seminar conducted via the World Wide Web at a specific date and time, dedicated to a specific topic, and with an unlimited number of participants. Webinars can be used for new product releases and press conferences.

Wiki

A collaborative Internet project that allows users to contribute and manage content. The best-known Wiki is Wikipedia, the online encyclopedia established in 2001.

W-LAN

Wireless Local Area Network. This is a local radio network to transmit data over short distances. In many countries, it is also referred to as Wi-Fi.

Word-of-mouth marketing

A form of marketing that utilizes the positive recommendations shared by satisfied customers within their own social groups or networks.

www.ingramcontent.com/pod-product-compliance
Lightning Source LLC
Chambersburg PA
CBHW050702280326
41926CB00088B/2427